CORNELL INTERNATIONAL INDUSTRIAL AND LABOR RELATIONS
REPORT NUMBER 14

MAKING MONDRAGON

The Growth and Dynamics of
the Worker Cooperative Complex

WILLIAM FOOTE WHYTE

KATHLEEN KING WHYTE

88-1598

ILR PRESS
New York State School of Industrial and Labor Relations
Cornell University

Copyright 1988 by Cornell University
All rights reserved

Cover design by Kat Dalton
Text design by Susan Baker

Library of Congress Cataloging-in-Publication Data
Whyte, William Foote, 1914-
  Making Mondragón.

  (Cornell international industrial and labor
relations report ; no. 14)
  Bibliography: p.
  Includes index.
  1. Producer cooperatives—Spain—Mondragón.
I. Whyte, Kathleen King. II. Title. III. Series:
Cornell international industrial and labor relations
reports ; no. 14.
HD3218.M66W48   1988   334'.6'094661   88-8809
ISBN 0-87546-137-9 (alk. paper)
ISBN 0-87546-138-7 (pbk. : alk. paper)

Copies may be ordered from
ILR Press
New York State School of
Industrial and Labor Relations
Cornell University
Ithaca, NY 14851–0952

Printed on acid-free paper in the United States of America
5 4 3 2 1

Contents

Contents

Tables and Figures

Preface

Until Mondragón came to my attention, I had believed that worker cooperatives reflected noble ideals but had little prospect for long-term survival and growth in modern industrialized economies. My introduction to Mondragón occurred in 1974, when I noticed an article by Robert Oakeshott (1973) on a bulletin board at Cornell University.

The discovery of Mondragón excited me, as it had Oakeshott, and I decided I had to see the Basque cooperative complex for myself. Kathleen King Whyte and I thus set out for Mondragón in April 1975 to conduct our first field study. This trip was supported by a travel grant from the German Marshall Fund.

At that time, the research problem was to explain Mondragón's extraordinary record of dynamic development, survival, and growth. That theme was pursued particularly by Cornell graduate student Ana Gutiérrez-Johnson, who accompanied us on the 1975 trip, remained after we left, and returned for two more field trips before completing her master's and doctoral theses (1977 and 1982).

In the 1980s, the research problem was to determine how the Mondragón cooperatives were coping with extreme economic adversity. The cooperatives had to struggle simply to hold their own in the Spanish economy, which was much more severely affected by the recession than were the economies of other Western industrialized nations.

In October 1983, Kathleen and I made our second trip to Mondragón. That visit began a much more intensive research process during which our personal project developed into a highly collaborative relationship with Mondragón people and colleagues and students from Cornell. This enabled us to follow at close range the painful but extraordinarily successful struggles of the cooperatives to reorganize without sacrificing their human values. As we left the field in 1986, it appeared that Mondragón was gaining new economic and technological strength and again entering a period of dynamic growth. In fact, that year, when unemployment in the Basque provinces remained higher than 25 percent, the Mondragón cooperatives had added 500 jobs to reach an all-time-high employment level of more than 19,500.

The appendix describes in detail the evolution of the research process and the roles of the organizations and people who helped us in so many ways. The publication of this book is the culmination of our long and rewarding collaborative relationship with the people of Mondragón.

WILLIAM FOOTE WHYTE
December 1987

PART ONE

Mondragón in Context

1 The Importance of Mondragón

Mondragón is still far from a household word in the United States or elsewhere, but for growing numbers of researchers and activists, this cooperative complex based in a small Basque city of Spain is a fascinating example of success in a form of organization for which failure is the general rule. The story of Mondragón is the most impressive refutation of the widely held belief that worker cooperatives have little capacity for economic growth and long-term survival.

A negative judgment on worker cooperatives was first rendered early in this century by the prestigious social scientists Beatrice and Sidney Webb. Their verdict has been the conventional wisdom ever since:

> All such associations of producers that start as alternatives to the capitalist system either fail or cease to be democracies of producers. . . .
> In the relatively few instances in which such enterprises have not succumbed as business concerns, they have ceased to be democracies of producers, managing their own work, and have become, in effect, associations of capitalists . . . making profit for themselves by the employment at wages of workers outside their association. (Coates and Topham 1968, 67)

It is now clear that the Mondragón cooperatives have met both tests posed by the Webbs. Besides their employment growth—from 23 workers in one cooperative in 1956 to 19,500 in more than one hundred worker cooperatives and supporting organizations—their record of survival has been phenomenal—of the 103 worker cooperatives that were created from 1956 to 1986, only 3 have been shut down. Compared to the frequently noted finding that only 20 percent of all firms founded in the United States survive for five years, Mondragón's survival rate of more than 97 percent across three decades commands attention.

3

Nor have the Mondragón cooperatives lost their democratic character. They continue to operate on the one-member one-vote principle. Many of the cooperatives employ no nonmembers, and, by their own constitutions and bylaws, no cooperative may employ more than 10 percent nonmembers.

THE SIGNIFICANCE OF A UNIQUE CASE

Responding to the first report on Mondragón at the 1976 annual meeting of the American Sociological Association (Gutiérrez-Johnson and Whyte 1977), a discussant dismissed the case as simply a human-interest story. His argument was that the success of Mondragón depended on two conditions: the unique nature of the Basque culture and the genius of the founder, Father José María Arizmendiarrieta. Because neither of these conditions could be reproduced anywhere else in the world, he felt the Mondragón story was without scientific or practical significance.

The most general answer to such a critic is that the criticism is itself unscientific. It is one of the fundamental principles of science that, on discovering an exception to a law or generalization, one does not rationalize it away and reaffirm the general principle. On the contrary, one concentrates one's attention on the exception, in the hope that it will lead to a modification of the previously accepted generalization, or to a more basic reformulation, opening up new avenues of scientific progress. Nevertheless, we are now grateful to this critic for forcing us to think harder, both about Mondragón in the context of the Basque culture and about the general scientific and practical implications that can be drawn from this case.

QUESTIONS FOR RESEARCH AND PRACTICE

The salience of the questions we raise throughout this book depends in part on the time period we are addressing. Mondragón experienced rapid growth from 1960 through 1979. Employment leveled off from 1980 through 1986, while Spain was mired in a severe recession. There were slight drops in employment in 1981 and in 1983, and then small increases again from 1984 through 1986.

Although questions regarding economic success and failure are relevant for both periods, the primary question for the years through 1979 is, How did Mondragón manage such rapid and sustained growth? For the later period, the question is, How has Mondragón been able to survive—and even resume modest growth—in the face of extreme economic adversity?

While seeking to answer these questions, we will probe the Mondragón experience for what it can teach us about the problems and possibilities of creating worker-owned firms and of maintaining worker ownership and control through periods of growth. We will learn about efforts to achieve economies of scale while maintaining local autonomy and grass-roots democracy. We will examine unique systems for stimulating and guiding entrepreneurship, for providing cooperatives with technical assistance, and for intervening to assure the survival of a failing cooperative. We will also analyze the process of technological and organizational change as it was carried out within Mondragón's individual firms, with the stimulus and guidance of an industrial research cooperative.

We make no claim that Mondragón has all the answers to the problems of worker cooperatives. In fact, its members and leaders tend to be more critical of their organizations than admiring outsiders are. Nevertheless, Mondragón has had a rich experience over many years in manufacturing products as varied as furniture, kitchen equipment, machine tools, and electronic components and in printing, shipbuilding, and metal smelting. Mondragón has created hybrid cooperatives composed of both consumers and workers and of farmers and workers. The complex has developed its own social security cooperative and a cooperative bank that is growing more rapidly than any other bank in the Basque provinces. The complex arose out of an educational program begun in 1943 for high school–age youth. It now includes college education in engineering and business administration. These various cooperatives are linked together in ways we will explore.

Although any cooperative program must be developed in the context of the culture and political and economic conditions in the region and nation of its origin, Mondragón has such a long and varied experience that it provides a rich body of ideas for potential adaptation and implementation elsewhere. Such ideas apply most clearly to worker cooperatives and other employee-owned firms, but Mondragón also provides fruitful lessons in regional development and in how to stimulate and support entrepreneurship, whatever the form of ownership. An expanding mini-economy, the cooperative complex is far from self-contained, yet the network of mutually supporting relationships on which it is based provides an important key to regional development.

We also see possibilities for private companies to learn from Mondragón as they seek to foster labor-management cooperation. In fact, the learning can go in both directions if we think more generally of the conditions necessary for participation and cooperation in any organization devoted to the management of work.

THE GROWING INTEREST IN WORKER OWNERSHIP

Interest in Mondragón has grown in response to the explosive growth of worker cooperatives and employee-owned firms in recent years, especially in Europe and the United States. Of the 11,203 worker cooperatives in Italy in 1981, half had been established since 1971. Of the 1,269 in France in 1983, 66 percent had been created since 1978. And of the 911 in England in 1984, 75 percent had been founded since 1979 (Centre for the Study of Cooperatives 1987).

The most impressive worker cooperatives in the United States have been the plywood firms in the Northwest (Bellas 1975), but the most spectacular growth of worker ownership in recent years has been in the form of employee stock ownership plans. In 1970 employee ownership was exceedingly rare. By 1986 Corey Rosen, executive director of the National Center for Employee Ownership, estimated that about seven thousand firms employing 9 million employees had some form of shared ownership. In most cases, to be sure, employees own only token amounts of stock and have no influence on management. Rosen estimated, however, that in 1986 employees owned a majority of the stock in as many as five hundred firms, and in an unknown but apparently growing number, employees have become involved in decision making.

THE DECLINE OF ABSOLUTIST IDEOLOGIES

For many years, the field of economic organization and management was locked into the intellectual prison of the two-valued orientation: the choice between private versus government ownership and control of the means of production. Ideologists on either side of this debate might have conceded some minor defects in their preferred system but countered by pointing out supposedly greater evils in the opposing system. The protagonists implicitly agreed on one proposition: There were only two basic ways to organize and control economic activities.

Over the years, this dogmatism has been fading in the face of experience. Faith in government ownership and control has been weakened by the ever-more-apparent rigidities and inefficiencies of such systems—plus, of course, the dictatorial political control that tends to accompany them. Decades ago Yugoslavia abandoned full government control in favor of labor-managed firms, yet this deviation from orthodoxy received little attention beyond a few intellectuals devoted to the study of offbeat topics. Now even the popular media feature accounts of emerging private businesses or cooperative firms in the Soviet Union and the People's Republic of China.

At the same time, supporters of private enterprise were beginning to entertain the idea that the apparent deficiencies of such a system, as it operated in their countries, had deeper roots that could not be fixed by tinkering. Without denying the demonstrated potential of a private firm to produce and distribute goods at a high level of efficiency, they began to focus seriously on the limitations of a system that relied chiefly on the profit motive and individualistic competition to distribute wealth and provide full employment.

The choice is not simply between acceptance or rejection of the profit motive. The choice may be between considering the pursuit of profits as the sole or primary driving force or considering profits as a necessary limiting condition—a means to other ends. Inherent in the latter option is a recognition that the generation of an economic surplus is essential for long-term growth in employment under socially acceptable conditions.

This shift away from absolutist ideologies has accompanied the sudden rapid growth of worker cooperatives and employee-owned firms. Abandoning formerly popular ideologies, increasing numbers of people around the world are experimenting with unorthodox ways of organizing and controlling economic activities. Some people may see cooperatives as a panacea that will solve the problems of capitalism or socialism by supplanting them, but probably many more of us look forward to economies in which diverse forms of organization will test themselves in the marketplace and in the minds and hearts of those who work in them. It is in support of this more pragmatic and pluralistic view that we turn to Mondragón to learn what it can teach us about social and economic development.

THE BASQUE COUNTRY. The three provinces of Guipúzcoa, Vizcaya, and Alava make up the autonomous Basque government, with its capital at Vitoria. The province of Navarre and the adjoining area of France also have large Basque populations.

2 The Basques

To outsiders, the first contact with the Basque country may be puzzling, for although all but a few old-timers speak Spanish like the natives they are, and economically and politically the Basques are part of Spain, they are culturally distinct from other Spaniards. Without romanticizing or exaggerating this distinctiveness, it is important for one's understanding of Mondragón to view Basque culture in the context of regional and national economic and political development.

SETTING THE BACKGROUND

The most distinctive aspect of Basque culture is the language, Euskera, which is unrelated to any other. Although Euskera is spoken by only 25 percent of the Basques, more than 56 percent of the people of Guipúzcoa, the province where Mondragón is located, are competent in the language (Tarrow 1985, 248). In recent decades, competence in Euskera has been emphasized in Basque schools, especially private schools founded to preserve and strengthen Basque culture.

Basques are found along the coast of the Atlantic Ocean (the Bay of Biscay) and on both sides of the Pyrenees, but predominantly in Spain. The Basque country in Spain consists of either three or four provinces depending on whether one accepts the legal definition or that espoused by some Basque nationalists. Following the reinstitution of democracy after the death of Franco, the provinces of Alava, Guipúzcoa, and Vizcaya joined to form the semi-autonomous regional government. Many citizens of northern Navarre consider themselves Basques, but, because of their ancient attachment to the Kingdom of Navarre and greater acceptance of Spanish culture, Navarre remains outside the Basque regional government. Including the four provinces, the Basque population in Spain is estimated at 2.7 million. Geographically, the cooperatives in the complex are most heavily concentrated in Guipúzcoa, followed closely by Vizcaya, which, like Guipúzcoa, is directly on the coast. The complex includes small but growing numbers of cooperatives in Navarre and Alava.

The Basque region in Spain is generally mountainous and moist. Historically, the Basques have supported themselves precariously by sheep herding and by farming the generally unfavorable terrain, but early in their history they moved into seafaring, shipbuilding, and iron mining and steel fabrication.

As early as the fourteenth century, Basque coastal cities were the main Spanish centers of shipbuilding, and they remained important through the eighteenth century. As shipbuilding declined, iron and steel continued to develop. Steel for the famous Toledo swords came from a mine and workshop near Mondragón. As we learn from the distinguished expert in Basque studies, Julio Caro Baroja, "By the middle of the 17th century the village of Mondragón is known not only for its swords but also for the 'arms of all types' that were coming from its workshops" (1974, 170).

These industrial pursuits had a major impact on the countryside. As Caro Baroja said (1974, 172), "Shipyards and foundries are schools of artisanship, their influence spreads throughout the country."

The region developed autonomously until the political consolidation of the nation during the reign of Ferdinand and Isabella in the fifteenth century. The history of the region since then must be seen against a background of struggle by local leaders to preserve their autonomy and the efforts of the Crown first to accommodate that autonomy and then to suppress it.

The Basques took advantage of the political struggles of the kings of Navarre and Castile against the feudal lords in the thirteenth and fourteenth centuries. Up to this time, allied with the King of Aragon, the lords had controlled the countryside, and fighting among them had retarded the growth of commerce.

In their struggle against the King of Aragon and the feudal lords, the kings of Navarre, and later Castile, encouraged the growth of urban centers. To migrants to the towns and cities, the Castilian Crown offered freedom from the serfdom owed to feudal lords. The monarchs saw freeing the townspeople from the control of the feudal lords as a means of extending central control, whereas the Basques saw it as enhancing opportunities for local autonomy.

This struggle for autonomy was supported by the development of a distinctive Basque myth. By the fifteenth century, the Basques had persuaded the Spanish king to declare all inhabitants of Guipúzcoa *hijosdalgos* (people of known parentage or, literally, "sons of something") and thus "noble" and "equal" in relation to each other. (*Hidalgo*, a shortened form of the word, was a title given in Spain to members of the minor nobility.) Ironically, the myth did not base egalitarian claims on the virtues of the common man but rather on the comforting fiction that, because they were all of noble blood, Basques were equal among themselves and superior to other peoples.

Democratic local governments expressed the egalitarian spirit. In the sixteenth and seventeenth centuries, every male head of a family was entitled to vote for members of the municipal government, and in Guipúzcoa and Vizcaya municipalities elected representatives to a provincial government. The general assemblies in these two provinces codified the common law into what were called *fueros* (laws to govern and administer the provinces as autonomous units). As the bases for local democracy, the *fueros* are looked on with nostalgia by many Basques. From the seventeenth century on, the Spanish Crown withdrew much of its support of local autonomy and restricted the right to vote in municipal elections to those who met a wealth requirement, thus halving the number of voters.

Basque members of skilled crafts and professions struggled to maintain their values of equality and democracy within their occupational associations, while seeking to gain monopolies on their particular economic activities. The rising power of the merchants, who needed free trade and cheap labor for mines and factories, undermined the preexisting restrictions on immigration and also the monopolies on crafts and professions. In rural areas, families expressed their sense of equality and social solidarity by joining together to exchange labor and mutual aid.

The Basque guilds were health and welfare organizations, as well as units of production. They protected their workers and helped orphans and widows. They opened hospitals and sanitariums. They formed networks of skilled workers, which bid for jobs, distributed the work among the guilds, and delivered the finished products.

The guilds were characterized by strong internal solidarity but were closed to outsiders. Although the guilds lost their monopoly powers when large industry developed, the guild tradition survived in the region. Some of the largest guilds, such as those of firearms producers, formed producers' cooperatives in the twentieth century. This form of organization found acceptance among the small industries in the interior of the region—and indeed in other parts of Spain as well. In 1972, there were 193 registered producers' cooperatives in the Basque country (Gorroño 1975). Of these, 144 were independent of the Mondragón complex.

The growth of industry and commerce undermined the basis for Basque solidarity across social classes and led to strong and militant unions. Nevertheless, Basque values supporting the dignity and worth of all labor withstood growing social stratification.

> During the Ancien Regime in Castile, it was inconceivable for a nobleman, even a mere *hidalgo*, to dedicate himself to industry or commerce. The only acceptable positions for him were in public administration, in the militia, in the priesthood or in managing agricultural properties. But in the Basque provinces our ancestors, gentlemen of noble orders with titles, not only themselves worked in foundries and shipyards but also bought and sold merchandise and did business with outsiders. Thus one can say that by the middle of the 18th century there existed in Guipúzcoa and Vizcaya a social class that did not resemble the great aristocracy of Castile and Andalucia, who held sway over immense estates. Nor did they resemble the impoverished *hidalgos* so familiar to us in the classical literature. Rather this [social class] could be compared to what in England was called "the gentry" constituted by wealthy families, of more or less obscure or mixed ancestry, that increase their wealth generation after generation, and live very comfortably, taking advantage of all the opportunities and fashions of the moment. (Caro Baroja 1974, 161)

General statements about the Basques' views on the dignity of labor and equality need some qualification. Working with one's hands in industry or commerce is not looked down on in the Basque country as it is in some other regions of Spain. Social distinctions in the prestige of occupations are of course recognized, but Basques seek to separate the respect due to the person from the status of his occupation. Thus social distinctions are minimized at work, in public affairs, and even in interpersonal relations. In fact, groups of men formed in school sometimes continue their friendly association in later years even though the members are now in occupations with considerably different status.

THE FRANCO ERA: 1939–75

Following their victory in the Civil War (1936–39), General Francisco Franco and his Falange party organized the Spanish government along the lines of Mussolini's corporative state. The Falangists lost power in the following decades and there was a loosening of government control from the 1950s on, but the structure of the state under Franco remained intact until the dictator's death in 1975.

The Franco government sought to exercise direct control over all Spanish organizations of any political or economic importance, except the Catholic Church. The pre–Civil War government had instituted various social reforms, including the disestablishment of the Catholic Church, which previously had been partially supported by the state. Franco sought to gain indirect control over the Church by reinstituting state support and by requiring that the pope's nominations for top offices in the Church be subject to government approval. These officials were required to swear an oath of loyalty to the government.

Before the Civil War, the Basques had been predominantly opposed to Franco, although they were ideologically divided between Basque nationalists and socialists and communists. Because Franco had rallied support by appealing to fellow generals, Basques in those regiments that responded to his appeal were ordered into action. Desertion and execution if apprehended was the only alternative, so many Basques fought under Franco against the Basque army. In this divisive period, the Franco forces at one time were in control of Mondragón while the Basque forces controlled the surrounding mountains.

In the early months of the new regime the government acted, especially in the Basque country, to remove priests and higher Church officials not considered loyal to Franco. The Basque archbishop, Mateo Mugíca, was deported, along with a number of priests (Azurmendi 1984, 38). Mugíca's successor, Archbishop Francisco Javier Lauzurica y Torralba, publicly stated, "I am one more general under orders from the Generalissimo to smash [Basque] nationalism" (page 39).

Nevertheless, the Church maintained some degree of autonomy, particularly in the Basque country. During the Franco years all public meetings were prohibited except those specifically approved by the government. This meant that the Catholic Church was the only institution that could provide shelter for discussion and organizational meetings of people sympathetic with unions or cooperatives. At some personal risk, a priest with pro-labor and democratic sentiments could facilitate and guide emergent opposition or independent organizations.

The Franco government mounted a vigorous cultural repression focused particularly on Euskera, the Basque language. If children were caught speaking Euskera, their parents were subject to financial penalties and, because they were strongly suspected of being unfriendly to the government, they were often the targets of police surveillance. Basque parents reacted in opposite ways to this repression. Some stopped using Euskera at home so as not to expose their children to the possibility of being caught speaking it in public. Others took special pains to emphasize the speaking of Euskera in the home, while cautioning their children against using the language elsewhere. After many years, the cultural repression eased, and in 1968 it became legal to speak Euskera and to publish in the language.

INDUSTRIAL RELATIONS UNDER FRANCO

As part of its attempt to control political activity, the Franco government outlawed free unions and banned strikes. The government substituted the corporatist model of the Organización Sindical Española, which meant that managers as well as workers were organized by industry in so-called vertical unions: "Labor conflict, most importantly in the form of strike activity, was made illegal, but in return workers were granted a high degree of job security" (Gunther et al. 1986, 23).

Collective bargaining was initially outlawed. Wages were set by the Ministry of Labor. As a substitute for collective bargaining, the government authorized the creation in each plant or company of what was intended to be a consultative body: the *jurado de empresa* (literally, jury of the firm). The *jurado* consisted of a president or chairperson appointed by management plus no more than ten members elected from the ranks of the administration, technicians, and workers, in proportion to their numbers in the work force (Amsden 1972, 109).

In 1958 the government legalized collective bargaining but only through the *jurados de empresa* at the firm level. When several firms negotiated jointly with representatives of their employees, meetings took place in the provincial, regional, or national offices of the Organización Sindical Española. When the *jurado* initiated collective bargaining, the management-appointed chairperson no longer served in that role. Negotiations were then carried on by equal numbers of employee representatives and management representatives.

The creation of the *jurados* faced former free trade union leaders and activists with a dilemma: to boycott the *jurados* as management-dominated organizations (which they generally were) or to seek to infiltrate them so they could be taken over by union-minded people. In some cases, the union activists chose the second alternative and gained some success in using the *jurados* as if they were unions. (This situation parallels that of the campaign of the Steel Workers' Organizing Committee [SWOC] to unionize the giant U.S. Steel Company. Management had organized company unions in each plant. Leaders of SWOC countered by urging their members to get themselves elected to leadership positions in the company unions. When this infiltration strategy had gained widespread success, the company was in effect organized, and the union could then bargain with management on a companywide basis. Of course, Spanish union activists had to maintain the formal fiction that they were simply *jurado* representatives.)

Although the laws and policies of the Franco government shifted power from workers to employers, the employers were not entirely happy under the existing conditions.

Under the original corporatist system of labor relations, workers were prevented from striking, and wage levels were established by the Ministry of Labor; but, in return, employers were prevented from firing their employees and could transfer them to new tasks only with great difficulty. Faced with new competition from foreign producers after 1958, employers came to believe that these job-security provisions undermined productivity to such extent that they more than offset the benefits derived from this system. Consequently, during the 1960s and 1970s employers entered into de facto collective bargaining with worker representatives, offering them better pay and fringe benefits than were officially sanctioned by the labor ministry, in exchange for greater flexibility in reallocating their labor forces and other productivity-related provisions. This paved the way for the reemergence of trade unions, such as the *Comisiones Obreras* (Workers' Committees), the *Unión Sindical Obrera* (USO), and the UGT, which in turn, facilitated the reemergence of political party activity. (Gunther et al. 1986, 26–27)

To understand industrial relations during the Franco era, one must distinguish between the official and the unofficial and also recognize political changes evolving over more than three decades. Officially, strikes remained illegal and free trade unions were banned throughout the period, yet strong unions grew up in some industries and in some regions. Officially, management had the right to denounce union leaders and have them thrown in jail, but where unions were strong, this would only precipitate a costly strike. Therefore, in many cases employers chose instead to bargain with the clandestine unions and even to sign written (but unofficial) contracts with them. Furthermore, successful strikes did occur, and, in some cases, rather than intervening against labor, government officials acted to resolve the conflict by forcing employers to grant some of the workers' demands. Union activists also formed *comisiones obreras* (workers' committees) throughout Spain, often loosely linked with the plant-level *jurados*. Though these *comisiones* were outside the legal framework, they became the most powerful form of labor organization, uniting workers with a wide range of political tendencies. The *comisiones* organized worker pressure so effectively as to force the government to yield in some labor conflicts—until 1967, when a government crackdown made open *comisiones* activities impossible (Fishman 1985).

Growing labor militancy during the Franco era must also be seen in the context of economic and political changes. Ideologically, and recognizing that economic and military support from Germany and Italy had made their civil war triumph possible, Franco and the Falange party leaders strongly sympathized with the Axis powers in World War II. Though they had declined to join their former allies, they probably expected the Axis powers to win. The Allied victory left Spain politically and economically isolated. Although it gave some opponents of Franco the false hope that the end of the dictatorship was at hand, the Allied victory also must have suggested the need to become more pragmatic and less ideological and have shaken the confidence of some government leaders.

Spain's first break from political and economic isolation came in 1949, when, in return for U.S. use of Spanish military bases, President Harry Truman gave Spain economic aid through the Marshall Plan. This infusion of U.S. funds helped fuel the economic expansion that served to stabilize the Franco regime. As the Spanish economy grew rapidly in the 1950s and 1960s, the challenge of managing an expanding economy and coping with inflation tended to bring to government men who saw themselves as professional administrators rather than as political leaders. During these years, the politicians of the Falange party slipped from power to near impotence, as technocrats rose to manage the economy and the state.

Over the years, the Franco government relaxed its tight controls over some other spheres of Spanish life as well as industrial relations. Press censorship continued to the end of the regime, but during a visit in 1975 we saw books by Marx and Lenin openly displayed in bookstores. (Until

1965, anyone caught buying or selling Marxist literature was subject to severe penalties.)

FROM DICTATORSHIP TO DEMOCRACY

By the 1970s, clandestine, but almost open, political activity had increased significantly. When it became known that Franco was in poor health and did not have long to live, political and union activists began positioning themselves to move into the open as soon as the dictator died. Basques who interpreted politics for us in the early 1970s used the metaphor of a pressure cooker. The temperature was steadily rising, ready to burst forth when the lid was removed.

In the early days of the post-Franco era, democratization proceeded with amazing rapidity. Free elections were promised, and all political parties (including the Communist) were legalized. Free collective bargaining was also legalized in 1977, two months before the first parliamentary elections.

The democratization process opened up for the Basques the possibility of achieving some level of regional autonomy within the Spanish state. After some months of tension-filled negotiations, an autonomous Basque government was established, with its capital in Vitoria, a city about twenty miles south of Mondragón. Though the powers of the regional government have been limited, it has had considerable scope in cultural activities and economic development. It has gone beyond the acceptance of publications in Euskera, granted finally under Franco, to the active promotion of the language, including financial support for elementary schools in which Euskera is taught.

Since the reestablishment of free elections, the Basque Nationalist party (PNV) has been the leading party, followed by the Socialist. Committed to achieving greater autonomy for the Basque provinces, within the government of Spain, the PNV was seriously weakened in 1986 by factional splits. Another party, Herri Batsuna, remains committed to achieving Basque independence from Spain, but it has never polled more than 16 percent in any election.

Whenever foreigners enter into a discussion of Basque politics or even of Basque cooperatives, they want to know about ETA, the clandestine entity whose terrorist activities have been publicized around the world. To satisfy this curiosity, we provide this brief background, although ETA has had very little impact on the Mondragón cooperatives.

ETA (in Euskera, the acronym stands for "Basque homeland and liberty") has not been a single organization but a loose grouping of factions linked by a fanatical dedication to the goal of freeing the Basque country from Spain. Under the dictatorship, ETA necessarily acted clandestinely and has remained clandestine, but it is reportedly linked to the legal political party Herri Batsuna.

ETA began in the 1950s but resorted to violence only in 1968, when it directed its attacks at prominent government leaders, military officers, and members of the Guardia Civil, the national police organization. ETA also targeted wealthy Basque business leaders, threatening them and their companies with violence unless they paid "revolutionary taxes." (Apparently the Mondragón cooperatives were not targets of such extortion. We have not heard of any protection money paid to or demanded by ETA.)

No one can say what level of popular support ETA has in the Basque country. Support seems to have declined sharply since the restoration of democracy, as evidenced by anti-ETA demonstrations, some even in the Basque region.

It is generally believed that the number of ETA militants has dropped substantially since the end of the dictatorship, but a few desperate men with modern armaments can cause enormous damage. These days most Basques probably believe that independence from Spain would be economically disastrous, even if it could be achieved politically. In this context, ETA violence is increasingly seen as a negative force holding back the economic and political development of the Basque country.

COOPERATIVES BEFORE MONDRAGÓN

The cooperative movement in the Basque country developed in intimate association with the labor movement, political parties, and the Catholic Church (Olibarri 1984) and appears to have arisen out of the formalization of practices of cooperative labor traditional in the countryside and guilds of craftsmen. Olibarri has reported that there may have been several consumer, production, fishing, housing, and mutual aid cooperatives as early as 1870. The first documented founding of a consumer cooperative was in 1884, organized among the steel mill workers in Baracaldo. The first documented agricultural cooperative was formed in 1906.

The cooperative movement in the early twentieth century arose out of five sources of organizational initiative and support. In keeping with the paternalistic orientation of many employers, some companies established consumer cooperatives for their employees. The employer contributed capital to these organizations, but generally the workers were allowed to run them.

The Catholic Church was active in developing cooperatives but limited itself to organizing consumers, farmers, and credit cooperatives. The Socialist party sponsored consumer cooperatives and also contributed to the early development of worker cooperatives by working closely with labor unions. Basque nationalists, working with and through ELA, the labor union of Basque solidarity, stimulated the development of consumer cooperatives and created worker cooperatives. They also joined cooperatives together by organizing the Central Sindical Solidaridad de Obreros Vascos (SOV), which held its first congress in 1929. Finally, groups of individuals who maintained independence from employers, political parties, or the Church formed consumer and housing cooperatives.

Although the Basques appeared to be more inclined to organize cooperatives than people of other regions, developments in the Basque country should nevertheless be seen against a background of growing interest in cooperative organization in other parts of Spain. The Unión de Cooperativas del Norte de España (Union of Cooperatives of the North of Spain), which included cooperatives beyond the Basque provinces, was founded in 1914. By 1922 the Unión had established a credit union, which survived until 1936. A national organization, the Federación Nacional de Cooperativas, was organized in 1928. In 1917, the Catholic Church had established the Confederación Nacional Católica-Agraria, which united 21 federations of 1,500 locals and a total of 200,000 members. All, or nearly all, of these locals were either consumer or farmer cooperatives. The growth of farmer cooperatives had been stimulated by a national law passed in 1906. Another national law, passed in 1931, provided a legal framework for further development of cooperatives.

Until 1920, worker cooperatives tended to be limited to very small organizations of bakers and furniture makers. The principal forerunner to Mondragón—Alfa, Sociedad Anónima Cooperativa Mercantil y de Producción de Armas de Fuego (Cooperative Corporation for Marketing and Manufacturing Firearms)—was established in 1920. Alfa grew out of a long strike during which the unionized workers pooled their resources to establish their own firearms organization. They were strongly supported by their metal workers' union (Sindicato Metalúrgico de Vizcaya), which contributed 45,000 of the original 300,000 pesetas of capital. For the times, Alfa had an extraordinary record of adaptation and survival. In

1925, facing an economic crisis in which their firearms were no longer cost competitive with U.S. imports, the leaders of Alfa managed to shift the operation to manufacturing sewing machines. Alfa survived and prospered until the beginning of the Civil War in 1936. At that time it had 5 to 6 million pesetas in capital and was supporting a thousand families.

Although the Church, political parties, and unions were all involved in various ways in supporting and developing cooperatives, they were not in competition with one another. The Church had strong links to the socialists and labor unions, and leaders of ELA used Pope Pius XI's encyclical *Quadragesimo Anno* (1931) to support the ideal of cooperativism: the elimination of the wage system. The 1933 ELA congress in Vitoria passed recommendations calling for labor support and the effective linking of cooperatives of consumers, workers, and credit unions. The third congress of ELA was scheduled to meet in 1936 with a mandate to find the best ways to strengthen relations among cooperatives of various types so as to promote the movement as a whole. The outbreak of the Civil War aborted this meeting.

Clearly, the Mondragón movement developed out of a rich and diverse culture, representing broad interests and many organizations within the Basque country. The Alfa case was well known to the founder of the Mondragón movement, Father José María Arizmendiarrieta. His nephew was a friend of Toribio Echevarria, the organizer and leading spirit of Alfa, but he had no personal contacts with the Mondragón movement. Following the Civil War, Echevarria went into exile in the United States. Direct contacts between the two men were not established until 1966, when they began exchanging letters. We know from one letter from Echevarria that he greatly admired Don José María and the Mondragón movement, but apparently Alfa did not provide a model for that movement. According to Joxe Azurmendi, who was the leading student of Don José María's life and works:

> One cannot deny some indirect influence [of Alfa], more or less hidden: Arizmendiarrieta has never concealed his admiration for the personality of Toribio Echevarria. But he has also made clear that the Mondragón experience was not begun by trying to imitate or continue an earlier model, but rather seeking its own model for the [cooperative] firm. (Olibarri 1984, 307)

The Basque country had been a fertile field for the growth of cooperatives before the Civil War, but very few had been worker cooperatives, and only Alfa had grown to substantial size. Under Franco the Catholic Church was the only organization of importance that maintained any freedom of action and that might have stimulated and guided the formation and growth of cooperatives. But the Church had no experience in creating worker cooperatives. Although it might have been anticipated that priests would continue to work to advance the cooperative movement, there was no basis for predicting that a priest would be the founder and guiding spirit of an industrial complex based primarily on the principles of the cooperative movement.

PART TWO

Building the Cooperative Complex

3 The Foundation

If a regional planner had been asked at the end of the Civil War to select the future site of the most important industrial complex in the Basque country, Mondragón would have seemed one of the most unlikely choices. A small and inconspicuous town (population of 8,645 in 1940), nestled in a narrow valley surrounded by steep hills and mountains, Mondragón, with its narrow streets and buildings dating back to the fifteenth century, had little space for industrial expansion or population growth. In fact, substantial expansion could be accommodated only by constructing multistory apartment buildings on the hills outside the town.

Mondragón is located inland from the two principal Basque cities on the north coast, about fifty kilometers southeast of Bilbao, one hundred kilometers southwest of San Sebastían. After its railroad line was abandoned in 1965, Mondragón was entirely dependent on poorly maintained roads for access to the outside world. Principal access to the major Spanish markets to the south was through the Basque city of Vitoria. Vitoria is only about twenty miles away, but the road from Mondragón, hemmed in by mountains, is winding and hilly. Even in the mid-1980s, when the road had been substantially improved, it remained two lanes for most of the distance from Mondragón to Vitoria, so that increasingly heavy truck traffic often slowed drivers to a crawl.

Mondragón did have one feature that favored industrial development: a centuries-old industrial tradition. The famous swords of Toledo were made from steel produced there. More recent history, however, appeared much less promising for industrial development.

From the early years of the twentieth century, Mondragón had been dominated by a large foundry and metalworking company, the Unión Cerrajera. Stock in that firm was closely held by family and friends, and no one outside the circle could hope to rise above a first-line supervisory position. The company had a history of conflict, climaxed in 1916 by a bitter three-month strike, which ended in complete defeat for the union. When the workers finally returned to their jobs, management refused to reemploy thirty-three workers presumed to be ringleaders. This meant that the thirty-three were also barred from employment in any of the forty factories and workshops in the area, because the firms maintained a common blacklist to exclude "troublemakers." As late as the 1950s, we were told, the blacklist against labor activists was still maintained by Mondragón employers.

The failed strike against the Unión Cerrajera fueled smoldering class conflicts. According to Don José María, the founder of the Mondragón cooperatives, "This was an active and restless town even before the war, and there was a considerable socialistic orientation. There had also been serious social tensions." (All quotations from Don José María are from personal interviews unless otherwise noted.)

Joxe Azurmendi (1984, 99) quotes an executive of the Unión Cerrajera who described Mondragón as "a difficult town and one of the most brutal. I remember going about with body guards, and there were frequent street fights and assaults in the pre–civil war period." By 1940 leaders of the political opposition and of militant unions had necessarily gone underground, but the spirit of political radicalism and social-class militance remained alive in the minds of the working people.

Mondragón was predominantly a working-class town. A few families formed the upper crust, and a very small group of shopkeepers, professionals, and office employees made up the middle class. A great gulf separated the masses of workers from the small upper strata.

It was generally assumed in Mondragón in that era that the son of a worker would be a worker himself—if he could get a job. Education provided no channel of social mobility. The public schools provided no training in industrial or craft skills. The Unión Cerrajera supported a training program, but enrollment was limited to sons of company employees. Higher education was out of the question. No son of a Mondragón worker had ever gone to a university.

José María Arizmendiarrieta took up his pastoral duties in Mondragón in 1941 during what was known later as "the hunger period." Working-class people were desperately poor and oppressed by unemployment, rundown and overcrowded housing, and an outbreak of tuberculosis. People speak of the spirit of hopelessness. They saw themselves as a conquered people, living under a regime that offered neither political freedom nor economic opportunity.

Don José María: From Family Farm
to the Priesthood

José María Arizmendiarrieta was born on April 22, 1915, in the village of Markina, about fifty kilometers from Mondragón. (Hereafter we will refer to him as Don José María or as Arizmendi, as he was commonly called in Mondragón. In the Basque country, any priest or professional person is referred to or addressed as "Don.") The eldest son of a respected farm family of modest means, José María and his younger sister and two brothers grew up speaking Euskera at home. At the age of three, he lost the sight in his left eye in an accident, but this did not dampen his inexhaustible curiosity about the world beyond the village. In the Basque country, the eldest son is expected to inherit and manage the family farm, but from his early years José María felt a calling for the priesthood, and, encouraged by his mother, he gave up his inheritance.

At the age of twelve, José María entered a preparatory school for theological studies and went on to study for the priesthood in the seminary at Vitoria. Throughout his studies, he displayed a special interest in Euskera and the Basque culture, so that he became known among his associates as someone who was especially dedicated to the culture and exceptionally well informed about it.

When the Civil War broke out in July 1936, Vitoria fell to the Fascists, but Arizmendi was on vacation in his village in the province of Vizcaya. Vizcaya and Guipúzcoa remained faithful to the constitutional government, and José María joined its military forces.

Because of his childhood injury, Arizmendi was ineligible for combat duty. Instead, he established and edited newspapers written in Euskera and published by the Basque military authorities. His duties and opportunities as a journalist provided him with a constant flow of information, and he was known among his friends as someone who viewed events in a more detached and reflective manner than his fellows. While remaining faithful to the Basque cause, he nevertheless had no illusions about the outcome of the war. One of his friends in that era quoted him as stating, "The ones who will win this war will be the military and the capitalists" (Larrañaga 1981, 30).

Following the fall of Bilbao in June 1937, there was no longer any possibility of armed resistance in the area where Arizmendi was serving. Because he could not escape the control of the Franco forces, he turned himself in to the authorities. He spent a little more than a month in prison, along with twenty-eight companions who had served with him in the Basque forces. Finally he faced the military interrogation that would determine his fate. There was one crucial question: How had he been supporting himself? After a moment's hesitation, he said that he had been a soldier in the Basque army. That answer saved his life. Classified as a prisoner of war, he was later released. A man who had worked with him on the newspaper identified himself as a journalist and was executed. (The library of Ikasbide, the educational center at the Mondragón complex, displays a document of the Franco forces that lists Arizmendi among those to be executed.)

Arizmendi returned to Vitoria to finish his studies for the priesthood. He read widely in the library, pursuing a strong interest in social problems and social movements, as well as theology. As he was approaching his ordination, he appealed to the monsignor to allow him to study sociology at the University of Louvain in Belgium. The monsignor denied his appeal and dispatched him to Mondragón with no other assignment than to serve under the more senior priests of the parish. By denying Arizmendi's petition, the monsignor deprived the Basque country of a sociologist with academic credentials and opened the way to the development of an applied sociologist whose extraordinary achievements would outweigh any set of credentials.

BEGINNING IN MONDRAGÓN

The arrival of Arizmendi in Mondragón on February 5, 1941, was distinctly unimpressive. His biographer reported (Larrañaga 1981, 65) that he had the difficult task of succeeding very experienced and capable men.

> The people, enthralled by the verbal brilliance of his predecessors, awaited the new priest. Don José María took up his new position, aware of his lack of oratorical talent and sure that he was to undergo a hard test before people accustomed to the phillipics of Don Luis Dolora and the subtle phraseology of Don Roberto Aguirre.
>
> Don José María's debut in the pulpit was a great disappointment to the people. He spoke in a monotone with intricate and repetitive phraseology difficult to understand. Away with this priest that the Monsignor has imposed upon us, he hardly even reads with any grace! That was the first reaction of the faithful.

Arizmendi continued to take his turn in the pulpit, but he never mastered the oratorical style of his predecessors. He was more comfortable and far more effective in dialogue and in small-group discussions. But even under these circumstances, people found him difficult to understand at the outset. Arizmendi was shaping his own social gospel, in marked contrast to the traditional preoccupations of most of his fellow priests, who were concerned with individual salvation. In Chapter 18, we will examine Arizmendi's social philosophy at length, but for now it is enough to note the central elements that shaped his vision and eventually the actions of his followers. In his sermons and writings, he stressed that work should not be seen as a punishment but as a means of self-realization. There should be dignity in any work. He spoke of the need for cooperation and collective solidarity. He combined a social vision with an emphasis on education for technical knowledge and skills.

His followers at the time thought of him as a socialist, and indeed some of the conservative townspeople referred to him as "that red priest." His vision focused on immediate matters as he searched for ways to guide people into action to solve the problems oppressing them.

In his pastoral work, Don José María gave special attention to the revival of two moribund church organizations, one for blue-collar youth and the other for the families of his parishioners. He worked with and through the church organizations to establish a medical clinic. He also worked to establish an athletic field and a sports league, beginning with soccer. These early organizing activities produced a social base for all future institution building and made it possible for Arizmendi to concentrate on his principal concern: providing the people of Mondragón with the technical skills necessary to support a social vision.

Arizmendi had been invited by the management of the Unión Cerrajera to provide religious instruction in the company's apprenticeship program. He took advantage of this opening to urge management to expand the apprenticeship program to include boys who were unrelated to employees. When the company rejected his proposal, he began working to establish an independent school to teach craft and industrial skills to boys fourteen to sixteen. He formed a parents' association to work with the young people to generate popular interest and support. The sponsoring association solicited contributions from local enterprises and also raised money through various cultural and social activities and sports events.

As the climax to the organizing campaign, the sponsors placed boxes on the principal street corners of Mondragón in which all citizens inter-

ested in the school could put slips of paper with their names and addresses
and a statement indicating what they were prepared to contribute in
money or personal services. Those entering their names became members
of the incipient organization and gained the right to vote for the officials
and determine policies.

This manifestation of democracy startled government officials, who were
bound to be concerned about the prospect of free elections for any purpose.
Some regarded Arizmendi as a demagogue and troublemaker. His super-
vising priest stood by him but advised Arizmendi to tone down his talks
and be more cautious about engaging in unorthodox activities. On the
other hand, some of the most militant Basque nationalists considered him
a collaborationist with government because he took pains to ensure that
all his activities were within legally prescribed limits.

About six hundred residents, approximately 15 percent of the adult
population of Mondragón at the time, responded with pledges of support.
Many small- and medium-sized enterprises joined, but the Unión Cerrajera
and the local government declined to participate. The school opened in
1943 with a class of twenty students.

As a branch of Acción Católica, the parents' association had no legal
standing, and the school was not eligible for national educational subsidies. The next project was to formalize and legalize the educational
organization the sponsors had created. At the time, most forms of organization were prohibited, but Arizmendi searched the statute books
until he found a nineteenth-century law that made it possible to charter
the parents' association under a new name, the League for Education and
Culture. The first organizational charter of the league, which was established in 1948, provided for four groups of members, each with voice
and vote: (1) any individual who had expressed the desire to join the
league; (2) active members who contributed either monthly dues or a
service, including teaching; (3) sponsors who gave annual financial contributions of at least 1,000 pesetas (about $89 at the 1948 U.S. exchange
rate; most of the small enterprises in Mondragón were sponsors); and (4)
honorary members (local authorities, who were legally required to be
represented in any association). Each membership group elected ten representatives to a general assembly, which in turn elected the fourteen-
member school board. Six board members were representatives of contributing enterprises, and one was the mayor of Mondragón.

The chartering of the school, the Escuela Politécnica Profesional, and
the presence of the mayor on its board indicated that the new cooperative

organization had gained at least grudging acceptance from political authorities. It was not until 1971 that the Unión Cerrajera closed its apprenticeship school and began making annual contributions to the Escuela Politécnica.

The school expanded its program, adding a new level as soon as the students had completed the previous one. Spanish technical education has three levels: *oficialia, maestria,* and *peritaje industrial. Maestria* is equivalent to a high school—level technical education. *Peritaje industrial* is roughly comparable to the first three years of a U.S. undergraduate degree.

The Escuela Politécnica Profesional provided the base for the creation and development of the cooperatives that would build the Mondragón complex. And, serving as a teacher as well as a preacher, Don José María infused the institution-building process with the social vision that would guide the Mondragón movement.

4 The First Worker Cooperatives

After completing the education available in Mondragón, some of the first graduates of the Escuela Politécnica Profesional went to work in the dominant private enterprise, the Unión Cerrajera, but they were determined to secure further education. At first this seemed impossible because there was no university in or near Mondragón, and none of the graduates could afford to give up their jobs to live and study elsewhere. After canvassing various possibilities, Arizmendi worked out an arrangement with the University of Zaragoza in the province of Aragón (outside the Basque country) whereby students from Mondragón could study in absentia. Eleven of the twenty young men in the first class of the Escuela Politécnica Profesional went on to receive degrees in technical engineering from the university.

While continuing their studies, some of these men were doing well on their jobs, advancing to skilled worker and minor supervisory or staff positions, but they did not feel at home in this environment. Labor relations in this period were distinctly adversarial, and the graduates of the Escuela Politécnica Profesional found that their sympathies were with the workers.

Meanwhile, these men continued to meet with Arizmendi every week for discussions. Between the time of his arrival in 1941 and the founding of the first worker cooperative in 1956, Arizmendi was extraordinarily active as a teacher and discussion leader. José María Ormaechea, one of his closest associates, remembers that "in the calculations we were making in 1956, we counted more than 2,000 circles of study that he conducted. Some for religious and humanistic orientation; others for social orientation" (Azurmendi 1984, 170).

Thus, from 1941 on, Arizmendi conducted at least one study session every 2.7 days, not counting holidays and vacations, in addition to teaching his regular schedule. As one of his former students told us, "He taught classes in religion and sociology—and really his religion classes were mainly sociology." Sessions with those who had been his first students focused particularly on discussions of conflicts between labor and capital, reform of private enterprise, and self-management and the participation of workers in ownership.

In the early 1950s, the management of the Unión Cerrajera decided to expand the firm's capital base by selling new stock. Arizmendi's disciples gained an audience with top management at which they urged that workers be given the opportunity to invest in their firm. When management flatly rejected this proposal, the disciples made one last attempt to reform the private enterprise system. They traveled to Madrid to propose to government authorities that a state-sponsored program be established by which workers would gain shares in ownership. When this proposal was rejected, they gave up hope of reforming capitalist firms. Five of these men—Luis Usatorre, Jesús Larrañaga, Alfonso Gorroñogoitia, José María Ormaechea, and Javier Ortubay—now told Arizmendi that they were determined to start a new company organized along the social and economic lines they had been discussing.

The five pioneers were guided by a social vision, but they were also responding to concerns about their own careers based on an assessment of current economic conditions. They knew that sons of workers would never rise above minor managerial positions in the Unión Cerrajera. They also concluded that, because Spain was economically isolated from other countries, any firm that could produce a useful and well-made product would succeed.

Establishing Ulgor

The five pioneers had no blueprint for the structure and legal form of the organization they wanted to create, but they envisioned it as a worker cooperative. In an economy that had no precedent for such a phenomenon, they were determined to be collective entrepreneurs. There were no legal provisions for collective savings accounts, so the five men put their savings in individual accounts and trusted one another to contribute these personal funds when the time came to make the collective investment.

To raise more funds, Arizmendi devised a strategy to reach the community that had supported the creation of the earlier social welfare and educational projects. He suggested that they use an old and well-established social custom, the *chiquiteo*. Every day after work groups of friends gather on the streets of Mondragón and move along from bar to bar, sipping wine and conversing with the patrons and bartenders in each establishment. Through these informal channels, the five men spread the word that they were planning a cooperative firm and that they were looking for help from the community in the form of loans. Arizmendi and his associates also used all their personal and organizational contacts to publicize the project. At this point they could not tell potential lenders what the firm would produce, where it would be located, or how it would be legally constituted. Nevertheless, they built on a record of successful community organizing and their great personal prestige as the first university-educated children of blue-collar workers. With nothing more to go on than the personal promises of these men, about a hundred people in the community responded with pledges, basically as an expression of faith in the five pioneers and in the guiding hand of Don José María. Including the commitments of the five founders, 11 million pesetas (about $361,604 in 1955 dollars) was pledged—an enormous sum at this time in a working-class community of Spain.

During this period, citizens in Spain were not free to create industrial enterprises. This was a privilege jealously guarded by the state authorities; working people without high-level connections had little opportunity to found their own firms. As Jesús Larrañaga commented: "In 1955, authorizations for permits to establish a factory were subject to rigorous control, and those who had the authorizations looked upon them as if they were made of gold" (1981, 124). Arizmendi suggested that they establish a foundry. One of the five men, Ormaechea, did a feasibility study and presented the proposal to the licensing officials, but it was buried in government files.

The first break came toward the end of 1955 when the five men learned that a private firm in Vitoria had gone bankrupt. The founders were less interested in the building and equipment than in the firm's license, which was extraordinarily broad in scope. The firm was authorized to produce a line of electrical and mechanical products for home use. By buying the firm, the founders gained rights that would have been inaccessible through any other channel.

After a year in the building in Vitoria, the five pioneers and eighteen associates moved into a new building in Mondragón that they had designed. The date of the move, November 12, 1956, is now given as the official date of the founding of Ulgor, the first worker cooperative in Mondragón. It also marks the beginning of what the founders call "The Cooperative Experience of Mondragón."

Ulgor (the name was taken from the first letter or two of the five founders' names) functioned for more than three years without a legal constitution or bylaws. The firm was simply registered in the name of one of its founders. As far as the government authorities were concerned, an individual controlled the organization. The faith the men had in one another and in Don José María enabled them to work together without knowing the form their organization would take. They held frequent meetings after work to discuss with Arizmendi the theoretical and practical considerations underlying the organization's design. This was a fruitful experience because it enabled them to combine what they were learning from working together with the social vision and legal research of Arizmendi. Arizmendi himself never held a formal position in Ulgor—or in any other cooperative organization in Mondragón—but had only the title of adviser. After the founding of Ulgor, he studiously avoided participating in official meetings of any of the organs of cooperative governance and shared information and ideas only in informal individual or group discussions.

Writing the Constitution

The constitution and bylaws of Ulgor, with several modifications, became the model for all the worker cooperatives created subsequently. (The structure of a Mondragón cooperative is illustrated is figure 4.1.) The document vests ultimate power in the general assembly of the cooperative (*asemblea general*), in which all members of the firm have not only the right to vote but the obligation. (Members who do not have a valid reason for missing an assembly meeting are denied the right to vote at the next meeting.) The general assembly meets at least annually. Meetings may also be called by the governing council of the cooperative (*junta rectora*) or petitioned by one-third of the members.

The governing council is the top policy-making body of the cooperative. In earlier writings we translated *junta rectora* as board of directors because its powers have something in common with boards of private firms familiar to us. That term masks the following differences, however, which suggest that "governing council" is a better translation.

1. The board of a private firm is elected by the stockholders, and each

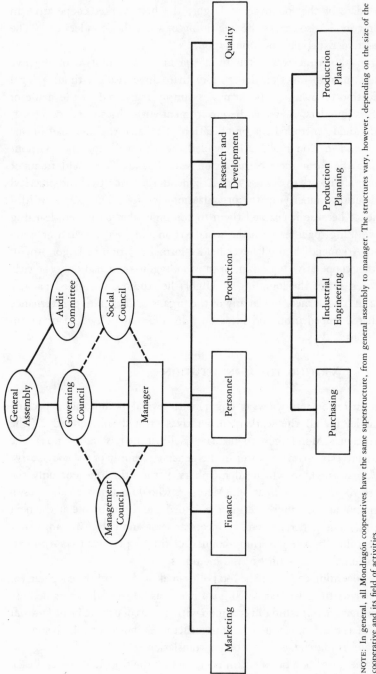

NOTE: In general, all Mondragón cooperatives have the same superstructure, from general assembly to manager. The structures vary, however, depending on the size of the cooperative and its field of activities.

Figure 4.1. Structure of a Mondragón Cooperative

share of stock entitles the owner to one vote, so that individuals or organizations holding large blocks of stock are likely to be able to control the company. The governing council in a Mondragón cooperative is elected by the members, who are all workers, and each worker has only one vote.

2. A board frequently includes members who are not employed by the company and usually one or more key executives. The governing council includes only worker-members; key executives may attend council meetings, but they are *not* members of the council. Mondragón distinguishes between *governance* and *execution* or management of operations. In a private company, this line is blurred because executives often both govern and manage.

3. In a private company, the titles of president or chairman of the board do not identify the chief executive officer unless a CEO is added. In Mondragón, the chief executive officer of a cooperative is called the manager (*gerente*). The manager is likely to be the most influential individual in the cooperative but is under the general control of the governing council, at whose meetings the manager has a *voice* but no *vote*.

The manager is expected to be a strong executive but also to work in close consultation with department heads. He or she is consulted by the governing council regarding the replacement of department heads but does not make such key personnel decisions, which are reserved for the governing council.

Members of the governing council are elected every two years for four-year terms. Members are not compensated for their council responsibilities but continue to be paid their regular salaries. The council has overall responsibility for management policies and programs. It selects the manager, who serves for a four-year term unless he is deposed by the council. It also appoints his immediate subordinates. The manager may be reappointed; but his performance must first be reviewed by the council. This policy contrasts with that of a private company, where there are rarely preestablished terms of office for CEOs or procedures for reviewing their performance and they therefore serve for an indefinite period until they retire, quit, or are deposed by their boards.

Ulgor began with two other structural elements that distinguish it from a private firm. An audit committee, required by law, consists of three people elected by the members of the cooperative. The sole, but important, function of the committee is to perform an internal audit of financial operations and of the firm's adherence to formally established policies and procedures. Ulgor also created a management council, which consists of the manager and chief department heads. In a private firm, such a body may exist informally, but the founders of Ulgor thought it important to formalize the process of executive decision making. The structural design of Ulgor and the determination of its constitution and bylaws were so thoroughly discussed and skillfully decided that only a few major changes were required later except those necessary when Ulgor became linked with other cooperative organizations.

THE SOCIAL COUNCIL

The first major change in the design of Ulgor involved the creation of a social council. Earlier publications (including our own) give the impression that the social council was born when Ulgor was created, but it now seems apparent that this was highly improbable. In a cooperative begun with twenty-three members, all of whom knew one another very well, why would they have felt that they needed both a social council and a governing council? In fact, the social council did not exist at the time Ulgor began, although a precursor was formed at a surprisingly early date. Records indicate that what was first called the social committee had an organizing meeting early in 1957 and its first business meeting on February 25, 1957, little more than a year after Ulgor began operations in the Vitoria plant. In February 1958, members of the social committee proposed that a formal constitution be drawn up to establish the social council. In early December of that year, the governing council approved the constitution and the chairman presented it to the general assembly for ratification.

As a social invention unique to Mondragón, the social council is of special interest. We wondered about its intellectual origins and the social influences that led to its creation. At one time we assumed that the rapid growth of Ulgor had created a need for participation beyond that provided by the annual meeting of the general assembly. That seemed unlikely, however, once we discovered that the first meeting of the precursor social committee was held when Ulgor had fewer than fifty members.

It did not occur to us before his death in 1976 to ask Arizmendi what led to the conception of the social council. We have since interviewed two members who worked closely with him in the early years. Both of them told us that the social council was Arizmendi's idea and that he had drafted the clauses describing its functions and responsibilities in the constitution and bylaws of Ulgor, submitted to the government in October 1958 and officially approved the following April. Regarding what the founder had in mind at the time, both men were unclear and uncertain.

Alfonso Gorroñogoitia thought the idea might have arisen out of Arizmendi's experience with including students in the system of participation at the Escuela Politécnica Profesional or from his reflections on the Franco-era *jurado de empresa*, the employee body elected to advise the managements of private companies. He noted that such a body had existed in Mondragón's dominant private company in this era but added that management's response to any advice from its *jurado* was always the same: "No! No! No!" Perhaps Arizmendi believed that an elected advisory body would fit better into a cooperative firm. In an interview in 1986 with Professor Davydd Greenwood of Cornell University, Gorroñogoitia emphasized at several points that the social council was not intended to be a countervailing power (*contra-poder*) in relation to management. It should not make demands on management, but rather should help integrate the cooperative by furthering the communications process. He conceded, however, that it was legitimate for such a body to question abuses committed by management. He commented that some members were inclined to influence the social council toward acting like a union, and he added that during the difficult process of economic readjustment in 1979 and 1980 the social councils of the cooperatives had gone beyond their legitimate functions. He rejected any parallelism with unions and insisted that the most similar organizational model was the *jurado de empresa*.

After 1958, some *jurados* did more than advise management; they engaged in collective bargaining. This suggests the difficulty of maintaining the distinctions on which Gorroñogoitia insisted and focuses our attention on the ambiguity of the role played by the social councils in the course of the evolution of the cooperatives. As Gorroñogoitia himself concluded, the social councils, like other elements of the cooperatives, continue to be products of experience and thus subject to change.

Although we cannot say what was in the mind of the founder when he conceived of the social council, we do know that in the December 1966 issue of *Trabajo y Unión*, the monthly publication of the Mondragón complex, he wrote under the heading of "Concept":

Leaving aside for the moment the characteristic of membership enjoyed by each member, we see that each one is a worker in the cooperative. . . . From the point of view of membership, we are all represented in the Governing Council, but if that were the only organ for representation, our participation in the firm would be very little, at least regarding the ordinary matters [of working life]. To avoid this passivity and to facilitate direct experience with many problems, what we call the Social Council came into existence.

Arizmendi then described the scope of the matters on which the social council had the right to advise the governing council and management. He included safety and health on the job, social security, systems of compensation, and social work activities or projects. On these matters the governing council and management were obligated to seek the advice of the social council before making decisions.

From the time of its creation, the social council has differed from the governing council in its system of representation. Whereas members of the governing council are elected at-large, members of the social council are elected from the departments or sections where they work. There are annual elections to the social council, and members serve staggered two-year terms. Reelection is permitted, but Arizmendi considered it unwise, wishing to encourage the maximum number of members to gain this experience.

The constitution provides that any member of the governing council holding a low-paying job (below an index of 1.6 in the system of compensation to be described shortly) is also automatically a member of the social council. Implicit in this policy is a recognition of the expectation (which proved correct) that members of the governing council would be drawn predominantly from management. The workplace basis of representation facilitated the election of more rank-and-file workers to the social council.

Initially, every ten workers (more or less) were to elect a representative to the social council. Arizmendi believed, however, that the council should never have more than fifty members, so that with growth the constituency of each representative was enlarged to maintain the size of the council within the prescribed limits.

To reinforce the concept of the social council as an advisory body, its chairperson was chosen by the governing council from its own members or from management. The social council was required to meet once a month and could be convened at other times by its chairperson.

Although the social council was not designed to function as a union, a review of the minutes of the social committee and of social council meetings for the first three years indicates a concentration on a number of issues typically pressed by unions in their relations with management.

Proposals were put forth for increases in pay and for reductions in the workday from ten to nine hours, without a reduction in pay. (In December 1959, the governing council agreed to the nine-hour day.) Discussions were held about additional paid holidays and about systems of incentive pay. What we call fringe benefits also figured prominently in discussions. In 1959, when Ulgor officially became a cooperative, its members were no longer covered by the Spanish social security system, so management and the social council had to plan to provide for the health care and retirement income of their members. In those early years, the social committee or council also devoted some attention, but much less than had been anticipated by Alfonso Gorroñogoitia, to such distinctly social questions as the functioning of the cafeteria, the sale of pharmaceutical products to members, safety on the job, and social work projects.

As in the case of the *jurado* of the Franco era, the independence of the social council was limited because management appointed its chairperson. Nor was the social council granted the right (conceded to the *jurado* in 1958) to negotiate with management. It was impossible to draw a sharp line between discussions and negotiations, however, so it remained to be seen to what extent the activities of the social council might evolve from discussion into what could realistically be called negotiation. Although the social council does not have the right to call a strike, it can, in the case of serious disagreements with the governing council, refer the issue to the general assembly, where the total membership of the cooperative makes the final decision.

RIGHTS OF WOMEN WORKERS

A second change in the constitution eliminated discrimination against married women workers. From the outset, single women had been hired without discrimination but had been required to leave the firm when they married. This policy reflected a traditional belief that the place of a married woman was in the home and also a concern with high unemployment. Men were considered the primary wage earners and thus deserved preference for continued employment. By the mid-1960s this policy had been abandoned. The women naturally demanded it, and in that decade the need for labor in the Mondragón cooperatives was growing so rapidly that economic necessity combined with egalitarian principles to eliminate overt sex discrimination.

VOTING RIGHTS

Another early change involved voting rights. From the outset, all full-time members of the general assembly had the vote, but Ulgor began with a system of weighted voting. Votes in the general assembly were linked with job classification, and managers and supervisors thus had more votes than the rank and file. Underlying this policy was the belief that those contributing more to the firm should have greater influence. In the early years this provision was abandoned. Because the number of workers lower on the pay scale far outnumbered those at higher levels, weighting the votes made no difference. The inequality of the original policy clashed with the cultural emphasis on egalitarianism, and the members recognized that it violated the traditional principles of cooperatives, which were well known in Mondragón.

FINANCIAL POLICIES

In the area of financial operations, one policy has remained inviolate from the outset. Neither members nor outsiders own stock in any Mondragón cooperative. Rather, a cooperative is financed by members' contributions and entry fees at levels specified by the governing council and approved by the members. It is as if members are lending money to the firm. Each member thereby has a capital account with the firm in his or her name. Members' shares of profits are put into their accounts each year, and interest on their capital accounts is paid to the members semi-annually in cash.

According to law, at least 10 percent of profits (or surplus over expenses) must be set aside each year for educational, cultural, or charitable purposes. In addition, a percentage determined by the governing council is put into the firm's reserve fund. Members share in the remaining profits in proportion to hours worked and pay level. In 1960, 10 percent of the firm's profits were distributed to members in cash. Twenty-five percent was distributed in 1961 and 30 percent for the years 1962–65; the remainder of the members' shares in profits went to their capital accounts. From 1966 to the present, all shares in profits have gone into members' capital accounts.

Those unfamiliar with accounting terminology might assume that a member's capital account consists of money deposited for the member in a savings bank or credit union (though in this case it could not be withdrawn until the member left the firm). On the contrary, capital accounts involve paper transactions between the members and the firm. Real money is, of course, involved because management is obligated to manage the cooperative with sufficient skill and prudence so that the firm can meet its financial obligations to members if they leave the firm or retire. In practice, however, the financial contributions of members are not segregated from other funds but are used for general business expenses.

We had earlier understood (Gutiérrez-Johnson and Whyte 1977) that no profits were ever distributed to members in cash. We had assumed that if the members had become accustomed to receiving profits in cash, it would have been impossible to persuade them later to forgo the immediate cash in favor of building up their capital. Now we see that, although the members never received *all* their share of profits in cash, they did, from 1960 to 1965, get some portion in cash.

It was a momentous decision to eliminate cash payments. If the decision had been to continue or increase such payments, it would have been impossible to build the strong and dynamic complex we see today. The decision was vigorously debated at the time, but we have no information on the process of decision making. The decision was made in 1966 during the first year after Ulgor joined other cooperatives to form the cooperative group ULARCO. Don José María and the leaders of Ulgor and of ULARCO must have persuaded a majority of the members that building up their capital was necessary to support the increased investments required to finance the rapid expansion of operations then in progress.

Those members leaving voluntarily before retirement age may withdraw all the funds in their capital accounts if, in the judgment of the governing council, their reasons for quitting are reasonable. In extreme cases—for example, if someone leaves to join a firm competing with the cooperative— the cooperative can retain 20 percent of the departing member's capital account. Those remaining to retirement receive all the funds in their accounts. This money is not equivalent to a pension, however, which is financed by deductions from members' pay.

From 1959 through 1969 the amounts allocated to the reserve fund fluctuated from 35 to 52.6 percent. Through the 1970s, the range was 10.8 to 29 percent. From the onset of the recession in 1980, ULARCO has been setting the amount at 50 percent to strengthen the reserve fund during this period when profits have been much lower. As some of the cooperatives experienced serious losses in the recession years around 1980, reserve funds became depleted and, in some cases, the members had to draw on their capital accounts to keep their firms operating. This led some of the cooperatives to increase substantially the percentage set aside in reserve funds when the cooperative again produced surpluses.

Wage and Salary Levels

Decisions governing pay in Mondragón were based on three principles: (1) solidarity with their fellow Basques, which meant that the starting rate for unskilled workers was fixed at approximately the prevailing rate for similar jobs in the private sector; (2) internal solidarity, which meant that the need to reward superior performance and service had to be balanced against the need to minimize status differences based on pay; and (3) openness with regard to pay, which meant that information on all salaries was available to all members.

In Mondragón, wages and salaries are called *anticipos* (money paid in anticipation of earnings). Originally the founders had established a three-to-one ratio between the lowest and the highest paid members. How did they decide on such an extraordinarily narrow margin? In the beginning they had no conception of how the firms would grow in size and complexity. They visualized a firm with a hundred or two hundred members in which the responsibilities and the complexity of the chief executive's job would not be far removed from those of the rank and file. As the cooperatives grew, compensation for higher management lagged far behind the salaries paid in Spanish private firms of comparable size and profitability. Leaders of the complex became worried as executives left to go to private firms, although we were told at the time of our first visit in 1975 that the turnover at the higher levels was still less than 10 percent a year. Furthermore, of those executives who left, few had gone through the Escuela Politécnica Profesional before beginning work in the complex. In other words, those who had been socialized into the cooperative way of life as youths found sufficient social and psychological satisfaction within the complex to outweigh the lure of higher pay elsewhere. Nevertheless, top managers in the large firms were becoming increasingly concerned as they recognized that the three-to-one ratio had been fixed when the founders thought of their enterprises as small and relatively simple. The growth of Ulgor, together with the creation of cooperative groups and supporting organizations, gave rise to a feeling of inequity, especially among those who had worked in the complex from its early years and had long held high managerial positions. It was not only the salary comparison with

Spanish private industry that hurt. They noted that nowhere else in the industrial world did such a narrow ratio prevail. Within management there was a growing belief that the three-to-one ratio was an anachronism that would eventually be abandoned. In that case, it would be unjust to maintain it until after those who had founded the complex and contributed so much to its growth had retired. Thus, the members eventually voted to allow executives whose responsibilities were especially high level and taxing and whose duties extended beyond the normal workday to receive a 50 percent premium over the base rate. In effect, the ratio is now 4.5 to 1.0—still extraordinarily small compared to firms elsewhere. In practice, those holding classifications above 3.0 are only a very small fraction of the executives in the total complex.

Some of the more technologically advanced firms in Mondragón have no members at the index level of 1.0 for unskilled workers, so that the actual pay ratio *within* the firm may still be substantially narrower than 4.5 to 1.0. When it is difficult or impossible to find an individual with skills and knowledge essential to the firm, a cooperative may hire someone from outside on a special contract and at a higher salary. The constitutions of the cooperatives prohibit them from having a work force that is more than 10 percent nonmembers, however, and few of the cooperatives even approach that figure.

For many years after the founding of Ulgor, pay rates were based on those prevailing in comparable private firms in the Basque country and were adjusted upward in response to the rising cost of living. Beginning in 1978, and responding to the worldwide recession, which had particularly severe effects in Spain, the Mondragón cooperatives went through the difficult process of changing the bases of the system of wage payments and capital contributions. We will tell that story in chapter 12.

GOVERNMENT RECOGNITION

Building a sound internal legal and financial structure was necessary, but not sufficient, to ensure the survival and growth of the Mondragón complex. After the members had decided on the governing structure, they still needed to gain legal recognition for what they had created. Arizmendi had already spent many hours searching the national legislation to find a niche into which to fit the organization. A 1942 law of cooperatives seemed an imperfect but possibly serviceable vehicle, although he and his associates were also concerned about legislation and administrative procedures of the Franco regime, which appeared to place all cooperatives under the guidance and potential control of the government agency Obra de Cooperación.

At this point, Arizmendi journeyed to Madrid to gain legal recognition. According to Arizmendi's biographer, the constitution of Ulgor contains

> concepts that are in flat contradiction with cooperative orthodoxy, but it was possible to save the situation through the collaboration of José Luis del Arco, advisor to the Obra de Cooperación in Madrid. José Luis del Arco yielded to the tenacious defense by Don José María of these socio-economic concepts. (Larrañaga 1981, 137)

José Luis del Arco had quite a different recollection of this meeting:

> In this first encounter I had with Padre Arizmendi, we were two people united in the belief in the economic and social possibilities of cooperatives, but I was the expert in legal aspects—I had devoted more than fifteen years to this task. Besides, I occupied in that period the key position, and Padre Arizmendi came to consult me on problems for which his reading of the text of the law did not provide any solution. I gave him the answers, because the letter of the law is one thing and the spirit of the law is that which can bring the letter of the law to life. In short, I did not surrender to Father Arizmendi, but I provided him with the solutions that he had not been able to find. (1982, 29)

Whatever happened in this encounter, the essential point is that del Arco's advice guided Arizmendi in devising the phraseology that would make the application for legal recognition acceptable to government officials. This encounter began a friendship between the two men that lasted until the death of Arizmendi, thus assuring the Mondragón cooperators of the support and guidance of a knowledgeable and influential figure on government policies for cooperative development.

EARLY EXPANSION

As Ulgor moved beyond its early struggles and entered a period of rapid and sustained growth, other groups of entrepreneurs organized worker cooperatives. These were stimulated both by the example of Ulgor's success and by the prospect of manufacturing products required by Ulgor. The worker cooperatives that followed Ulgor in the early years also arose out of the social and educational mobilization guided by Don José María.

Most closely related to Ulgor in their origins and subsequent history were Arrasate, Copreci, and Ederlan. A machine tool firm, Arrasate, founded in 1958, sold some of its output to Ulgor and went on to build its own national and international market. Copreci, founded in 1963, initially sold Ulgor nearly all of its output of valves, thermostats, and other components for home and commercial kitchens. By the 1980s, Copreci had increased production and marketing and was selling Ulgor only 20 percent of its output. Finally, Ederlan was formed in 1963 by combining the Ulgor foundry with Comet, a bankrupt private foundry.

The formative years in the history of the Mondragón complex were part of an educational process for the founders that began with their projects in community health, the building of the sports program, and particularly the campaign to establish the school. In their continuing dialogues with Don José María, the founders learned the importance of integrating into their social vision a high level of competence in technical and economic affairs. This linking of social, economic, and technological ideas was important not only in shaping the internal development of each cooperative but in beginning the development of a network of mutually supportive cooperatives.

In past studies of Mondragón, there has been a tendency to describe present structures and policies as if they were fully determined at the time the first Mondragón cooperative was created, implying that subsequent decisions were largely predetermined by the framework initially established. To be sure, some initial decisions were determinative in that, had they been made otherwise, the Mondragón movement would bear little resemblance to what we see today. The form of ownership and control is one such example: If control had been legally based on stock ownership—even if ownership had been limited to workers on a one-share-per-worker basis—it would have been almost impossible to maintain the character of the worker cooperatives in the long run. Rather, the initial financial policies included both fixed and variable elements. Ulgor was initially committed to establishing capital accounts and profit sharing for members, but until 1965 a fraction of profits was paid to members in cash. Allocation of all of the members' shares of profits to their capital accounts became a fixed principle years after the founding of Ulgor. Similarly, from its creation the cooperative was committed to setting aside in a reserve fund some proportion of the annual profits, but that proportion has varied substantially over the years in response to what the leaders and members have learned from experience. Finally, although the first social council was created in the very early years, the definition of its role was somewhat ambiguous from the outset, and, as we shall see later, leaders and members have frequently needed to rethink and redefine the nature of this important organizational element.

5 Supporting Organizations and Diversification

The early days of Ulgor were fraught with problems. The oil-burning heater then in production was a primitive model by later standards, but it nevertheless initially presented great difficulties for the inexperienced entrepreneurs. The corrosion of metal components was a major technical problem, and when they had overcome this difficulty, a fire broke out in the plant that inflicted fatal burns on one of the ten members at work. Members worked ten to twelve hours a day six days a week, without any thought of overtime pay. It was only as Ulgor gained strength and financial stability that it was possible to reduce progressively the hours worked—now 42.5 a week.

THE COOPERATIVE BANK

Before they had fully resolved their initial technical and marketing problems, Don José María began talking to Ulgor's leaders about creating a cooperative bank. His studies had convinced him that a credit union or cooperative bank was indispensable to any successful worker cooperative movement. He believed that a cooperative could not raise equity capital by attracting private investors, that private banks would be reluctant to make loans to worker cooperatives, and that a worker cooperative would lose its independence if it was indebted to a private bank. Through intensive study of national banking legislation, Arizmendi discovered an important opportunity that had never been exploited by the private banks. A program of *ahorro obrero* (savings for blue-collar workers) empowered a bank to pay .5 percent above the interest rates on other savings accounts.

This gave the cooperative bank an important advantage in attracting savings.

As Alfonso Gorroñogoitia later wrote (de Arroiabe 1984):

> The first suggestion to create a bank in the form of a cooperative he made to us in a sudden visit when we were having a meeting of the management council of Ulgor. Our initial reaction was one of annoyance, and we literally sent Don José María packing. . . . we thought that it was a visionary idea, that it did not have any relation to our knowledge, our background or mentality, which was far from the world of finance and banking and that it seemed to us just a fantasy and a bad one because of our total lack of knowledge of the field. (page 5)

Don José María did not allow this rejection to stand in his way:

> He continued patiently and alone preparing the constitution and bylaws. From time to time, smiling and almost timidly, he would come back and talk with us and insist on the necessity of this bank. I suppose that he thought, undoubtedly correctly as always in the case of his strategic conceptions, that he should give little attention to these ingenuous youths and he would have to get around this wall of incomprehension, maneuvering on his own and finding other routes to travel. (page 5)

We wondered how Don José María finally overcame the resistance of his young associates. In conversation with Simon Mz. de Arroiabe, who was writing a history of the bank, we learned that the founder did not persuade his associates. Instead, he presented them with a *fait accompli*. In consultation with José Luis del Arco, who had helped in the legalization of Ulgor, he paved the way for the official establishment of the bank, the Caja Laboral Popular. The first step required that the government be presented with the minutes of a preorganization meeting (*reunión preconstituyente*). The document described a meeting on March 15, 1959, at which the members approved a constitution and bylaws and designated a provisional governing council and audit committee. The document carried the signatures of Alfonso Gorroñogoitia and José María Ormaechea.

As Arroiabe explained to us in 1983, this was "the meeting that never took place." Furthermore, without their knowledge, Don José María had forged the signatures of Gorroñogoitia and Ormaechea.

We asked Arroiabe, "Weren't they angry when they discovered what Don José María had done without their permission?"

"They were a bit upset momentarily," he answered, "but they didn't think that the Caja would ever amount to anything, so it was not worth bothering about."

Before the cooperative bank was officially chartered, Arizmendi worked out an arrangement to handle the paperwork in two offices, one in the school, the other in the offices of Acción Católica, and to deposit the money with the Savings Bank of Guipúzcoa. In 1959, just three years after the founding of Ulgor, the Caja Laboral Popular secured charters in two provinces, Guipúzcoa and Alava. Arizmendi took this precaution so that they could continue to operate throughout the Basque country even if the authorities in one province decided to cancel the charter. There was no legal challenge in either province, but the strategy illustrates the care he took in preparing for all eventualities.

Don José María had hoped to persuade Gorroñogoitia or Ormaechea to take charge of the Caja, but the best he could do was persuade them to accept its existence when it was officially established on September 24, 1959. Don José María next turned to José Ayala to lead the new organization. Ayala had been one of the original disciples of Don José María and had been involved with him in various religious, athletic, and cultural activities. In 1943 he had become the first president of the youth sports club of Mondragón. As Arroiabe explained, in addition to his dedication to the founder's causes, Ayala dressed well and was married to a woman from a well-to-do local family, so that he reflected the social position of a banker and thus provided reassurance to depositors (see also de Arroiabe 1984, 2–4).

We were unable to interview Ayala, who died in 1982, but his wife told of their decision to follow Don José María into the Caja project:

> José had an office job with Roneo [a local private company]. To be employed in the office was to have a good position, one of the most sought after and secure. One was thus within the class of distinguished citizens, those with privileges, and those able to live well.
>
> But Don José María would harangue us about being satisfied with such a secure sinecure. Still, I must tell you sincerely that the theories of Don José María, in the early period, were not very clear, and I even have to call them ambiguous and ill defined. He was guiding us with good sermons in which he was mixing consumers cooperatives and credit unions and I don't know what other things. What is clear is that we were among those committed to the apostolic work and we cast our lot in this way more for the man, Don José María, than for his ideas. (Larrañaga 1981, 8–9)

Ayala launched the Caja loyally, remained in leadership positions for many years, and later was the manager of Lagun-Aro, the social security organization of the complex, until his death. Don José María appreciated the services of Ayala but felt that men with more entrepreneurial vision and skills needed to be in leadership positions. In 1961, he persuaded Ormaechea, then the head of manufacturing for Ulgor, to become chief executive officer of the Caja—at first on a part-time basis. A year later, Ormaechea left Ulgor to commit himself to the Caja full time. In the same period (May 1961), Don José María persuaded Alfonso Gorroñogoitia to serve as chairman of the Governing Council of the Caja. A month later Luis Usatorre and Jesús Larrañaga joined the council. Now the Caja had four of the five founders of Ulgor in key leadership positions. (The fifth founder, Ortubay, had left Mondragón to found a private business in Vitoria.)

This infusion of dynamic leadership by the founders of Ulgor marked a major shift in commitment toward the Caja and led to accelerating growth. It also contributed to making the Caja Laboral Popular one of the leading banking institutions of Spain.

At this time, credit unions were a familiar form of organization in the Basque country and elsewhere. Traditionally, credit unions have served the limited purposes of attracting personal savings and providing individual loans for consumer purchases. The main purpose of the Caja was to finance the creation and expansion of worker cooperatives and other cooperative organizations.

The Caja Laboral Popular was the first second-level cooperative of the Mondragón movement. Linking and supporting other organizations, it was founded jointly by the Ulgor, Arrasate, and Funcor worker cooperatives and by San José (a consumer cooperative not previously linked with worker cooperatives).

SOCIAL SECURITY

The Caja began its legal existence with two divisions: savings and social security. Because members of worker cooperatives were not considered employees under Spanish law, the national social security system did not cover them. The cooperatives therefore had to establish a program to provide for the health and retirement needs of their members. Payroll deductions supplied most of the funds for what became Lagun-Aro (the name comes from the Basque words for a protective program).

In 1967 Lagun-Aro became an independent cooperative with its own building and governing council. Membership on the council is drawn from the cooperatives, whose payroll deductions cover the social security needs of their members.

Lagun-Aro has grown rapidly as a result of the expansion of the base cooperatives to which it is linked. By the end of 1984, Lagun-Aro was linked with 140 cooperatives, and it was serving 18,266 members, 47,465 including dependents.

In recent years, Lagun-Aro has contracted out pension coverage of its members with the state agency Mutualidad de Autonomos. For many years Lagun-Aro maintained a modern and highly efficient clinic for its members and their families. On a fee basis, the clinic also served other citizens of Mondragón, thus extending its health care to the wider community. On January 1, 1987, the Basque regional government took over the financing and management of the clinic, which it has used as a model for clinics in other towns of similar size in the region.

The Mondragón cooperators have turned their exclusion from the national security system to an advantage, both financially and with respect to the quality of service they offer. As the chairman of the Governing Council of the Caja Laboral Popular, Alfonso Gorroñogoitia, told us, in 1983 the national social security system required each private firm to pay 420,000 pesetas (about $2,800) per worker per year. Lagun-Aro was providing superior coverage for only 240,000 pesetas ($1,600). According to Gorroñogoitia, many private firms do not pay for this coverage, and the government has not dared to intervene in cases where forcing payment could push a firm into bankruptcy. Nonetheless, the cooperatives have a substantial cost advantage over private firms that do pay their social security taxes.

In recent years, with the rapidly growing interest in the reform and redesign of work, doctors of industrial medicine at Lagun-Aro have been increasingly consulted on projects involving the development of new technologies or new ways of working.

THE STUDENT COOPERATIVE

As the initial two-year program of the Escuela Politécnica expanded into higher grades and enrolled rapidly increasing numbers of students, it became apparent that, unless other sources of revenue could be found, the tuition would have to be increased so much that many able and ambitious children of poor families would be unable to continue their education. Because it was against the principles of the cooperatives to restrict their benefits to those families able to pay, Don José María guided the members toward another social invention: Alecop, a worker cooperative in which most of the members were students of the Escuela Politécnica. Previously the League of Education and Culture had been helping students earn money for their education by arranging part-time jobs in the form of "contracts for apprenticeship" with private firms. Alecop brought this form of earning and learning through working into the cooperative complex itself.

From its creation in 1966, Alecop has had two shifts each working day. Students work four hours a day in the plant and attend classes for another four hours, which means that the school must maintain two equivalent instructional programs. Alecop started by producing components on order for other Mondragón cooperatives. While continuing this business, it has attracted increasing numbers of contracts from private firms. Emerging out of the Escuela Politécnica, Alecop has capitalized on its relationship to the school by developing a line of instruments and equipment for use in science and engineering classes in high schools and universities.

In designing Alecop, the leaders had to balance their desire to involve the student members in governance with a need to safeguard the economic strength of the firm by representing the interests, experience, and maturity of the small full-time staff of managers and technical specialists. The interests of the other cooperative firms that were contracting some of their work out to Alecop also had to be considered. A tripartite form of representation was therefore established. One-third of the members of the governing council is elected by the permanent staff, one-third by the student members, and another one-third by the contracting cooperatives. In 1984 Alecop provided employment, earnings for tuition and living expenses, and experience in work and in the cooperative processes of governance to more than 450 student members.

SERVICES AND AGRICULTURE

In the early years of Ulgor, the cooperative pioneers expected to limit their activities exclusively to industry. With the success of Ulgor, however, the complex attracted attention in surrounding rural areas. The younger brother of Don José María, who had taken over the family farm in Markina, came with some friends to ask Don José María to help them start a farmers' cooperative to market milk and timber and wood products from their farms. In general, agricultural cooperatives are controlled by the farmers who are members. Workers who operate a store to sell the necessary inputs and market the farm products are treated simply as employees. Believing that this practice violated the fundamental principles of his philosophy of cooperatives, Don José María persuaded the farmers to establish a hybrid cooperative in which the workers in the store would have equal membership rights with the farmers. Thus the first Mondragón agricultural cooperative, Lana, was established with offices in Markina— and in other locations, as the organization expanded. Lana began in 1961 with twenty-five farmers and one store worker as members. By 1982, its membership included 300 farmers and 120 workers who were involved in the sales, distribution, and processing of its products.

Management worked out a formula for distributing income to the two groups of members whereby the farmers would be paid the market price of the materials they brought to the cooperative and the workers would be paid an amount based on the value added in transforming and marketing the raw materials. We will return to Lana in chapter 16 when we discuss the growing importance of agriculture and services in the cooperative complex.

At the time the Mondragón complex was developing, there were several consumer cooperatives in the Basque provinces and the founders of the movement did not intend to create them. By the late 1960s, however, nine of these cooperatives were encountering increasing financial and organizational difficulties. Jointly, they appealed to the Caja Laboral Popular to reorganize them and integrate them into the cooperative complex. At the time, no one within the Caja had any experience with consumer cooperatives, so management established a study team to consider extending the scope of the Mondragón complex into this field. In addition to examining the literature, members of the study team visited successful consumer cooperatives in France and Switzerland.

At the time, Spanish law prohibited cooperatives from selling to non-members. The study team concluded that it would be impossible to achieve the volume of sales necessary to support growth if they remained within the letter of the law. They therefore decided to open membership in Eroski, the new consumer-worker cooperative, to anyone who paid a trifling amount. This meant that a new customer could sign up at the cash register by paying several pesetas extra with the bill. To simplify the paperwork in serving its expanding volume of members, Eroski from the outset eliminated dividends on purchases. Members were attracted by Eroski's moderate prices and its program of consumer information and cultural activities. In recent years, Eroski has been publishing a monthly consumer magazine with information on product quality, nutritional standards, and health care. This free publication rivals America's *Consumer Reports*.

Among the cultural activities sponsored by Eroski are vacation trips and vacation housing rentals, which are available to members at moderate prices. Eroski also conducts an extensive public consumer education program.

In the conventional consumer cooperative, membership is limited to consumers, and each member has one vote for the board of directors. Eroski from its beginning has been a hybrid organization with two categories of membership, one for workers and one for consumers. To balance the interests of the two groups, the governing council consists of equal numbers of elected consumers and workers. According to the Eroski constitution, the chairman of the governing council must always be a consumer.

In the early years of Eroski, the leaders of the cooperative complex saw it as a relatively unimportant sideline, but, especially in recent years, it has grown explosively and has gained importance both because of its volume of business and because it has accelerated the growth of the complex. We will address this topic again in chapter 16.

HOUSING AND CONSTRUCTION

The growth of the cooperative complex increased migration into Mondragón and surrounding areas from other Basque provinces and even from outside the Basque country. As the population of the city of Mondragón nearly tripled between 1940 and 1970, the leaders of the movement became concerned about providing adequate housing for workers and their families in a town surrounded by hills and mountains. This problem led to the formation of cooperative housing projects and the concomitant creation and expansion of construction cooperatives. In 1982, five construction cooperatives employed 1,511 members, and by 1984, the complex had created seventeen housing cooperatives (mainly in high-rise apartments).

Throughout the period of expansion, Mondragón's leaders did not simply apply the principles of the Rochdale pioneers. They created a number of social inventions, from the organizational structure of their worker cooperatives, to the hybrid forms of agricultural and service cooperatives and Alecop, to the design of second-level cooperatives that linked the growing network of mutually supporting organizations. Their vision was not limited to the building of individual cooperatives. Rather, they were dedicated to developing a cooperative way of living and working. It was this vision that guided them to discover novel ways of solving the practical problems of organizational development.

6   Cooperative Groups

By the early 1960s, Ulgor had overcome its initial technical and marketing problems and was well on its way to becoming one of the hundred largest industrial companies in Spain (Gorroño 1975, 155). The founders had not anticipated the extent and pace of this growth. Their ideal had been to create small organizations in which all members would know one another, thus facilitating interpersonal and organizational adjustments. Success undermined this vision.

When a private company grows with the dynamism of Ulgor, management tends to respond by establishing a divisional organization or subsidiary companies in which all units are under the firm control of top management. This arrangement has the advantage of concentrating financial resources, achieving economies of scale in production and marketing, and providing support for projects in strategic planning and research and development. It has the now-recognized disadvantages of a large, unwieldy bureaucracy, which is likely to discourage flexibility, initiative, and creativity at lower levels and to alienate workers from managers.

The social vision of the leaders of Mondragón ruled out this model of growth. Their objective was to achieve the advantages of growth without succumbing to bureaucratic rigidities.

With the continuing guidance of Arizmendi and by studying their own experiences and the growth problems of other cooperative and noncooperative firms, the founders of the Mondragón complex devised a set of principles designed to balance growth with organizational autonomy. To expand employment and at the same time limit the growth of existing organizations, they established a policy that whenever any line of production reached the point where its manufacturing and marketing were so efficient that it could become an independent organization, it was to be separated from its original firm. This policy promoted growth through

58

a complementarity of interests. That is, in the beginning, new firms were created to meet the needs of Ulgor for component parts in manufacturing or for machines used in its plant. The new firms had an initially assured market with Ulgor but were free to sell their products wherever they could find buyers.

The leaders were applying a policy that on a national scale is called import substitution. One way for a nation to expand its industrial production and develop its human resources is to manufacture products that previously have been imported. The same logic applies to city economies (Jacobs 1984). The economy of a city or area does not grow simply by adding unrelated manufacturing and commercial organizations. Jacobs argues that the base for the healthiest and most sustainable growth is the development of increasing numbers of firms that buy from and sell to one another as they create a labor market with increasingly skilled workers and technical and professional people.

In planning spin-off firms, the leaders of Mondragón had to consider how to link them without unduly limiting the autonomy of the individual firms. They had to devise a process for creating a new organization from a department of another firm. They also had to balance the interests of members of the new firm with those of the members remaining in the parent company. The planners recognized that, even with the experience achieved within the department of the parent firm, the costs of developing its own manufacturing and marketing organizations would probably make the new firm initially less profitable than the parent firm. On the one hand, it seemed inequitable to expect members to sacrifice profits when they left a firm to form a new one. On the other hand, if the profits of the parent company and the new firms were pooled and allocated to all members in the group based simply on hours worked and their level of compensation, members of the original firm might well feel that they were being forced to subsidize the new firms. The leaders also recognized that forming a group of firms would facilitate planning for future growth. A question remained, however: How should this planning be carried out?

FOUNDING ULARCO

It was Don José María who worked out the basic design for the organization of the first cooperative group, ULARCO, and guided the members in studying and implementing its creation. (To distinguish the names of individual cooperatives from those of cooperative groups, the latter are printed in small capital letters.) The name ULARCO was taken from the first two letters of the first three cooperatives at Mondragón: Ulgor, Arrasate, and Copreci. Arrasate had emerged to manufacture machine tools for Ulgor, and Copreci had been created to manufacture components for Ulgor's gas stoves and heaters. The fourth component of the original group, Ederlan, was formed when a privately owned foundry was taken over and combined with the foundry at Ulgor. Fagor Electrotécnica, which produced electronic components and equipment, was created out of elements of the first three cooperatives and formed the fifth firm in the group.

GOVERNANCE STRUCTURE

Establishing a general management for the cooperative group required that a new structure be devised with several organizational levels. Membership would be drawn from the five cooperatives, but procedures also had to be established so that individual members could vote directly on any proposal to change working conditions.

The structure of the cooperative group is similar to that of individual cooperatives, but procedures for selecting individuals to fill the various positions necessarily differ. The General Assembly of ULARCO is made up of all members of the governing councils of the constituent cooperatives, all managers and members of the management councils of those units, and all members of their audit committees. The general assembly is responsible for approving all accounts and budgets, for making decisions on the admission and expulsion of individual cooperatives, and for framing general policies.

The Governing Council of ULARCO (*consejo rector*) originally consisted of three members from each cooperative. As new cooperatives were created within ULARCO, the representation from each dropped to two and then to one.

The General Management (*dirección general*) of ULARCO, whose members are chosen by the Governing Council of ULARCO, is responsible for planning and coordination, for reviewing and recommending annual and long-range plans for each constituent cooperative, and for coordinating commercial policies. It is responsible for studying and establishing common systems of administration and administrative structures, for acquiring manufacturing licenses, for maintaining relations with outside organizations, and for overseeing the creation of new firms and new services. It provides personnel, legal, accounting, and some commercial services to the constituent organizations. The centralization of personnel functions facilitates the transfer of members from one cooperative to another within ULARCO. Thus, when one cooperative must curtail its production, some of its workers can be transferred temporarily or permanently to a cooperative that needs additional workers. This has proved to be an important means of stabilizing employment.

The Central Social Council (earlier called the Permanent Commission) was first made up of two representatives from the social councils of each cooperative firm; now each firm has a single representative. The Central Social Council (CSC) is responsible for studying and evaluating management's plans. This means that management is responsible for keeping the CSC informed and for consulting with its leaders on major plans. The CSC then reports back to the social councils of the constituent cooperatives.

POOLING PROFITS AND LOSSES

Since at least 1970, all members of the constituent cooperatives of ULARCO have been compensated on the basis of the pooling of profits and losses of all the firms in the group. This arrangement was worked out in stages. Because it had been formed from other units at the time ULARCO was created, Fagor Electrotécnica agreed to pool 90 percent of its profits for the first year (1966), with the understanding that its contribution would decrease by 10 percent in each of the following years. Copreci, Arrasate, and Ederlan began by pooling 20 percent of their profits, with a commitment to increase their contributions by 10 percent in each of the following years. Ulgor pooled 100 percent of its profits from the outset. In 1970 a policy was ratified that required all the cooperatives of ULARCO to pool 100 percent of their profits, although a report prepared for the Governing Council of Ulgor (May 31, 1985) indicates that this policy was actually implemented in 1968. The sequence of decisions from 1966 to 1970 reflects the complicated process of adjustment to the new organizational structures and policies and the need throughout the discussions and negotiations to balance the interests of the individual cooperatives with those of the emerging cooperative group. One hundred percent pooling was clearly the ideal arrangement for ULARCO. Interestingly, this objective was achieved around the time when the contributions of Copreci, Arrasate, and Ederlan matched the decreasing contributions of Fagor

Electrotécnica and long before the ascending contributions of the three cooperatives would have reached 100 percent.

The ULARCO cooperative group was an unprecedented form of organizational development. Years later, stimulated by the Caja, most of the Mondragón cooperatives had joined to form such groups.

7 Applied Industrial Research

According to conventional wisdom, even if worker cooperatives can overcome the problems of democratic management and save or borrow the funds necessary to expand or survive during a recession, they are doomed to fail in the long run because they are small and lack the capacity for research and development. Even if they start with up-to-date technology, they remain competitive only until private firms modernize their technology and products. The solution in Mondragón was to create an applied industrial research cooperative that would support and be supported by the industrial cooperatives.

Ikerlan emerged out of the Escuela Politécnica Profesional under the leadership of Manuel Quevedo, an instructor in charge of shop operations. In 1965, Quevedo and others began discussing the possibility of conducting industrial research, and some activity was already under way in 1966. Initially, the purpose of the research was to observe the technology and production practices of the cooperatives so as to strengthen the teaching program in the school. After several months, however, Quevedo expanded his vision to include research that would contribute to increasing the efficiency in the cooperatives. The research department was founded with this purpose in 1968, and Quevedo and two of his associates were relieved of teaching responsibilities.

In 1968, six faculty members (including Quevedo) secured a leave of absence to spend six months at French universities learning about industrial research. They arrived in Paris just when the universities were temporarily paralyzed by the student uprisings. They found out, however, what was going on in the laboratories, continued to read, and later made other study trips abroad. Their goal was to learn as much as they could about research abroad and how some of the leading research institutions were organized and managed.

At about the same time, Quevedo proposed that the school establish an automation laboratory. When the director of the school, Javier Retegui, told him that the school had no funds for this purpose, Quevedo volunteered to do extra teaching in the adult education program and to contribute those earnings to the school. In 1972 the automation laboratory took on its first contract work with the industrial cooperatives.

In 1974 Don José María surprised even his close associates in the school by deciding that Mondragón was ready to launch a more ambitious industrial research program. Initially, capital investment of about 112 million pesetas ($2 million) was used to construct a new building with offices, laboratories, and a machine shop. The investment was a very heavy commitment for the cooperative complex. One of the Ulgor pioneers, Jesús Larrañaga, commented, "We opposed this idea as we did other ideas when Don José María first presented them to us, but he always succeeded in convincing us." The 1974 meeting to discuss Don José María's proposal brought together the leaders of the Caja and of those cooperatives most likely to benefit from industrial research. The Caja and a number of worker cooperatives promised support, and the proposal was accepted. Ikerlan moved into its new building early in 1977.

THE INFLUENCE OF DON JOSÉ MARÍA

Don José María's closest associates credit him with giving Ikerlan its general orientation—a recognition of the need for Mondragón to escape from dependency on private capital and on technology produced elsewhere. His vision of the future was not limited to the social and economic. He read voraciously on a wide range of topics and had a strong interest in the latest developments in industrial technology. The director of the school, Retegui, said that on several occasions Don José María had told him and his associates about some new technology or manufacturing process they had never heard of, whereupon Quevedo would look for sources of information on the topic and find that Don José María had pointed them in an important direction.

Apparently, Don José María and Retegui jointly made the decision to appoint Quevedo as the head of Ikerlan, but, in a sense, the decision made itself. Having created the automation laboratory in the school, Quevedo became the logical person to lead the new organization.

FINANCING IKERLAN AND SERVING
THE COMMUNITY

Initially, Ikerlan was supported entirely by the Mondragón cooperatives, but in 1982 the Basque government began contributing half of Ikerlan's annual budget. In 1984, 38 percent was paid by firms with contracts for projects. Most of these were cooperatives, but government support opened the door to private firms, and by 1984 two corporations had project contracts. Twelve percent of the budget came from annual contributions based (in 1983) on fees of 2,600 pesetas ($17.50) per member of any supporting organization.

Ikerlan aims to keep the fee as low as possible to broaden organizational membership. Member cooperatives and private firms receive a monthly bulletin reporting on new technologies and manufacturing methods being developed within Ikerlan or elsewhere. Furthermore, when any staff member thinks of a possible application to the work of a supporting organization, he or she informs its leaders. In this way member firms are assured of being fully informed about the latest developments.

Cooperatives or private firms that are not members of Ikerlan are required to pay 50 percent more than member organizations for the same contract. For an additional 50 percent, private firms may have exclusive rights to the results of a project for a two-year period. If the firm wishes to maintain this proprietary right forever, Ikerlan charges a 100 percent premium.

Staff sometimes contract to work on a problem that they are not at all sure they can solve. If they are unable to solve it, Ikerlan shares the expense with the client firm on a fifty-fifty basis. The half charged to Ikerlan is considered part of its learning process. The arrangement encourages firms to spend on high-risk research.

The government contribution is not a grant to Ikerlan's general fund. It is used to award competitive fellowships to advanced students of engineering, physics, and energy-related specialties. Each year a public announcement is made of the fellowships available at Ikerlan and at two other research institutes. Fellows selected by Ikerlan work as interns for eighteen months or two years, giving them the basis for their doctoral theses. As projects and money become available, some of the fellows are invited to become full-time staff members.

Ikerlan's financial arrangements reflect the original vision of Mondragón's founders that the cooperatives should serve both their members and the broader Basque community. In this spirit, Ikerlan offers private companies membership and contract rights on the same basis as the cooperatives. Even before the Basque regional government came into existence, Quevedo proposed to leaders of two other Basque institutes that they jointly attempt to enlist government support for their organizations. As a result of their efforts, they persuaded government officials that a fellowship program was essential if the Basque country was to expand its capacity to pursue applied industrial research.

The Basque government has been providing 100 to 120 fellowships annually for advanced study abroad. Workers at Ikerlan are eligible for fellowships to study for a doctorate at the University of Toulouse in France or may pursue advanced studies elsewhere.

At the time of our 1983 visit, we witnessed another example of Ikerlan's mission to the Basque country. An exhibition was being prepared for viewing and demonstration of robots developed at Ikerlan as well as elsewhere. Invitations to the exhibition were sent to supporting organizations and also to other firms for which robotization might be relevant.

GOVERNANCE AND WORK ORGANIZATION

As a second-level cooperative, Ikerlan has had to balance the interests of its own staff with those of the supporting organizations. Staff members make up about 40 percent of its eighty-five-person general assembly, and, based on one vote for every three hundred employees, supporting cooperatives now represent 30 percent. The other second-level cooperatives (the school and the Caja) are also represented by one vote for every three hundred employees, but with the provision that their representatives not comprise more than 30 percent of the general assembly. The twelve-person Governing Council of Ikerlan includes four Ikerlan workers, six representatives of industrial cooperatives, and two representatives of the second-level cooperatives. Elections take place every two years, and representatives are elected for four-year terms.

By the end of 1984, Ikerlan had a staff of ninety: fifty-four permanent staff; thirteen fellows; and nineteen students and four professors from the Escuela Politécnica who worked half time. There were four research departments: microelectronics, mechanics, computer science, and robotics.

Ikerlan has a highly decentralized structure. Instead of having a program director who is responsible for several projects and assistants who work on them, each full-time member of Ikerlan has full responsibility for two projects.

On projects for a cooperative or private firm, the policy is to establish a joint team made up of one or more members of the client firm and several people from Ikerlan. This design ensures that there is a smooth flow of information back and forth between the cooperative and the research organization and thus facilitates the development and introduction of new technology. Quevedo reported that projects develop more efficiently when the client organization has its own industrial research staff. Ideally, research to improve current manufacturing methods is done by the cooperatives, and Ikerlan concentrates on more advanced technologies.

It is the policy of Ikerlan to divide its projects evenly between those for which there are specific contracts and those that staff have developed to meet future needs and interests. A member of Ikerlan manages one project of each kind.

In just a few years, Ikerlan has gained a reputation as one of the leading industrial research institutes in Spain and has won increasing international respect. How has this come about?

Here again we see the seminal contributions of Don José María and the school he founded. The conventional strategy for creating an industrial research organization is to recruit a chief executive officer with an advanced degree. As is typical in Mondragón, the leaders opted instead to build from within, without concern for social prestige or educational qualifications. It did not trouble them that Quevedo lacked high-level academic credentials. They realized that he had risen to the challenge of each new task, building a team to work with him, and they expected him to continue to grow with increasing responsibilities.

While concentrating on the tasks at hand, Quevedo and his team members have developed Ikerlan mindful of their vision of the future. This is illustrated particularly in the way they secured financial support from the Basque government, a pursuit they began many months before the government came into being. Furthermore, by forming a coalition with two other research institutes, they ensured that Ikerlan would not only serve Mondragón but contribute to the socioeconomic and industrial development of the entire Basque country. Finally, basic decisions in Ikerlan were not guided simply by the opportunities of the moment. On the basis of their study of research institutes elsewhere and continuing analysis of their own experience, Ikerlan's leaders crafted a systematic strategy of organizational development.

8 The Central Role of the
Cooperative Bank

When the Caja Laboral Popular began operating in 1960, it employed two people. Within the next quarter-century, it had grown to become one of the most profitable savings institutions in Spain and was playing a central role in strengthening the Mondragón complex. The relationship between the Caja and individual cooperatives is now so strong that the bank determines their norms and guides their development.

ORGANIZATION AND CONTROL OF THE CAJA

The General Assembly of the Caja is structured so as to represent the interests of the cooperatives it serves, as well as those of its own worker-owners, who are outnumbered two to one. Only workers in the Caja, however, elect representatives to its social council.

The governing council has twelve members, eight representing the cooperatives and four representing workers in the Caja. The eight tend to be top-management people from the most important cooperatives. According to its chairman, Alfonso Gorroñogoitia, given their numbers and prestige as top industrial leaders of the complex, they usually dominate the council. He acknowledged that the Caja is thus in the very unorthodox and supposedly unsound position of being controlled by its principal borrowers. If a private bank were so controlled, one might expect the principal borrowers to look after their own interests instead of those of the bank, thus resulting in decapitalization. As we shall see, however, the bank has substantial powers to intervene in the affairs of its borrowers, thereby protecting its own long-term economic viability. In fact, Gorroñogoitia refers to the governing and management structures of the Caja as "embodying an Arabesque of equilibria of powers." As we examine its

Entrepreneurial Division, we will see how the bank manages to balance these powers.

Until shortly before 1983, Gorroñogoitia was chairman of the governing councils of Ulgor, ULARCO, and the Caja Laboral Popular. Although this position reflected the enormous prestige he enjoyed, Gorroñogoitia thought he had an unsound concentration of leadership responsibilities. He had managed to maneuver himself out of the chairmanship of the board of Ulgor and told us that he was hoping to be relieved of the chairmanship of either the Caja or ULARCO in the coming months. Another of the five Ulgor pioneers, José María Ormaechea, had been general manager and chief executive officer of the Caja for many years.

CONTRACT OF ASSOCIATION

The contract of association between the Caja and individual cooperatives governs not only the relations between the contracting parties but also major internal policies and structures of the associated cooperatives. For our purposes, it is the general nature of the contractual relationship rather than detailed provisions that are important. Rather than following the contractual relationship over the years, we shall simply summarize the provisions prevailing in the 1980s.

The democratic rights of the members of individual cooperatives must be exercised within the norms and structures specified by the contract of association. In other words, workers who want to form a cooperative and contract with the bank are not free to organize in any form they wish. It is this normative control lodged with the Caja that makes Mondragón a complex whose cooperatives are tightly bound together rather than a loose association.

The contract requires each member cooperative to make an initial contribution to the bank's capital and to conduct all its banking with the Caja. The Caja has the right to perform an audit on member cooperatives once every four years. (During the recession of the 1980s, the Caja performed such audits every other year.) The audit covers what the Caja calls "social and entrepreneurial aspects" as well as matters that are strictly financial. There is no charge for the audit.

A cooperative must not discriminate in employment on the basis of sex or political or religious beliefs. Anyone willing to assume the work and financial responsibilities of a member is free to join, but selection, of course, is based on a cooperative's organizational needs. In principle, all workers must become members after a probationary period. In practice, as discussed earlier, nonmembers may be employed, but they must not exceed 10 percent of the total membership.

Each cooperative must establish a system of democratic governance on the basis of one member one vote and in its constitution and bylaws must provide for the institutional structures first created by Ulgor.

To join a cooperative, a member must make a capital contribution and pay an entry fee. The contribution, which may be paid through payroll deductions, cannot be less than 80 percent or more than 120 percent of what the Caja requires from its own members at the time they join. The entry fee cannot be more than 25 percent of the obligatory contribution.

The contract also outlines the policies to be followed in allocating income to social work projects, the reserve fund, and members' shares of profits. The latter must be deposited in members' capital accounts and not distributed in cash. Clearly, even the policy for paying interest is weighted to favor the accumulation of capital over personal income. Interest to members' capital accounts is credited to those accounts semi-annually at the prevailing rate established by the Bank of Spain, plus an additional 3 percent—if authorized by the cooperative's governing council. Only 6 percent may be paid to members in cash, however, regardless of the amount of interest allocated to them. (In some years Spain's prevailing interest rate has been more than twice as high as this 6 percent figure.)

The objective of each member cooperative is to create jobs, within the limits of its financial capacity. Furthermore, the contract states that lack of capital shall not limit the entry of new members who might otherwise be employable. The cooperative should expand employment if it can reach the market profitably by undertaking additional production, even if new investments are required to do so. In effect, expansion should be made possible either by assessing its members for additional capital or by borrowing from the Caja. The policy also states that the cooperative should cover its investments principally from its own resources. To make the principle more concrete, the contract states that the cooperative should maintain an "independence ratio" of two or more, meaning that its own capital should be at least twice as much as its borrowed capital. Although it would be difficult, if not impossible, for the Caja to force a cooperative to invest simply to create additional jobs, this policy expresses an important commitment of the Mondragón complex.

In compensation policy, the cooperative agrees to adhere to a maximum ratio of three to one between the top salary and the rate for unskilled labor, although there is the possibility of extending the range to 4.5 for a few who have very special responsibilities and talents. Nonmembers may be hired on contract and paid more when they are essential to the firm.

The cooperative agrees to establish its pay scale at between 90 and 110 percent of the prevailing rate in the Caja. The rate may drop below 90 percent if the cooperative is experiencing financial losses. In setting the compensation rates for particular jobs, the cooperative agrees to apply the methods in the job evaluation manual prepared by the Caja.

Our first impression was that the Caja played such a central role in the Mondragón complex because the services it performed for member co-operatives gave it substantial influence over them. Clearly, the technical assistance, credit, and other services the bank offers provide the base for its power and influence. In addition, because of the contract of association, the Caja has strong legal controls over the cooperatives. The contract spells out in detail the norms and processes to be followed regarding not only the internal structures and processes of the member cooperatives but also the obligation to build a strong capital base and to extend employment. When we examine the experience of the Caja and the member firms in coping with the recession of the early 1980s we shall see the importance the Caja places on building a strong capital base to support as many jobs as possible.

THE ENTREPRENEURIAL DIVISION

The Mondragón pioneers began building the cooperative movement with the necessary entrepreneurial talents and drive. Through their studies and experience, they were acquiring knowledge beyond that of their fellow citizens. They were guided, however, not by individualistic competition but by their social vision. As David Ellerman (1982) has pointed out, they were building a system of *social entrepreneurship*. Nothing like this system had ever existed anywhere before.

In the early years, while they were creating new firms, the pioneers were skillful improvisors and opportunists, but they were never content with ad hoc solutions to problems. Through discussion and study, guided by Don José María, and by reflecting on their own experience, they were constantly striving to discover the basic principles required to build their movement and the organizational structures and social processes needed to put those principles into practice. The Caja Laboral Popular provided the leadership during this process, and in recent years the cooperative groups, beginning with ULARCO, have become increasingly active.

In the early years the Caja worked only with preestablished social groups, so that cooperatives were built on a base of existing ties. That is still the strong preference, but because the Caja's resources have grown much more rapidly than the number of such groups able to draw on them, and important needs and opportunities have arisen without such a social base, the Caja has initiated the process of organizing such groups. For example, following a failed effort to build a milk and beef production cooperative with an association of farmers in 1983, the Caja recruited young men with some technical agricultural education to create the organization.

From the beginning, the Caja had been a development bank. According to its constitution, it was dedicated to creating jobs in cooperative enterprises. As the Caja took in more savings and profits than the growth in demand for loans, its leaders could not afford to sit back and wait for borrowers to come to the bank. They had to develop an active program of reaching out into the cooperatives and into the communities to locate potential groups of entrepreneurs. This imperative led to the formation and expansion of the Entrepreneurial Division.

Although the 116 staff members of the Entrepreneurial Division represented only about one-tenth of the bank's total personnel in 1982, the division is of special interest because of its involvement in creating cooperatives and in providing consulting services and emergency assistance to existing cooperatives. In 1981 the division was reorganized into six study and action areas, some of them having two or more departments. At that time, the structure was as follows: (1) research, including the Department of Research and the Library and Documentation Center; (2) agricultural/food promotion; (3) industrial promotion, divided into a producers' area and a promotion and intervention area; (4) consulting, including consultants in exports, marketing, production, personnel, administrative and financial affairs, and legal affairs; (5) auditing and information, including auditing and information control; (6) urban planning, including areas of urban planning, industrial buildings, and housing.

To meet the growing need for assistance to cooperatives in serious financial difficulty, intervention was removed from the industrial promotion area in 1983 and established as an area of its own, equal in rank and importance to the other six. We will deal with the intervention program when we consider Mondragón's reactions to the severe recession of the early 1980s.

The industrial promotion area is most involved in the creation of new firms. The products area works on the development and improvement of a "product bank" based on prefeasibility studies of promising markets and of a variety of related products within each market. The potential entrepreneurs need a feasibility study on the particular product they choose to manufacture, but prefeasibility studies enable them to narrow down the possibilities in advance. Previously, it generally took two years to complete an adequate feasibility study, but the availability of prefeasibility studies shortens this time.

When the project begins with a preformed group of potential entrepreneurs, they approach the Caja, or respond to the Caja's informational and promotional activities. The group proposes that one of its members be the future manager, and he becomes responsible for the feasibility study. If the products area is satisfied with the qualifications of the manager and with the commitment of the founding group, the Caja takes the prospective manager into its products department and covers his salary for eighteen months to two years, provided the group agrees to consider this salary a loan to members of the group personally or to the firm they hope to create. The personal assets of members of the founding group or of their co-signers serve as collateral for such a loan. (If the cooperative is not created, group members become individually responsible for repaying the loan.)

If the group emerges from an existing cooperative or cooperative group—ULARCO, for example—that organization may agree to back the loan. The products department then assigns a staff member to serve as sponsor or Godfather (*Padrino*) to work with the prospective manager in carrying out the feasibility study and developing the business plan. The Godfather remains with the firm in an advisory role during startup until shortly after the firm reaches the breakeven point. During this period, he sits on the governing council of the new cooperative.

The Caja has found that it takes at least three years for a firm to become established, pass the breakeven point, and begin to yield profits. The Caja covers the losses within this period, but, again, these losses must be paid out of future profits.

Ellerman (1982) estimated that, although the Entrepreneurial Division requires new firms to repay the loans advanced them, these payments cover less than half the total costs of the division, which is constantly engaged in research on products, technologies, markets, and urban and regional development. Of course, the Caja recovers much of this subsidy by serving as the bank for new firms.

In 1975 the initial equity provided by the founding members made up about 20 percent of the capital required to start a cooperative. A Ministry of Labor program, which provided low-interest loans to any new firm, based on the number of jobs created, contributed an additional 20 percent. The balance of 60 percent was loaned by the Caja. With continuing inflation, the initial payments of members (entrance fees plus capital contributions) rose from about $2,000 in 1975 to about $5,000 in 1981. As the costs to create jobs continue to rise, the Caja has been considering extending the repayment period on loans to new members from two to four years (Ellerman 1982).

In spite of these rising costs, Ellerman (1982) estimated that the initial contributions of new members had dropped from about 20 percent to close to 10 percent of the cost to create new jobs. The Caja has increased its loans to the firm to make up the difference. In other words, the policy has been to limit the increase in members' contributions by shifting the additional burden to the Caja.

If the losses of the first two to three years were charged against the balance sheet for the new firm each year, the startup burden could wipe out the equity provided by the founders. In this case, new members could enter the firm with their capital contributions intact while the founding members had little or no capital in their personal accounts. To avoid this obvious inequity, the Caja has established a policy of charging only 30 percent of the losses of the firm to current expenses during the startup years and of capitalizing the remaining 70 percent, to be paid off over a subsequent seven-year period (Ellerman 1982). If the accumulated losses of the cooperative in the startup period totaled 1 million pesetas, for example, 300,000 would be drawn out of the capital accounts of founding and other current members and 700,000 (advanced by the Caja) would be added to the cooperative's debt to the Caja.

Until the 1980s, the Caja had supported only one outright failure. This occurred in fishing, an industry with which the Caja had had no experience. In this case, the government provided 71 percent of the loan, the Caja 24 percent, and the workers only 5 percent. In the view of the Caja, the fishermen squandered their working capital, and the firm became insolvent. The staff at the Caja thought that a reorganized firm could still succeed if the fishermen would put in more personal capital and develop a sounder business plan, but the fishermen declined to take the further risk and the Caja closed the business.

In other cases in which a firm has been unable to reach the breakeven point and current operations have not seemed promising, the Caja has imposed drastic changes, such as reorganizing the management and developing new business plans. In one such case a potential failure was avoided when the Entrepreneurial Division completely changed the product line. Workers were sent home on furlough while the old machines were torn out and new machines installed. This intervention created a viable firm.

The Caja has frequently been called upon, especially in recessionary periods, to manage the process of converting a financially troubled private firm into a cooperative. But even with experienced personnel, an existing plant and equipment, and a position—however precarious—in the market, such a conversion, people at the Caja tell us, is generally much more difficult to effect than the creation of a new cooperative. The problem, as they see it, is not so much the material resources as the difficulties of resocializing managers and workers to the culture of the Mondragón complex. Nevertheless, some conversions have been successful.

The following two cases are described to illustrate the startup process. The first was carried out in 1965, long before the Caja had reached its current level of entrepreneurial development.

Starting the Women's Cooperative

The story of Auzo-Lagun is based on the work of Ana Gutiérrez-Johnson. It is of special significance because it provides further examples of the creative influence of Don José María while illustrating the changing role of women in the cooperatives.

In an earlier era in Mondragón, industrial work, with the exception of a few white-collar jobs, was considered an exclusively male domain. The expansion of the Mondragón complex created such a demand for labor that women were allowed to become industrial workers.

At the time Auzo-Lagun was founded, in 1965, women in Mondragón were discharged from jobs in cooperatives when they married and were substantially behind men in education and training. A survey conducted in 1977 indicated that 48 percent of the women of Auzo-Lagun had not finished elementary school and could only read and write and do simple arithmetic. An additional 35 percent had finished elementary school. Only 10 percent had finished high school. Six percent had had some post–high school education, and only 1 percent had college degrees.

By the early 1960s, Don José María recognized that a growing number of married women—both Basques and immigrants from other provinces— needed to help support their families and were interested in at least part-time work. He began discussing with groups of these women how they could fit their needs and interests into the prevailing labor market. He pointed out that there was a demand for services using their skills as housewives: preparing and serving food, housecleaning, and so on.

This matching of interests and needs with market demand was not universally welcomed. Some of the Basque men objected to this apparent threat to the traditional family, as did some of the more traditionally minded women.

The founding group persisted, however, and in 1965 Auzo-Lagun was registered as a cooperative. Formed to give part-time work to married women, the new firm began on a small scale. It provided food service to one cooperative factory and opened a small restaurant in Mondragón. The food service expanded as contracts were secured with other cooperatives and with some private firms.

During this period, Auzo-Lagun operated a food-preparation service out of a church parish house. The women also drove their own trucks to deliver food to factories where other members set up steam tables and handled the serving and related activities. Over the years, Auzo-Lagun has added new departments, including an industrial cleaning department, which dispatches women and trucks with cleaning equipment to the various client organizations.

Another department, Services to Third Parties, arose out of a request from ULARCO for women to perform temporary industrial jobs. Before opening the department, Auzo-Lagun worked with ULARCO in carrying out a survey of the labor market of married women interested in such jobs. Convinced that a sufficient number of women were interested, Auzo-Lagun then opened the new department, which soon employed approximately half its members. Throughout its existence, this department has employed the most women, but it has also been the most problematic.

Because of the statute in the constitutions and bylaws of the firms in the ULARCO group which requires that laid-off members be paid 80 percent of their regular pay, firms could not afford to take in new members during a temporary upsurge in demand. In providing part-time unskilled labor to the industrial cooperatives, the new department solved this problem for ULARCO but saddled Auzo-Lagun with the heavy responsibility of providing continuing employment, health care, and social security for its members when they were no longer needed by ULARCO. This problem was solved by having ULARCO pay Auzo-Lagun somewhat higher rates per part-time worker than Auzo-Lagun paid the women. Thus Auzo-Lagun could build up a reserve fund in times of high demand for temporary workers. This solution eased financial burdens but did not eliminate the problem of financial instability.

In the same period, the leaders of Auzo-Lagun were grappling with another problem: the need for child care. Women with children below school age could not work even part time unless they could arrange with relatives or friends to care for their children. Thus a child-care center was established in 1976 to provide professional care for small children during working hours. A small fee was charged for members and a somewhat higher fee for nonmembers.

Up to this time, Auzo-Lagun had grown piece by piece in response to particular opportunities. Now the women saw the need to reorganize the firm to make it more businesslike and to plan more effectively for the future. The Governing Council of Auzo-Lagun thus approved a proposal to create the job of general manager to reorganize the firm. Some of the founding members left the cooperative and the transition was difficult, but every step was approved by the governing council and also by the social council.

The firm now proceeded to develop a more systematic business planning process, with the assistance of the Caja Laboral Popular. The Caja conducted a study of local market conditions to help Auzo-Lagun become less dependent on ULARCO's fluctuating demand for part-time labor.

To make expansion possible, Auzo-Lagun built its own plant in an industrial park near Mondragón. In addition to the activities noted, the new plant now provides space and facilities for the subcontracting from ULARCO of minor assembly jobs that can be done within Auzo-Lagun and under its direct control.

By the late 1970s, Auzo-Lagun was providing approximately 1,500 meals per day in and around Mondragón. With the investment of $180,000 in the new space and facilities, the department expects to expand its volume to 5,000 meals daily and to serve other cities.

By 1977, Auzo-Lagun was providing more than 400 part-time jobs to its members. By 1982, as the recession reduced ULARCO's needs for part-time workers, employment at Auzo-Lagun was down to 352.

Auzo-Lagun proved to Mondragón that women could effectively manage a workers' cooperative. In the twenty years since Auzo-Lagun was created, women have gained substantial influence in staff positions in other cooperatives and cooperative groups, but until recently Auzo-Lagun was the only firm in which women had important line-management positions. By 1987, a woman had been appointed to the second highest line-management position in Mondragón's largest cooperative group and women were in positions as second-level supervisors and plant superintendents.

STARTING A COOPERATIVE FROM
INSIDE THE CAJA

This account of a recent startup is from an interview with Juan María Iraeta that took place in October 1983. He grew up in San Sebastián and took his degree in engineering there, then worked in Ulgor for about fifteen years and in the Entrepreneurial Division of the Caja for two and a half years. He shifted to the Caja because he was interested in assuming more general responsibilities.

Iraeta became interested in setting up a cooperative in Zarauz, a small coastal city near San Sebastián, because there was no worker cooperative there. A few years ago, it had several furniture factories, but they all went out of business, and "Zarauz [was] becoming an enclave for tourists."

He got together with nine friends from Zarauz to talk about launching a cooperative. They liked the idea and approached the Caja, which accepted them warmly. When it came time to elect someone to investigate the idea within the Caja and then to manage the establishment of the cooperative, they elected Iraeta—hardly surprising, since he had conceived the idea and was already working in the Caja.

Iraeta had been on this project in the Caja for a year and eight months when we met him. He devoted the first five months to exploratory work on lines of products for which the Caja had prefeasibility studies ready: agricultural machines, soaps and detergents, and frames for eyeglasses. Throughout this planning process, he met monthly on weekends with the other nine members. In February 1982, they decided that they wanted to concentrate on producing and marketing frames for eyeglasses and sunglasses.

He proceeded with a systematic study, which involved gathering information on the market: worldwide, European, and in Spain. The market prospects looked encouraging, so he began developing a five-year plan for 1984 to 1988, including such specifications for the firm as what products it would produce, how it would establish its sales organization, the structure of the firm, the finances, and the personnel.

In February 1983, Iraeta presented the study and proposal to the Caja for financing. Weeks of discussion and revision followed until July, when the Governing Council of the Caja approved the project. The business, Ikus, was opened in 1984.

The founders of Ikus decided to go into the high-priced end of the market, which required a prestigious brand name. The plan was to postpone production until a market had been established, by selling the products of a French firm that uses Yves St. Laurent designs. This meant that the firm would start with only two or three members in Zarauz, plus its salespeople. To select salespeople, Iraeta placed advertisements in the areas where the firm wanted representation.

Which of the nine group members would fill the two or three jobs? Iraeta discussed the nature of each job with the members of the group individually and invited each to indicate whether he wanted to be a member of the new firm. Although everyone had been interested in forming the new cooperative, only two men were seriously interested in working for it. These men went to the Caja for psychological testing. In addition, a marketing director was transferred to the new firm from another cooperative.

Iraeta explained that the decision to delay production until the marketing operation was well established had not been imposed by the Caja. He and his friends were worried about the financial obligations they would incur if they moved right into production, building a plant, buying machines, and so on.

The Caja financed the project with a loan at zero percent interest through the end of 1984, 8 percent during 1985 and 1986, and 14 percent in 1987. (Loans at such concessionary rates were established in the 1980s to stimulate entrepreneurship in a difficult economic period.) The Caja also provided a Godfather to attend all the meetings of the Governing Council of Ikus and to monitor and advise on the progress of the firm.

The government of the Basque country put up a grant of 300,000 pesetas (approximately $2,000 at the time) for each job established. The national government also had loan money available, at an interest rate of 10 percent, to be repaid over seven years. The group decided not to apply to the national program at the start but to submit a proposal later when more jobs were being created. Although the group could have received more than one loan for the startup process, Iraeta thought it would be more difficult to get a government loan after they had already received one and decided to wait until the firm had expanded before applying for funds. The entering members put up 525,000 pesetas (about $3,500) as capital and contributed an additional 105,000 pesetas as a reserve fund.

We asked Iraeta if there was any guarantee that he could return to his job in the Caja if the new cooperative failed. He said there was no guarantee whatsoever but that he hoped this would not be necessary. His wife had previously been general manager of the women's cooperative. She was now working in a government office in Vitoria, the Basque capital. When the cooperative was established in Zarauz, it would be impractical to commute between Zarauz and Vitoria, so his wife would leave her job. She hoped to work in a government office in San Sebastián, an easy commuting distance, but that was not assured. In other words, there was an additional risk. (In fact, she got the job.)

We asked Iraeta about his motivation for undertaking this risk. He said that for some time he had been interested in starting a firm and decided that this was the time, before he had too many family responsibilities and was older. His affection for Zarauz had not been his primary motivation, although it had determined the firm's location. By 1986, Ikus had grown to twenty-seven members.

Alfonso Gorroñogoitia told us that in 1983 the average investment required for each job created was 5 million pesetas (then about $33,000). With such a heavy up-front commitment, the Caja now prefers to follow a strategy of establishing the market before investing in buildings and manufacturing equipment.

CREATION OF NEW FIRMS BY
COOPERATIVE GROUPS

Entrepreneurial activities within the complex are not limited to the Caja. Cooperative groups are becoming increasingly involved in this endeavor, and it is the Caja's policy to foster such decentralization of entrepreneurial activities. In a meeting on worker cooperatives in Montreal (August 1984), Iñaki Gorroño, general technical secretary of the Caja, stated that Mondragón was too heavily dependent on the Caja's Entrepreneurial Division and needed to develop a more decentralized strategy.

Among the cooperative groups, ULARCO leads in the creation of worker cooperatives. Within the first decade of the founding of Ulgor, ULARCO and Ulgor were active in creating new firms by spinning off product lines, but the new cooperatives thus created remained within the ULARCO group. From this stage, it was just one more step—but an important one—to the creation of firms that would not be part of ULARCO.

In the late 1970s, leaders of ULARCO became concerned about an apparent slackening of the entrepreneurial drive among young Basques. Such a trend may have occurred not because of changes in the Basque culture but in employment opportunities. In the early days of the Mondragón movement, few jobs were available anywhere in the Basque country. As the complex expanded, it employed not only growing numbers of Basques but also migrants from other parts of Spain. Able and enterprising young people could build successful careers within a cooperative. The cooperative route also offered guaranteed employment, unavailable to those who founded a private company.

In an effort to stimulate entrepreneurship, the leaders of ULARCO created what was in effect an industrial incubator. It works in this way. Suppose a native of San Sebastián who has been working for some years within ULARCO has an idea for a new product and would like to start a firm in his home town. If the management of ULARCO has faith in the individual and thinks his product is promising, they encourage him to work on his plans. Furthermore, they make major personnel adjustments to support the project. For up to two years, they rotate the entrepreneur through a range of managerial positions to provide him with the range of experience necessary to lead the new enterprise. During this period, he divides his time between performing his regular job and planning the new project. Management also encourages him to bring into ULARCO two or three relatives or friends from San Sebastián—people he hopes will form the nucleus of the new cooperative with him. ULARCO gives them a similar combination of management experience and study and training opportunities.

When the plans for the new firm are ready, management does its own feasibility evaluation. If the initiator of the project and his fellow workers have won the confidence of ULARCO's management and the proposal still seems promising, ULARCO will assist in financing the project or guarantee loans from the Caja.

The salaries provided during the two-year training period are not a gift from ULARCO to the members of the new firm. Rather, the money ULARCO invests during this period is part of the loan to the new firm, which also includes funds for land, plant and equipment, and working capital.

During a 1983 visit to Azpeitia, a small city about thirty miles northeast of Mondragón, we saw the early efforts of another cooperative group, URKIDE, to create a new worker cooperative. URKIDE had been formed three years earlier by four cooperative firms that produced furniture, one that produced woodworking machines and tools, and one that produced machines. The group was formed only a short time before the devastating impact of the recession, particularly on Zubiola, a machine and tool firm. (In chapter 15 we deal with the rescue and rehabilitation of Zubiola.)

The need to reduce the work force of Zubiola gave special urgency to the formation of the new firm we observed in progress. Although a good supply of pine was available in the Basque country, the URKIDE furniture cooperatives had not been successful in using this variety of pine and had therefore limited themselves to other woods. If the technical and production problems of working with pine could be solved, it would be possible to create another furniture cooperative that would not compete with the existing URKIDE cooperatives. Under the direction of a man trained in wood chemistry and technology, several former members of Zubiola were working on research and development when we visited in 1983. Only a few of those workers who had had to leave Zubiola were employed, but the hope was that a new firm might eventually hire more of the workers who had lost their jobs.

The project director had consulted people from the Entrepreneurial Division of the Caja in planning research and development. As he and his pilot production group worked on the technical and manufacturing problems, others within URKIDE were assessing the marketing prospects for pine furniture, and still others were estimating the costs of a building and equipment for the firm. When the results of the feasibility study looked promising to the general management, URKIDE presented a five-year business plan and a request for financing to the Financial Division of the Caja. Leroa, the new cooperative, began operating in 1985 and employed twenty-four members by the end of 1986.

CONVERTING PRIVATE FIRMS

Worker cooperatives can be created either as new firms or by converting private firms. Leaders of the Caja clearly prefer to concentrate on startups. Former chairman of the Governing Council of the Caja Alfonso Gorroñogoitia told us about one conversion that required about six times as much work as the average startup. Rafael Hidalgo, head of the promotion department of the Entrepreneurial Division, stressed how difficult it is to resocialize the former employees and managers of the private firm: "If concrete sets hard in 28 days, people are set in their ways in about 18 years" (Ellerman 1982, 36).

Although a large majority of the Mondragón cooperatives have been created as startups, one of the earliest cooperatives, Ederlan, was formed in part by a conversion in which a private foundry was taken over and combined with a foundry spun off of Ulgor. Conversions have continued to occur from time to time, and, especially in the recession of the 1980s, the Caja has been beset by growing numbers of requests to save failing companies by converting them to cooperatives. It is therefore important to examine the potentialities and problems of such an undertaking.

There are several potential advantages of conversion.

1. The feasibility study can be based on solid facts and figures drawn from analysis of the past record of the private firm in production, financing, and marketing. In the case of a startup, no such record is available.

2. The private company may have several key executives whose technical expertise would be essential to the cooperative.

3. The workers already have some of the skills the cooperative needs. Thus the need for technical training is minimized.

4. If the private firm is in serious financial difficulties, it may be possible to buy its buildings, machines, and patents or licenses at a price below what it would cost to buy such assets in the open market.

None of these advantages can be gained unless the parties involved in the conversion project can overcome the problems of negotiating the transfer of ownership and accomplish the restructuring and resocializing required for creation of a viable worker cooperative. Let us first examine the problems involved in negotiating the transfer of ownership. (Here our field work is strengthened by an intensive case study detailed in Gutierrez-Marquez 1985.)

In a conversion, the challenge is to satisfy the interests of the entrepreneur-owners, the workers, and the Caja, which offers financial and technical assistance. Furthermore, in the Basque country it has been common for entrepreneur-owners to provide stock to some—but not all—of their employees. Thus substantial differences in interests can potentially divide those in the private firm into three groups: top managers with substantial stock, employee-owners with small holdings, and workers who are not owners. Selling at a high price is clearly in the interests of the top managers and against the interests of the nonowners, whereas the employee-owners are likely to be ambivalent.

These differences also affect the management of the negotiation process. In an ordinary sale of a private firm, those acting for the principal owners control and represent the firm. In a conversion, the Caja takes the position that the nonowning workers (who are to become members of the cooperative) must have their own representation in the negotiation process.

The legally protected rights of employees in the private firm also become a subject of negotiation. As Gutierrez-Marquez points out (page 176), a conversion involves "a drastic change in the legal situation of the workers according to Spanish Labor Law and Cooperative Law. As a result of this change, cooperative members would not have the same right to a lump sum compensation in case of lay-off or plant shutdown that other workers and employees have."

Workers can agree to give up their claims to some portion of the lump-sum payment so as to facilitate the ownership conversion, but their legal rights give them some bargaining power they would not otherwise have. Conversion also requires legal and contractual relations to be worked out. The new cooperative must be registered with the Ministry of Labor. In the case examined by Gutierrez-Marquez, it took the ministry eight to ten weeks to approve registration, after receiving the official papers. Working out relations with the Caja necessarily takes much longer. Caja financing will be authorized only if the bank officials are satisfied with the conclusions of a systematic feasibility study and have confidence in the business plan prepared by the leaders of the potential cooperative. Caja officials also must have confidence in the proposed managerial leadership, particularly the chief executive officer. The survival of the firm may depend on retaining the technical expertise of one or more key officials of the private firm, yet the Caja may believe that none of these individuals has the capacity to provide the managerial leadership the cooperative will require. In such a case, can such technical experts be retained as advisers rather than as executives? And, if the necessary managerial leadership is not immediately available within the firm, can the Caja official who has been working on the case be persuaded to assume the chief executive role on a transitional basis? Obviously, issues of this scope and complexity cannot be resolved simply and quickly. The process is bound to take considerable study, discussion, and negotiation among all the parties involved.

Finally, there is the problem of assessing the value of the property and determining the selling price. In addition to the usual complexities involved in such an accounting and estimating problem, the process must provide especially for protection of the interests of nonowners. In the city of Azpeitia, for example, workers employed by the firm that was eventually converted into the cooperative Maiak sought assistance from the management of URKIDE, the cooperative group in that city, in the face of an impending shutdown. URKIDE's studies indicated that the workers were prepared to pay far more than the property was worth to save their jobs. URKIDE's involvement resulted in a substantially reduced selling price. In other cases, involvement of the Caja is essential to ensure that the new cooperative is not so heavily burdened with debt as to have little chance of survival.

The purchase transaction may be further complicated by the financial losses sustained by the private firm during the conversion process. In one case, for example, the apparent value of the equity of the firm owners at the start of the process had been practically wiped out by two years of financial losses, and the principal owners naturally had difficulty accepting a financial settlement far below their original expectations.

Resocialization must begin during the conversion process and continue through the early months and years of the new cooperative. We have noted the problem of securing a chief executive officer who is not only technically competent but also capable of leading a cooperative. Inevitably structural and systems changes are also required. In many cases, the private firms that seek conversion into cooperatives are initially successful because of the technical or marketing expertise of a single entrepreneur. Although he may be respected by workers and other subordinates for his technical expertise, he may be unable to delegate responsibilities and build an effective organization. When such an individual leaves the cooperative or is shifted to a role as a consultant, the new CEO has to begin the organization-building task. This requires that considerable training be given those people taking on enlarged managerial responsibilities and those workers who are assuming the rights and responsibilities of cooperative members.

Reviewing this long list of problems makes it clear why Caja leaders are reluctant to get involved in conversions. Nevertheless, conversions do take place. An examination of the record enables us to draw some conclusions regarding the conditions to be considered in deciding whether to undertake them.

Size. The larger the private firm, the more complex and difficult the conversion is likely to be.

Location. In response to the rapid growth in the city of Mondragón, policy makers give special emphasis to expansion in other areas. This does not mean that cooperatives are established in areas remote from other cooperatives. Rather, the preference is to undertake conversions in areas where a cooperative group already exists (Maiak in Azpeitia) or that are near Mondragón cooperatives (Urola in Legazpia).

Complementarity. The Caja will not support the conversion of a firm that will compete with an existing cooperative. On the positive side, the Caja will favor conversions when continuing production and marketing offers advantages to existing cooperatives. For example, Maiak produces a different line of furniture from the three other furniture cooperatives in the URKIDE group. Thus Maiak strengthened URKIDE's marketing program while adding another cooperative to share the costs of managing the group. In the case of Urola, a firm that produces plastic products and plastic manufacturing equipment, a well-established cooperative, Goizper, had a strong interest in the conversion because it would ensure the continued availability of products Goizper needed.

Social adaptability. This appears to be the most critical condition. Even if all other conditions appear favorable, Mondragón is unlikely to undertake a conversion if the prospects of resocializing managers and workers appear to be poor.

The Mondragón movement is based on a principle of solidarity in all relationships. Solidarity with the Basque community is expressed in a policy of not creating new cooperative firms in areas where they would compete with existing Basque firms. This policy was probably especially important in the early years, when survival depended on avoiding conflicts that would provoke political reprisals. Community solidarity is also expressed in the ever-expanding creation of Basque-language cooperative schools. Intercooperative solidarity is expressed in strategies to create cooperatives that can buy from and sell to one another and perform services for one another. Intercooperative solidarity is also expressed in the grouping of cooperatives under a common general management, thus providing for economies of scale without building large control bureaucracies.

The social vision of Don José María and the dedication of his followers to systematic and objective analysis of hard technical and economic realities have combined to build a movement of impressive dynamism.

PART THREE

Managing Change

9 Coping with Internal Conflict

The most serious conflicts experienced by Ulgor and ULARCO occurred in the early 1970s. These events must be seen in the context of internal and external changes. Throughout the 1960s and beyond, Ulgor experienced explosive growth. Its total membership surpassed 3,500 in 1974, burdening the cooperative with the constant task of assimilating hundreds of workers unfamiliar with the ways of cooperatives. This growth period coincided with the approaching end of the Franco dictatorship.

By 1970 Spain's dictatorship had lasted a quarter-century beyond the end of the Nazi and Fascist dictatorships. Franco had reestablished the monarchy. The Falange party retained little influence, and Franco had not created the organizational or political conditions for maintaining the dictatorship after his death. By this time the tight controls of the early Franco years had been weakened, and leaders of clandestine political parties and unions had learned how to mobilize popular support to push the regime as far as possible without inviting military and police repression.

When we first visited Spain in April 1975, the pervasive atmosphere was one of tension, anxiety, and impatience. It seemed that people of various political views were waiting for the death of the dictator, positioning themselves for more activity when he passed on. At the same time, they were worried that Spain would lapse into the strife that had led to the Civil War and Franco's victory.

Unofficial political mobilization was especially evident in the Basque provinces, although the Basques were by no means unified. Marked divisions existed along class lines, political ideology, and commitments to Basque nationalism. Resentment against the tight control of Madrid was generally shared, but Basques were divided between those who hoped for greater regional and local autonomy and those who pursued the ideal of an independent Basque state.

The most militant of the separatists supported the Basque organization ETA, but it too was sharply divided along ideological lines. Some supporters were simply committed to Basque independence without regard to political ideology, but increasingly ETA had been finding common ground with Marxists, who were themselves divided. Some were committed to their own brand of socialism, others embraced the Soviet Union's version of Marxism-Leninism, and growing numbers followed Chairman Mao.

ETA had no unified policy regarding the Mondragón cooperatives. Views ranged from those who regarded the cooperatives as a disguised form of capitalism, and therefore an obstacle in the way of the proletarian revolution, to those who saw the cooperatives as building blocks of socialism.

The unrest within Ulgor first came to public attention in March 1971. A small group in one of Ulgor's two plants attempted to organize a strike aimed at achieving changes in job evaluations. The strike call failed to gain widespread popular support. There were no discharges, but at the end of their probationary period three apprentices were not accepted as members of the firm—although efforts were made to get them into another cooperative.

The Governing Council of Ulgor reacted to this disturbance by enacting a rule to distinguish sympathy strikes in support of labor causes throughout the Basque country or the nation from strikes focused on internal problems. From that time on, internal strikes were defined as attacks on the cooperative itself, and strikers were subject to penalties, including discharge.

In April 1971, one faction of ETA circulated an attack on the cooperatives that included this statement: "We must take into account and be alert to recognize that cooperativism is an alienation (depersonalization and undermining of the conscience of the Basque working class) and therefore is inadmissable." The attack ended with an appeal to the workers to "rise up against this technocratic class that calls itself cooperativist" (Azurmendi 1984, 617).

In November 1972, the Maoist faction of ETA circulated an attack under the title of "What Is Happening in Mondragón?" It accused the cooperative movement of taking over all sectors of public life in Mondragón—work, sports, education, and local government. Mondragón was said to be "an island of peace and collaboration in an environment of social contradictions of all types." The attack denied that the cooperative movement was defending the interests of the working class. It was "simply an entrepreneurial adventure" (Azurmendi 1984, 624).

The attack focused particularly on the social council:

> The nature of the social council is clear. It is a faithful servant and legitimate child of the system which gives rise to it. The participation of the workers in this organ gives it a democratic aspect, but the demagogy of the leaders of the cooperatives manages to channel the interests of workers, converting this organization, in reality, into a sort of bourgeois parliament. We must accentuate the conflicts that must not be assimilated and that go against the working class with an instrument imposed by our own organizations. (Azurmendi 1984, 627)

THE NEW JOB EVALUATION PROGRAM

In this highly charged political atmosphere, leaders of ULARCO moved to develop and implement a major program of social and economic change in a most sensitive area of cooperative life: compensation. Job evaluation to establish pay rates had been established in 1965, but there had been no unified system. There was one system for blue-collar workers and another for white-collar workers and executives. Furthermore, under the blue-collar system, each job had a fixed rate, whereas under the white-collar/executive system a merit rating was included whereby the job holder could receive compensation beyond the job rate based on an evaluation by superiors of his or her performance. The systems also differed in the way job evaluations were administered among the ULARCO cooperatives. There had also been a considerable lag in evaluating newly created jobs.

One of the main advantages of group management was that members could be moved from one cooperative to another in response to shifting personnel requirements. The variation in job evaluation policies and practices among cooperatives complicated the problems of adjustment of workers who were shifted from one firm to another and the work of the people in personnel who were administering the diverse systems.

Growing dissatisfaction with current job rates and with the variations in policies and practices among the cooperatives led the management of ULARCO to set in motion a major program of job evaluation. The assignment was complicated, however, by a value inherent in the structures and policies of the complex. In private industry, it is customary for each plant or company to have its own job description and evaluation program and to have separate systems for blue-collar, white-collar, and managerial workers. Because separation into these three categories was incompatible with the egalitarian values of the members, ULARCO's planners were determined to apply the same criteria to all jobs. They thus decided to create a standard system to be applied to all 2,883 jobs in the five member firms.

The personnel department in ULARCO began what turned out to be a two-year process by studying current practices and policies in private companies in various European countries. ULARCO set up a Central Job Evaluation Committee (CJEC), and each of the five member cooperatives set up its own job evaluation committee (JEC). The JEC for each of the five cooperatives was composed of its personnel director, members chosen by its social council, and someone appointed by the personnel department of ULARCO Central Services. The JEC elected its own chairman. The CJEC was composed of the personnel directors of each cooperative, the personnel director of ULARCO, and the chairman of each JEC, plus several job evaluation technicians from ULARCO Central Services.

The process of evaluation was guided by two sets of criteria, arrived at through study and discussion, one for the job and the other for the job holder. Jobs were to be evaluated based on their requirements for theoretical knowledge, work experience, effort, responsibility for decision making and guiding the work of others, and (when relevant) physical hardships inherent in the job.

The job holder was to be evaluated for overall performance, including output, quality, organizing ability, initiative, sense of responsibility, and cooperation with other workers. Basically, the job rate was to be established by evaluating the particular job, but the supervisor was responsible for adding a merit increment of up to 15 percent according to his or her evaluation of the worker. And, for the first time, individual merit ratings were to be used for blue-collar workers.

As is customary elsewhere, the evaluation process began with the creation of job descriptions. A worker on each job was interviewed by a member of the JEC. This description was then supplemented by interviewing the worker's immediate supervisor. A staff member then used job evaluation criteria to arrive at a tentative rating. Finally, the rating was reviewed and approved (or modified) by the firm JEC and passed on to the CJEC for final action.

First-line supervisors reported the results of the evaluation to each

Table 9.1. Changes in ULARCO's *Job Classifications (in percentages) as Result of Job Evaluation, 1974*

	Upgraded	No change	Downgraded
Copreci	40	42	18
Ederlan	66	20	14
Fagor Electrotécnica	54	40	6
Fagor Industrial	92	6	2
Ulgor	56	22	22

SOURCE: ULARCO Central Services. Cited in Gutiérrez-Johnson 1982, 283.

worker. In cases of downgrading, the supervisor also informed workers that their pay would not be changed for two years if they remained on their jobs but that the rate would be reduced for a new worker.

As part of the process, the committees established an elaborate appeals procedure. Grievances were presented by the supervisor to the plant personnel department. The plant JEC carried out a reevaluation and sent its conclusions to the Central JEC, which reviewed the plant JEC's findings and sent its judgment back to the plant JEC. On the basis of all this information, members of the plant JEC discussed the job with the individual worker, reported its decision directly to the worker, and then informed the Governing Council and the Management Council of ULARCO. If the worker was still not satisfied, he or she could make a final appeal to the Governing Council of ULARCO.

The records show that the resulting job evaluations upgraded far more jobs than they lowered. As table 9.1 points out, of the five firms, Ulgor had the highest percentage of jobs downgraded—22 percent—and it was here that the major conflicts arose.

GRIEVANCES

There were 1,022 requests for reevaluation of jobs—36 percent of all the jobs evaluated. Because many workers performed the same job in the same plant or in different plants, we cannot assume that 36 percent of all workers voiced their dissatisfaction with the results. Undoubtedly, in some cases an individual protested his job rating while other workers on the same job raised no objections. Nevertheless, the 36 percent figure indicated a fairly broad and serious concern. Two hundred and twelve ratings (slightly more than 20 percent) were changed as a result of the reevaluation, which indicated the seriousness with which the committees took their responsibility for working out problems with the members. Committee members reported that in many cases workers did not express their dissatisfaction immediately. Many members initially seemed to accept the rating but then demanded a reevaluation after comparing their jobs with fellow workers given higher ratings. People in personnel explained that each worker had an intimate knowledge of his own job but only a superficial knowledge of other jobs, so that workers were often unaware of the reasons someone received a higher rating. In any culture, perceived inequities in rewards among people working together constitute one of the most delicate personnel problems. In the Basque culture they are likely to be especially difficult since Basques are inclined to value *comparison equity* (one's own rewards compared to those of one's fellows) over any abstract weighing of the relation of one's contribution against one's reward (Gutiérrez-Johnson 1978).

Those workers whose jobs were downgraded were of course the ones who appealed for reevaluations. Furthermore, they were not satisfied with the guarantee that their pay would remain the same as before the evaluation. They had come to look on their jobs as measuring their worth and considered it insulting to think that their individual worth had been devalued but that they would charitably be paid more than they were worth.

There was also widespread dissatisfaction with the "functional evaluations" (merit ratings). The results could have only a minor effect on an individual's earnings, since the merit rating could add only 0.15 to an individual's index on the 1 to 3 pay scale. Nevertheless, the merit system gave supervisors power they had not previously had. Many workers personally resented this change and considered the new policy to be in conflict with Mondragón's basic principle of emphasizing equality among members.

THE 1974 STRIKE

By 1974, widespread dissatisfaction had led to the formation of organized groups, and circulars advocating a strike were appearing in the plants. The protest movement was centered in Ulgor. The course of events we follow was reconstructed during a month-long seminar in the summer of

1985 by a ULARCO study group working in collaboration with Professor Davydd Greenwood of Cornell University.

In an effort to head off the strike, the chairman of the Governing Council of Ulgor called a special meeting of the social council on June 19. The purpose was to inform council members about the course of events so that no one would be in the dark about what had happened and what could happen. He also announced the moves management would make in the event of a strike. In the first place, a strike caused by internal problems would be considered a serious violation of the rules of the cooperative (*falta muy grave*) and would be sanctioned by expelling the strikers from the cooperative. On receiving notice of their expulsion, they would be informed of their rights to appeal to the general assembly.

The chairman stated that the governing council had information on who was organizing the strike and appealed to the members of the social council to make these individuals aware of the consequences of their actions. He emphasized that those trying to organize the strike had neglected to bring their problems to the Social Council of Ulgor, thus violating the rules and procedures of their cooperative. He took this refusal as an attempt to undermine the constitutional bases of the cooperative. He closed by saying that he did not wish to threaten anyone but believed it was important that the strike leaders fully recognize in advance what the consequences of a strike would be for them personally.

On June 20, 1974, an informally organized committee from the Ulgor refrigerator plant asked to meet with some member of the governing council. The secretary of the council received them and took note of their three demands. They objected to the differentiation of pay levels on the assembly lines and asked that the equal payment system be continued. They also objected to the use of merit ratings for workers engaged directly in production. Finally, they demanded immediate publication of the list of proposed pay levels for all members. They insisted that these demands be met by noon that same day.

By this point, the leaders of both parties had taken strong confrontational positions. The governing council denied that the committee represented Ulgor's workers and directed it to follow the officially established channels for appealing to management. The governing council ruled that, according to policies approved by the membership, complaints about job evaluation decisions first had to be presented to the social council. The governing council further ruled that the social council should meet as often and as long as necessary to deal with these problems. The first meeting of the social council was scheduled for June 27, the first workday following a holiday.

On the afternoon of June 27, while the social council was deliberating about the grievances, the leaders called a strike. Approximately four hundred members of Ulgor walked out, along with some members of Fagor Electrotécnica.

As we were told by a former striker at Fagor Electrotécnica (who in 1983 was a foreman in that plant), although the strike was organized and directed by people at Ulgor, every effort had been made to gain support in Arrasate and Fagor Electrotécnica. The leaders had marched to Arrasate with the intention of going through the building to recruit support, but members of Arrasate had barred the doors. From Arrasate, next door to Ulgor, the strike leaders then crossed the street and were able to enter the Fagor Electrotécnica plant and recruit a few members.

While their leaders were marching to the plants to round up support, other members of Ulgor remained at their work stations, trying to organize a sit-down strike. They were confronted by members militantly opposed to the strike. A period of tension followed before the strikers were persuaded to leave the premises.

The governing council responded to the strike by immediately expelling 17 worker members who were considered instigators and imposing fines of varying amounts on 397 who followed them out of the plants.

During the brief strike, the strike leaders presented to the managements of Ulgor and ULARCO, through a member on the Social Council of Ulgor, a set of demands for settling the conflict. Reiterating the demands made earlier, they added amnesty for all the strikers and claimed that they would continue the strike until their demands were met.

The governing council flatly rejected these demands and ratified the expulsion of the leaders and the fines. During the following several days, all except the seventeen discharged strike leaders returned to work. The strike was broken, but its repercussions were felt widely and for long thereafter.

POSTSTRIKE DEBATE IN THE COMMUNITY

In the community in and around Mondragón the 1974 strike provoked the sharpest attacks yet on the cooperatives. One faction of ETA circulated a manifesto containing the following paragraph:

To break with capitalism, we must place ourselves in the land of reality (the class struggle) and not that of wishful thinking. These errors start from one basic point: denying to the working class the role of agent for destruction of capitalism and of the bourgeois state; this means the cooperative project is trapped in its own laws (the laws of the capitalists) against which they should fight. We must not forget the role of the state as supervisor and driving force of capitalism and that of the working class as the only agent capable of destroying it. (Azurmendi 1984, 629)

Considering its source, the most serious attack came from the Church in the form of a statement of the social secretariat of the diocese of Vitoria, under the title of "Conflicts in the Cooperative Movement." This manifesto was read from the pulpit in all the churches. It did not attack the Mondragón cooperatives by name but the cooperative movement in general. Joxe Azurmendi said that the manifesto "constituted a frontal attack by the Church against industrial cooperativism itself, a surprising development for the Church in aligning itself with the most radicalized of the new left" (Azurmendi 1984, 632).

The social secretariat wrote that "as always, the workers have suffered under the elitist behavior of the cooperative leaders" and "the virulence and crudeness of the cooperative leaders greatly surpasses that of the firms that they disrespectfully call capitalist" (Azurmendi 1984, 632).

The attack focused particularly on the prohibition of the right to strike, described as a fundamental right in all democratic countries and recognized in Spain not only by workers but also by management. It argued that Ulgor

in 1971 established a prohibition of the right to strike in its internal regulations. . . . These articles reinforce the clauses against the strike of the much disputed Spanish labor legislation in this regard and give rise to an internal situation much more restrictive for labor relations than in any other type of firm. (Azurmendi 1984, 633)

The defense was written by Javier Mongelos, general manager of ULARCO, and Jesús Larrañaga, manager of Ulgor. Basically, they took the position that the cooperatives had highly democratic structures and open channels for the resolution of conflicts and that the strike had been an attack on the basic nature of the cooperative itself.

Don José María played no active role during the strike and did not join in the counterattack against ETA and the Church. Instead, he used the strike as a means of alerting the members to the problems of bureaucracy:

> Any system of organization which attains a certain size runs the risk of being undermined, if within it flourishes a typical bureaucratic and functionary spirit, a fearful illness which degrades any achievement no matter what its nature, as it blocks the dynamic agents which strive to maintain efficiency in response to changing conditions. (Azurmendi 1984, 630)

THE CAMPAIGN TO READMIT THE STRIKERS

In the course of the following months, the discharged members and their friends signed up enough members to meet the one-third requirement for calling a special session of the general assembly to reconsider the expulsion decision. In a hotly contested meeting on November 23, 1974, the discharged members claimed that their decision to strike was their only recourse for expressing their disapproval of the job evaluation system given that the institutional channels designed for resolving such questions (the social council) were ineffective.

Members of the governing council defended their decision on the grounds that the strike was an open and conscious defiance of the institutional channels established by the cooperatives for handling such problems. Strikes had been explicitly prohibited in the legal regulations democratically approved by the membership. The meeting ended with a vote; 1,775 (62 percent) supported the governing council's action and 1,077 supported the petitioners.

In the regular annual meeting of the general assembly on March 26, 1977, the agenda included a petition to readmit the expelled members. Neither the governing council nor the social council took a position for or against the motion. Nevertheless, the vote went against the petitioners. A total of 1,505 (61 percent) voted against readmission, 939 voted in favor, and 20 votes were invalid.

In the following annual meeting of the general assembly, held on April 1, 1978, the governing council, in response to a request from the social council, included in the agenda a proposal to readmit the expelled members. The governing council supported a motion to readmit. The arguments presented suggested that the tensions and bad feelings could not be resolved otherwise, that the serious disagreements maintained divisions within the cooperative, and, equally important, that the discharges had not been well understood and accepted in the surrounding community. The governing council also praised the manner in which the petitioners had sought to gain reconsideration. This time the vote for readmission was 1,587 (67 percent) in favor, 712 (30 percent) opposed, and 50 votes invalid.

Following this vote, the majority of those who had been expelled from Ulgor presented their individual requests for readmission and were readmitted. Fagor Electrotécnica made the same decision.

REFLECTING ON THE STRIKE EXPERIENCE

The conflict had taken four years to resolve and had been such a matter of dispute both within the cooperative and outside during that period that ULARCO and Ulgor were in a major institutional crisis. Now that the conflict was over, there was a general feeling that the cooperatives had to learn from the bitter experience.

In 1985 the ULARCO study group reviewed the attacks on management by the strikers and their supporters. The group came to the following conclusions:

It is true that the cooperative, in facing the market, does share some of the conditions imposed by the capitalistic system.

The potential for conflict between technocracy and participation is an undeniable risk not sufficiently dealt with in the period of our concern by the dynamics of the organs of governance and participation.

The accusation of social class conflict lacks any real foundation but the climate of division created in that situation, which translated itself into "those on top" and "those on the bottom," led to this interpretation.

Concerning the minority position, it is possible that the institution could have adopted postures more open to dialogue. However, both parties adopted positions of antagonistic confrontation that were hardly reconcilable.

The cooperative should embody an advance in the development of the labor movement, and in the emancipation of the worker.

The study group thus ended with a resounding affirmation of the values on which the cooperatives were based. Nevertheless, the group's conclusions raised questions about the way management had handled the conflict. Although the political climate in the community in 1974 had clearly fueled the conflict, the study group did not defend the cooperative by simply attacking outside agitators. They recognized that the strikers had real problems and that the organs of participation were not functioning effectively at the time.

Could management have avoided the strike? Of course it is impossible to answer this question, but it appears that confronting the potential strikers with the penalties awaiting them intensified the conflict. Management was demanding that the dissidents take their problems to the established channel of the social council, whereas the dissidents were arguing that the social council did not really represent the workers. At the time, management was not open to dialogue with the protest leaders regarding the deficiencies they perceived in the social council.

10 Rethinking the Systems of Participation

The 1974 strike sent shock waves through the cooperative complex. It precipitated a series of discussions, centered on questions of internal policies and procedures, designed to discover what went wrong and to devise measures to avoid future breakdowns. As the oldest and largest cooperative and the locus of the most serious conflicts, Ulgor naturally assumed a leadership role in this process.

In Ulgor, the review and planning activities were concentrated on the social council. After a number of meetings and considerable study, in February 1975, the council had prepared an extensive report that analyzed its own weaknesses and proposed remedial steps (Gutiérrez-Johnson 1982, 369–79).

The report began with a flat statement: "There is no question that the S.C. has fallen short of fulfilling its role—even of knowing its real function in the firm." It went on to state that the social council had done little to integrate the needs and interests of the members as workers with decision making by management.

Because it responds passively to the inherently aggressive character of the management policy. It:
(a) limits itself to transmitting information from above to below, and vice versa.
(b) is a rubber stamp body for decisions already made.
(c) discusses "effects" without looking into "causes."

While recognizing that the social council did not understand "its real function in the firm," the report did not clarify the council's role. Instead, it focused on staffing, training, structure, and social process.

Council members recognized that the size and rapid growth of Ulgor had enormously increased the problems of coordination and communication. A committee without staff support and the time and resources to study problems could not make as effective decisions about economic and technological issues as full-time managers supported by ample staff and resources.

Before the strike, steps had been taken to cope with the communications problems attendant on organizational growth. Divisional social councils had been formed in each of Ulgor's two plants and in the Department of Central Services that worked with them. Representatives elected from each of these units formed the Central Social Council (known at the time as the Plenum), which in turn elected its executive committee, the Permanent Central Commission (PCC), from among its own members. None of the members of the PCC, however, devoted full or even half time to social council functions. The report urged management to increase substantially the time key members of the PCC could devote to such business.

The report urged the formation of mini-councils (*consejillos*) in the various departments to facilitate communication from the rank and file to management and vice versa. To improve the performance of the elected social council representatives at plant and firm levels, the report urged the formation of a training program that would focus on both social and business skills. Finally, the report recommended a major change in the leadership of the Central Social Council. From the time the Central Social Council had been established, a member of the governing council or a top management official had chaired it. The report recommended that the Central Social Council elect its own chair, who would also serve as an ex-officio member of the governing council.

Management responded positively to some parts of the report. Key members of the social councils were authorized to devote more time to council duties, but neither full- nor even half-time positions were endorsed. Management also established the *consejillos* and carried out a very extensive training program designed to improve the performance of members of the social councils.

Management rejected the proposal to allow the Central Social Council to elect a chair from among its members, arguing that having the same person chair both the governing council and the Central Social Council fostered better coordination between the two bodies. In other words, management favored coordination over the full independence of the Central Social Council.

In spite of the serious attention paid to the problems of the social councils in the 1975 discussions and reports, the basic problems appeared unresolved. Throughout 1981 and most of 1982 the Permanent Central Commission again discussed the functions and powers of the council, and in a report issued in September 1982, entitled "Restructuring the Social Council," the Permanent Central Commission presented an extensive analysis of the problems that had impeded functioning.

> The most important conclusions reached through this analysis have been the following:
> 1) Lack of fit between functions and responsibilities.
> 2) Division (insufficient interrelation) between the Social Structure and the Technostructure.
> 3) Excessive size of the Social Council.

After reflecting on the social and cultural changes that had fostered expectations for more active member participation, the report focused on the need to overcome the following two sets of "contradictions":

> a) the techno-entrepreneurial evolution, whose complexity tends to advance beyond the comprehension of the workers, and the psychological conditions needed by the workers in order to assume the responsibilities of cooperative members.
> b) The concentration of decisions at high organizational levels, as influenced by technical specialization, and
> The need for drawing together of human groups, as expressed in the new socio-cultural values.

The report commented on the growing "manifestations of lack of interest and hostility" expressed in recent meetings of Ulgor's general assembly and attributed this condition to a "lack of dialogue between person and institution." The desire to share in the profits appeared to be the main reason members were attached to their cooperative. The objectives of the firm, its control, the style of leadership, and the decision-making process should have been of great interest to the workers, but they were becoming less involved in these matters, leaving the dual role of member-worker underdeveloped.

The report found that "in general, one has the impression that line management devotes little time and attention to its leadership functions, justifying this neglect by the urgency of its operating tasks."

While this study was going on and following the circulation of the report, management responded positively to some of the report's recommendations. Management decided to strengthen the divisional social councils by giving them increased responsibilities for the concerns of their own units. Each of these units elected its own representatives (*vocales*) to the divisional social councils, and members of these divisional councils served also as representatives on the Central Social Council. To strengthen the performance of the Central Social Council as a deliberative body, management reduced its membership from 110 to 50 and based divisional representation on the number of members in each unit. Management vetoed the recommendation that each divisional social council elect its own chair. Following the same argument it had used in the 1975 report, management ruled that the manager of the plant or service should serve as chair.

Management responded in part to recommendations that social council members be trained in business methods being developed by management (for example, management by objectives, strategic planning, and zero-based budgeting). Management made no concrete response to the recommendation that key members of social councils be granted additional time during working hours to participate in meetings, to study problems, and to consult with constituents. By this time Tomasa Zabaleta was serving as administrative secretary of the Central Social Council of Ulgor and of the Social Council of ULARCO, devoting half time to each position, but this appeared to be considerably less time than the report had urged. Furthermore, the role of the administrative secretary was defined as being a facilitator of communication rather than an organizational leader.

Management did take two steps designed to provide more staff support to the Social Council of Ulgor. The council was given the right to secure technical assistance from ULARCO. The Governing Council of Ulgor also took steps to clarify and strengthen the relationship between the personnel department and the social council. To determine how this might be done, the governing council established a joint committee between the personnel department and the social council. The joint committee reported that "in practice one finds a lack of connection between the functioning of Personnel and that of the Social Council, thus also a lack of established channels of intercommunication."

The committee observed that personnel functioned at two levels:

definition of policies or general guidelines

implementation of these policies and guidelines

The Social Councils have the ability to act on the first level but have little possibility for impact on the second. This often leads to a failure to monitor the implementation of their recommendations.

For operating purposes, the committee therefore recommended that personnel be considered the "executive arm" of the social councils in discussions with management on working conditions, organizational improvements, and labor relations.

Finally, the 1982 process resulted in a significant change in the legal status of the social councils in ULARCO. According to Article 53 of the Ulgor bylaws, the social council was established as an advisory and consultative body to the management and the governing council. The scope of its mandate was to provide "guidance in everything related to accident prevention, safety and health on the job, social security, systems of remuneration, administration of social services and personal assistance."

This suggests a relatively narrow field of activity bounded by traditional conceptions of the functions of personnel departments. The 1982 revision eliminated the list of topics cited above and extended the scope of responsibility to serving as "the spokesman for the social aspirations and concerns of the members." It goes on to state that the social council provides "guidance on all general matters of a societal or labor character that affect the work community."

This more general wording legitimated the involvement of the social councils in advising management on such broad matters as organizational structure, the organization of work, and the nature of managerial leadership. Their duties in carrying out these responsibilities were not clarified, however.

ROLES OF UNIONS AND POLITICAL PARTIES

In the years following the 1974 strike and the end of the Franco regime, the leaders and members of Mondragón became increasingly concerned about relations with external organizations, such as political parties and labor unions. Although some people had remained clandestine members of political parties and labor unions during the dictatorship, it was impossible for anyone openly to represent illegal organizations, and the cooperatives thus did not need any policies or procedures for dealing with them. With the legalization of unions and political parties early in the regime of the first post-Franco government, the cooperatives came face to face with this issue. Members knew that before the Civil War and in other countries cooperatives had grown up in association with and attached to unions and political parties, so that the question of the possible involvement of such organizations in the cooperatives naturally became a subject for discussion.

Many of the members of Mondragón became involved in political parties after the dictatorship, and the values on which the complex were built supported the labor movement. Thus, for the first time in the history of Mondragón, members openly identified themselves as members of political parties and of unions. The question was, Should Mondragón now give some formal recognition to such "groups of organized opinions," as they came to be called? Because this was a policy question involving all firms in the ULARCO group—and with potential impact on other cooperatives—the scene for discussion and debate now shifted to ULARCO.

Questions regarding the relationship of political organizations and unions to the cooperatives had been raised in earlier meetings of the social councils, but the formal decision-making process did not begin until May 1979 with a meeting of ULARCO's Permanent Central Commission. Discussion continued until a decision was reached in December 1980. The PCC began by consulting with its constituent social councils. The May report of the commission stated that questions had been arising regarding "the possible structural relationship of the Social Councils of the cooperative with unions and political organizations." Four points were listed that supported consideration of the question and even indicated the possibility of major changes:

(a) Our status as workers, which relates us to the world of labor, especially in our region.

(b) The need to clarify the role that these unions and political organizations should play at the institutional level.

(c) The concrete form for their insertion and action in the cooperative structure and the relation with the organs of social representation of the cooperative.

(d) The possible change from representation in terms of groups of workers (based on physical proximity) to grouping by unions, political parties, or nonaligned groups, which would reflect a more ideological conception and might promote more strongly expressed contrasting views within the basic rules of the cooperative.

The May report outlined seven possible steps for arriving at a decision. The first step was for the PCC to refer the question for discussion and recommendations to all the social councils of the ULARCO group to determine whether the PCC should develop a proposal for change. If the constituent social councils supported such action, the PCC would study the question further and propose a tentative plan. The plan would then be submitted to representatives of unions and political parties for their comments and then to each social council for discussion and recommendation. The revised proposal, along with the regulations for its implementation, would be submitted to the governing councils of the constituent cooperatives and to the General Management of ULARCO. The final decision would then be made by the Governing Council of ULARCO.

To carry out the first step, the PCC circulated a survey with two questions: Did the members of the social councils want to proceed with discussion and potentially with decision making on this issue? If so, did they approve the seven-step procedure proposed by the PCC? The results of the survey indicated sharp differences of opinion on the first question. Members of the Social Council of ULARCO Central Services and of Fagor Electrotécnica voted unanimously in favor of proceeding, and Copreci registered only one negative vote. Ulgor proved to be so divided that the issue had to be referred for discussion to the small councils in each plant and department. The final vote from Ulgor was thirty in favor and twenty-five opposed. Arrasate was strongly opposed (twenty-three to eleven), and Ederlan even more so (twenty-four to three). At the time these votes were compiled, Fagor Industrial and Lenniz had not completed the discussion and voting process.

The ULARCO PCC report summarized the arguments on both sides. There were three general arguments in favor:

> Since the presence and informal actions of the unions and political parties in the cooperatives are now realities, it does no good to ignore them.
> The open discussion of the theme can give rise to a clarification of positions and mutual enrichment.
> The theme is of interest because we form part of the base of working people.

Those opposed also had three arguments:

> There was no felt need among the members for such a change.
> The change could polarize the economic and social activities of the cooperatives.
> This could lead to difficult confrontations.

The PCC then sounded out opinions at the level of the constituent social councils to see whether the information on how members in other co-operatives had voted would lead to a firm decision. In this further consultation, all the social councils except that of Arrasate supported continuing the exploratory discussions within the PCC.

Following further consultation with the social councils of the member cooperatives, the ULARCO Permanent Central Commission arrived at a series of decisions and explained them in a report dated December 31, 1980.

After summing up the arguments for and against recognizing "groups of organized opinions," the report cited this basis for the new regulations:

> In the face of these divergent opinions, this regulation proposes simply to focus the question and to authorize *de jure* recognition of a *de facto* condition.
> . . . The continuation of the *present situation of non-legality* for the unions and political parties can only give rise at best to ridiculous situations or at worst to the promotion of irresponsibility.

Having presented the pragmatic argument, the report went on to place the new policy in the context of the values of the cooperative complex:

> On the other hand, the cooperative community must be open, by definition, to all creative and efficient ideas for improving both economic and social management, received from whatever quarter. Therefore, we see no obstacle to providing these organizations with opportunities to make their contributions within the cooperative. If experience demonstrates that in practice they do not serve these ends, either for reasons of the existing culture or for the prevailing interests of these groups, there will be time to make a correction and eliminate this regulation.

The new regulations formalized the right of representation for unions and political parties. They were to have the same rights to information from management, the governing councils, and the social councils of any ULARCO cooperative as any individual member—but no superior rights. If a member of a union or political party was elected to one of the organs of governance, he or she had a right to speak for such an organization. If the group did not have any representative on an organ of governance, the group could ask to be heard by that organ. The individual representing the group would have the right to speak at the meeting of the body but would not have the right to vote. The social councils were also authorized to propose to the Central Social Council of ULARCO that a representative of a group seeking such a hearing be invited to its meeting.

These groups were also accorded the right to communicate proposals directly to the Permanent Central Commission of ULARCO and to the permanent commissions of the member cooperatives. They were given the right to place notices on official bulletin boards, and each cooperative was requested to provide space for this purpose. On request to the management of a cooperative, such groups were to be given space in its building for meetings after working hours.

To implement these regulations, the PCC invited any union or political party wishing to have official representation to name an authorized spokesperson and an alternate. In other words, after January 1, 1981, any group wishing to be recognized within ULARCO could easily obtain such recognition.

Interest in the issue seemed to subside following announcement of the new regulations. In fact, very few organizations went to the trouble of choosing an authorized spokesperson. Because any individual member had the right to secure information from the representatives and authorities of each cooperative and of ULARCO, and the highly democratic structure of governance gave individuals opportunities to express their views to the authorities, even when they were not officially elected as representatives, the "groups of organized opinions" may have concluded that there was no advantage to securing formal recognition. In practice, there was nothing to prevent an individual from speaking up for such an organized group in a meeting of a cooperative's general assembly or social council.

Do the results indicate that the lengthy process of discussion and decision making was a waste of time and effort—and a waste of money, since members were paid even though they were not doing their regular jobs? If the Permanent Central Commission of ULARCO and the constituent social councils had flatly denied recognition to unions and political parties, members of dissident minorities would have felt discriminated against, which could have caused considerable friction.

It is noteworthy that the PCC was prepared to consider making a change—even one so drastic as shifting the base of representation for social councils from members who work together to groups defined by organizational or political ideologies. The process of consultation and discussion made it clear that there was little support for such a change.

Finally, even though unions and political parties made little formal use of them, the new policies legitimated the right of such groups to be involved in the decision-making process. As we shall see, the new policies came to play a significant role in discussion of, and debate over, the changes required later to meet the problems of the worldwide recession.

The process was long and difficult, in part because members were confronting problems for which there was no precedent in Mondragón— or in the history of any other cooperative organization familiar to them. Because a cooperative, in principle, is a completely democratic and self-governing organization, unions and political parties, it could be argued, had no place within it. ULARCO's achievement was that it could reject a dogmatic reaffirmation of principles and instead devise pragmatic solutions based on them.

Rethinking and decision making in these two cases had quite different outcomes. On the one hand, the question of participation of unions and political parties in the governance of the ULARCO cooperatives was settled for the forseeable future. To this writing, the issue has not come up again for serious discussion. On the other hand, issues regarding the role of the social councils in ULARCO were not resolved, namely whether the social councils should confine themselves to advising management and facilitating communication between management and the workers or whether they should have the power—like a union—to challenge management and negotiate for the sharing of power in decision making. We will reflect further on this dilemma as we assess trends and problems in the cooperative group in the latter half of the 1980s.

11 Changing the Organization of Work

Until the early 1970s, worker participation in the Mondragón cooperative complex was limited to governance: from the general assembly of each cooperative to the election of members of governing councils and social councils. Participation had not been extended to the organization and management of work, which continued along lines characteristic of private firms.

According to José Luis Olasolo, who served as personnel director of ULARCO from 1974 to 1979, the program to introduce new forms of work coincided with a shift in the organizational structure of ULARCO. From its founding in 1965 through 1969, ULARCO had a collegial form of management in which power was shared by the managers of each of the constituent cooperatives. In 1970, with the appointment of the manager of Fagor Electrotécnica, Javier Mongelos, as general manager, a more unified style of management was adopted.

Shortly after Mongelos assumed the top position in ULARCO, his personnel director left to take a post outside Mondragón. For some months Mongelos served also as personnel director. A physicist by training, Mongelos had no formal education in personnel administration, but after taking on the position of director, he immersed himself in the literature of personnel and human relations. Reflecting on this reading, combined with his experience working in and managing cooperatives and discussions with associates, Mongelos came to three general conclusions:

1. The personnel department in cooperative organizations should play a leading role in linking the economic and technological objectives of the firm with the social concerns of the members.

2. The growing tensions in the workplace revealed the inherent contradiction between the democratic system of cooperative governance and

the rigid and authoritarian system for organizing work relations according to the scientific management principles of Frederick W. Taylor.

3. Management should explore possibilities of creating new forms of work organization that would be economically efficient yet more in harmony with the social values on which the cooperative movement was based. Personnel officials should share major responsibilities with line management in developing the program.

During this same period, other managers and members were becoming concerned about workers' dissatisfaction with their jobs and their relations at work and were wondering whether it would be possible to organize the workplace so that it was more compatible with the principles of cooperativism.

Mongelos initiated a series of meetings within ULARCO on new forms of work and encouraged the managements of the individual cooperatives to set up committees to study and plan for the introduction of such changes. The first such committee was set up in Copreci in March 1971, and the first change was introduced there in May 1973.

Mongelos saw the introduction of new forms of work as extending and strengthening the program of participative management by objectives. (In the United States, management by objectives and participative management are viewed as two different concepts, whereas the policy in Mondragón is to link them.) He presented his rationale to us in this way: "We had spent six to seven years with courses to implant the philosophy of participative management by objectives. The formation of work groups represents an extension of this idea to the bottom level."

When Olasolo became the personnel director of ULARCO in 1974, he had already read about innovations in the design of work, from the Tavistock Institute in London to the work democracy movement in Scandinavia. That same year, he had taken a study trip to Scandinavia with Jesús Catania, who was then production manager of Copreci. They had visited the Volvo Kalmar plant, which represented a radical departure from conventional automotive manufacturing technology, and had attended an international conference on new forms of work. On these travels, they had met Einar Thorsrud, leader of the work democracy movement in Norway. Later, Thorsrud had made several visits to Mondragón. He was fascinated by the cooperative complex, and Mongelos spoke of him as "a guide and inspiration for us regarding the bases of new work forms."

Although the leaders of Mondragón recognize how much they learned about new forms of work from reading and personal contacts with Einar

Thorsrud, work redesign projects were in fact under way in ULARCO several years before Olasolo's and Catania's trip to Scandinavia and their first encounter with Thorsrud. Furthermore, although the labor disturbances of the 1970s added a sense of urgency, the movement to make jobs more socially rewarding began well before the 1974 Ulgor strike and even before the smaller-scale work stoppage in Ulgor in 1971. In other words, the initial impetus toward work redesign arose in anticipation of the problems that had not yet become acute and in recognition of the inherent contradiction between Tayloristic work organization and the social philosophy underlying cooperative governance.

BEGINNING IN COPRECI

Why did the process of redesign begin in Copreci? Mongelos explained that although Ulgor was beset with the most serious labor problems, it was nonetheless out of the question as a place to start. Ulgor consisted of long assembly lines, where the large frames of stoves and refrigerators were suspended on steel hooks from overhead chains that moved at a mechanically determined speed. Clearly, no major changes in the organization of work could be introduced until Ulgor was prepared to make the enormous investments necessary to tear out the old assembly lines and build a completely new sociotechnical system.

Copreci appeared to have the best prospects for launching the new program. The product lines (components for gas and electric equipment and machines) and the technology imposed few physical or economic obstacles, and people in management—particularly the director of production, Jesús Catania, and the personnel chief, José Luis Gonzalez—were receptive and eager to experiment with the new ideas.

To determine where the changes should be introduced, the personnel department conducted a job satisfaction survey, which revealed substantial dissatisfaction in two work sections. Reorganization in one of these sections appeared particularly appropriate, since it made a thermostat, the simplest product assembled in Copreci. Workers sat on both sides of a conveyer belt that, at a machine-controlled speed, moved the parts of the components to be assembled at each work station. It would be easy to pull out the assembly line and substitute work tables.

The beginning of the change process in Copreci was formalized on March 7, 1972, by a management committee consisting of the director of production, the chief of personnel, the production superintendent, the foreman of the department selected for the first project, and six workers elected by their fellows. As the work progressed, representatives from the departments of engineering and quality control were added to the committee.

Before the intervention began, the management committee studied and discussed the productivity and quality problems in its operations, production requirements, and the relations among workers and between them and management. In the course of the project, the committee met frequently to monitor progress. During the first two years of the program, the committee met outside regular working hours and the members received no extra pay. Later, as the program was extended to more sections and the number of committees grew, meetings were held either during working hours or after working hours and the members were paid for their time (without overtime premiums).

Before the changes were introduced, plans were discussed with the workers to elicit their opinions and attitudes and to determine who would volunteer for the first experimental group (no one was required to participate). The eight members of the first group were selected by the committee based on their understanding of the project and their familiarity with all of the tasks to be performed.

The experiment began with the removal of the 7.5-meter-long conveyer belt and the substitution of a 2.8-meter-long work table. Workers were seated around the table and could now set their own work rhythm and freely exchange information and ideas. The table provided more work stations than workers so that people needed to move around from time to time to advance work on lagging operations and to avoid delaying interrelated tasks. All workers were expected to perform all the tasks and could rotate tasks as they themselves decided. As they gained skill and confidence in this new way of working, the workers began to take over such supervisory and staff functions as requisitioning tools and materials and recording their output.

The first work table experiment began in May 1973, a little more than a year after the initiation of the discussion and study process. To rule out the possibility that the performance of the workers had improved simply because of the way in which they had been selected, the management committee, in August 1973, selected *at random* members of a second work group. Again a conveyer belt was removed and a work table substituted. One assembly line operated for some months as a basis of comparison between the old and the new work organizations.

Nine months later, the program established a work group for a more complex product. This time, the members of the group requested and were granted such additional responsibilities as repairing defective pieces and analyzing the causes of the defects. At this point, assembly lines had been eliminated throughout the section and all the workers were at work tables, organizing and monitoring their own work.

A 1985 study by the personnel department of ULARCO (on which much of this chapter is based) reported the following lessons drawn from the Copreci experience:

> It is not necessary to prepare a minutely detailed plan of action before introducing such changes. It is sufficient to have a general plan and clear ideas, and be open to modifications that suggest themselves in the course of practical application.
>
> The initial selection of a (simple) product encourages members to move on to more complex situations.
>
> The rigidity in the flow of work (into this section) and the instability of programs and work groups make it difficult to achieve higher levels of (work group) autonomy.
>
> Work tables permit improved integration of the work processes and thus a reduction in inventory in process.
>
> It is possible to increase productivity per hour per person, due to a reduction of idle waiting time.
>
> Quality improves in direct relation to the complexity of the apparatus being assembled, due to better information regarding the work. Feedback is the basis for group self management.
>
> Changes proceed slowly. It is dangerous to create exaggerated expectations.

The study also noted that changes in work organization required changes in classification and pay. Because all group members were now performing the same tasks, they all had to receive the same pay. Furthermore, the mastery of a number of different tasks justified a higher pay classification.

The study recognized that it was difficult for the first-line supervisor to adjust to these changes. On the one hand, he had to avoid intervening in ways that would undermine the group's autonomy, and, on the other, he needed to help the group relate effectively to other parts of the department and firm. Insofar as the group became self-managing, the supervisor's disciplinary responsibilities also changed.

When we visited Copreci in April 1975, we observed the work tables in operation. Chief of personnel José Luis Gonzalez pointed out a work station at which an individual worker was performing a vertically enriched job which previously had been performed by several workers. He told us that the woman in question had insisted that she preferred to work alone. She sat performing assembly operations with components she placed on a large cylinder that rotated at a speed she herself controlled. Gonzalez told us that the next step in Copreci would be to experiment with a product-based organization: In certain work sections the production and assembly operations would be located together to give workers a better sense of the significance of their work and to improve coordination between these operations.

The personnel department of ULARCO Central Services, in a 1987 review of developments in Copreci, reported that the changes planned in 1975 had been fully implemented. In effect, Copreci had shifted its work organization from a function base (all similar machines or processes were grouped together in the same section) to a product base, in which the production and assembly of similar products were located in the same section under the same supervisor. This reorganization involved nearly all the products produced by Copreci.

This reorganization appeared to have the following major positive effects both on the quality of working life and on technical efficiency:

1. Workers could more readily visualize their contribution to the total product.

2. The above served to improve relations between production and assembly workers.

3. As workers and managers increasingly concentrated on the total product, it was possible to respond with greater flexibility to customers' needs and thus to improve the planning process.

4. The inventory of work in progress was reduced because production and assembly operations were integrated.

5. The research and development process was strengthened, which facilitated the introduction of automated processes involving entire work sections.

The only negative effect appeared to be that assembly workers were now much closer to the noisy production machines.

As top management became preoccupied with the challenges imposed by the 1973 and 1975 oil price increases, the management committees guiding the new program became inactive. The changed forms of work remained in place, however. In fact, when Fred Freundlich of Cornell

University interviewed a number of managers and shop-floor workers in 1986, he found them overwhelmingly in favor of the new ways of working. They spoke of their relieving the "terrible monotony" of assembly line work. The work groups increased workers' self-esteem and made individuals feel responsible to the group for their performance. Workers welcomed the opportunity to learn new skills and the improved relationship with their supervisors. Workers and managers both commented on how the management committees and the work groups increased contacts between the shop floor and higher management. Managers and workers (who were now keeping track of their own performance) believed strongly that the program had improved productivity and quality and had reduced scrap and stocks (inventory in process).

The management of Copreci revived the work reorganization program in 1984 by extending it to new sections and introducing new group-based activities.

Extending the Changes to Other Cooperatives

As Copreci moved steadily ahead in its work redesign program, other firms of ULARCO became involved in the process. A 1985 ULARCO report states that 83 work groups involving 632 members were actively involved at some time from 1973 to 1983. The most active years were 1976, 1977, and 1978, suggesting that the program lost momentum after that. Some of the other firms made progress, but none proceeded as far or as firmly as Copreci.

In 1973, Ederlan, a foundry that cast iron and aluminum, began an ambitious work redesign project in its grinding department. The position of foreman was eliminated, and work groups assumed some responsibility for the planning and control of production, quality inspection, and maintenance. These major changes were not adequately supported by training of managers and workers, and important structural changes in the organization produced instabilities that undermined management follow-through. These conditions led to abandonment by the group of their newly acquired functions, which, in turn, required the second-level supervisor to take over the responsibility of foreman.

In Fagor Electrotécnica, which produces semi-conductors and electronic controls, the process began in the television components department in 1974 with a survey that suggested that the large body of workers needed to be divided into small work groups. With this change, work groups assumed responsibility for rotating tasks, organizing their own work, making quality inspections, and requisitioning materials and tools as needed.

Early results showed increases in quality and productivity, as well as greater job satisfaction. The ULARCO report commented that the nature of the technology and production in the firm had facilitated the formation of effective work groups.

In spite of the technological limitations noted earlier, beginning with seminars in each plant late in 1975, Ulgor undertook to introduce changes in the final stages of assembly, where only limited space could be provided for small work groups. The changes involved taking some of the work off the assembly line, lengthening the work cycles for operators, instituting some job rotation, and having workers make quality inspections. These changes proved to be neither far-reaching nor enduring. Supervisors and staff seemed to be too occupied with managing the long assembly line to give adequate attention and support to small innovative efforts. In addition, there was not enough work space and it was difficult to coordinate the work groups with the main assembly line.

In 1976, Arrasate, which produces machine tools, planned an ambitious program, centered in the assembly department. The plan was to increase worker participation by having biweekly meetings of worker representatives with line managers and service personnel to exchange information and plan the work. As a group, the workers also took on new responsibilities for the allocation of tasks, quality inspection, and control of their tool supply. The position of quality inspector was thus eliminated, and the foreman was replaced by a worker who served as group leader.

While this program was being organized, management of Arrasate committed the firm to a major shift in the organization of production: from function-based (all similar machines are in the same work section) to product-based (machines used in the production of a particular product are placed in the same work section). This change was based on a purely technical study under the guidance of a consultant.

Major problems ensued in integrating the technology-driven change in the organization of production with the human organizational changes planned and guided by people in personnel. For some months, the worker participation program was stalled while management moved machines about and carried out the work necessary to provide adequate space and facilities for the product-based organization. Management planned to review developments during 1980 in order to revive the participation program, but by this time Arrasate was suffering from the recession that affected the machine tool industry particularly drastically. When a Cornell University team interviewed foremen and managers of Arrasate in the fall of 1985, no one was talking about work redesign. They were all preoccupied with the struggle to ensure the survival of their cooperative.

Lenniz, which produces kitchen cabinets and equipment, also undertook an ambitious redesign project. In 1977, foremen in one department were eliminated as sixty-one workers in fourteen groups were organized into three production units, each with a production technician. The project was a complete failure, and some months later the former work organization was reestablished. In 1986, José Luis Olasolo, who was personnel director of ULARCO at that time, explained the failure to us:

> In the case of Lenniz, there were two problems. The equipment and machines were brought in from Germany, and the technical personnel did not have sufficient understanding of the manufacturing process. Also the plant was designed for fewer models than what had to be produced later. . . . If you reduce the number of operators and yet you don't have enough technical knowledge in the system, it is impossible, or very difficult, to operate successfully.

The 1985 ULARCO report confirmed this interpretation.

Fagor Industrial, which produces machines for commercial use (ovens, dishwashers, washing machines), lagged in starting worker participation programs but began to change with the next wave of innovation: quality circles and total quality programs, which were also becoming popular in the United States in the late 1970s and early 1980s. The head of the quality department attended a seminar by a consulting concern and persuaded his management to contract with the firm for a seminar on modern methods of quality control. Management people from the Caja and from other ULARCO firms attended along with the management of Fagor Industrial.

The firm then contracted with the consulting organization to guide Fagor Industrial in the development of the quality circle program. The head of quality control became coordinator and assumed responsibility for explaining it to the social council. There followed a training program for foremen and other management people who were to lead in the development of quality circles.

In the early stages of the program, two circles were formed, each with six to eight members, one in machining, the other in assembly. The foreman served as moderator in each case, and the worker members were volunteers. The circles met weekly during working hours.

A NEW WORK ORGANIZATION
FOR A NEW FACTORY

The first opportunity to integrate the design of work with the design of a new factory arose when Ulgor decided to produce automatic dishwashers for domestic use. A new factory was built in Vergara, about ten miles from Mondragón. As Mongelos explained, building a new plant for a major new product involved strategic planning, and engineers in ULARCO Central Services therefore worked closely with Ulgor engineers in designing and implementing the project.

As we saw when we visited the plant in 1983, the work organization in Vergara contrasted sharply with the prevailing technology and work flow in the Ulgor refrigerator and stove plants. There were no assembly lines. At the beginning of the assembly process, workers set the frames of the dishwashers on stands, which they attached to a cable under the floor of the factory. The cable moved at a uniform speed from one work station to the next, but the pace of work at each station was determined by the work group. Operators worked in groups of six to ten. When the cable brought the frame to their station, members of the group uncoupled it and moved it manually to their adjoining work area. They then allocated and rotated the tasks as they themselves decided. Each group was responsible for the quality of its work, so the tasks included testing and registering the group's judgment that the quality was satisfactory. When the work was completed, members of the group attached the stand and frame to the cable, which propelled it to the next work station.

There are no foremen in the Vergara plant. The only official between the workers and the plant manager is called a *gestor* (in this context, a groups manager). He is responsible for overseeing seven work groups. He is not expected to give individual workers detailed instructions, but he is responsible for forming the groups, for observing progress and intervening when problems arise, and for seeing that the workers have materials and tools.

Has the new plant been a success? As Mongelos sees it, "Now the program in Vergara is well established. And the workers like it, as we have found from our surveys. Also, whenever a worker is transferred to another plant, he always wants to return to Vergara."

Until 1986 the Vergara plant was not a financial success, but its financial problems could hardly be blamed on the new work organization. As Olasolo pointed out, the plant was designed before the recession to produce 100,000 dishwashers a year. It went into production during a severe recession, when the market could absorb only about 30,000.

THE AMBIGUOUS ROLE OF THE SOCIAL COUNCILS

We had assumed that the social councils would be deeply involved in the design and implementation of the new forms of work and were surprised to find that they were involved only peripherally. In 1983, engineers in Ulgor presented their preliminary plans for a reorganized refrigerator plant to the social council. Members pointed out that the plans called for installation of new machines but maintained the long assembly line, and they persuaded the engineers to go back to their drawing boards to devise more socially acceptable alternatives. This placed the social council in the reactive position of not being involved in the detailed work of developing the plans but of criticizing them after they were shaped by the engineers. José Luis Gonzalez informed us that two members of the social council had been involved in the design process by virtue of having served on a committee that met from time to time with the engineers. Nonetheless, this occasional participation of two individuals was clearly not enough to involve the council strongly.

We asked Mongelos for his interpretation of why the social councils were only minimally involved in work redesign. He commented that their interest in participation had been focused exclusively on such major issues of governance as strategic entrepreneurial questions, on which it was difficult for rank-and-file members to participate effectively. He added:

> Just last week when X and I were together in a meeting, I said to him, "In the General Assembly of ULARCO, you focus on participation constantly, claiming that we do not provide sufficient participation." And I, a bit irritated, asked him, "Why is it that in the last ten years the social organs have never taken a position in favor of real participation of the members— that is, in matters concerning their work?"

Mongelos answered his own question by pointing to changes in the political environment during the last years of the Franco regime and following the introduction of free unions. He noted that this period had been one of intensified union and political activity. Perhaps social council members feared that militant union people would see the participation of members of cooperatives in work redesign as manipulation of the workers by management.

We checked this interpretation with the man who had been involved in the conversation with Mongelos. He confirmed the interpretation. There was indeed sufficient uncertainty within the social councils about their roles to prevent them from taking initiative in the process of restructuring work.

A recent publication of the Caja Laboral Popular includes the following statement in a list of legitimate functions of the social councils: "To study and analyze experiments in new forms of organization of work in order to overcome Taylorism and the dependent relations it involves, and to achieve full participation through self managing work teams" (Juan Larrañaga 1986, 19). Since the author of this essay made no reference to any controversy on this or any other point in his exposition on the history and functions of the social councils, readers might assume that such a statement reflects common beliefs and practices. In fact, there is no such clear-cut understanding or practice within Mondragón's oldest and largest cooperative group.

DON JOSÉ MARÍA'S LACK OF INVOLVEMENT

Insofar as Don José María played such a leading role in shaping the development of Mondragón, we expected to hear of his influence in the restructuring of work. But, as we learned from Mongelos and Olasolo, and as was confirmed by others, the founder was not involved at all. He did meet Einar Thorsrud and undoubtedly knew what was going on. He listened on occasion to descriptions of plans but neither criticized nor made suggestions. On the other hand, he did not express any disapproval. His interests and attention were focused on the broad structural questions of governance and on the creation of the network of mutually supporting organizations. Furthermore, nowhere in the writings of the founder did Joxe Azurmendi, who has made the most intensive study of his writings, find anything on work redesign. If, on one hand, this lack of involvement indicates a limitation in the vision of the founder, on the other, it speaks

to the strength and creativity of those who assumed leadership positions
in the organizations that he played so prominent a role in designing.

ASSESSING THE SUCCESS OF THE
WORK REDESIGN PROGRAM

During our first visit in 1975, we were impressed by how successfully
the new work forms had been implemented in Copreci. At the time of
our second visit, in 1983, we had the impression that, except for the new
dishwasher plant in Vergara, the work redesign program in ULARCO had
lost momentum. Perhaps management was resisting changes or at least
had lost interest in the program.

Our own field work during later trips, reinforced by the 1985 ULARCO
report, has persuaded us that our impressions in 1983 were misleading.
We need to distinguish between the social values and ideas guiding work
redesign and the market forces influencing industrial operations. The
ULARCO report noted that the economic adjustments Copreci was forced
to make because of the sudden and sharp increases in oil prices in 1973
and 1975 had led to a loss of momentum even though the firm had carried
out the most successful work redesign projects. The severe recession, which
began in Spain in 1979, naturally caused management to shift its attention
away from the redesign of shop-floor work toward the more urgent problems of carrying out major structural and economic policy changes. These
changes will be discussed in part 4.

It now is clear that the management of the cooperative group remains
strongly committed to developing new forms of work. Further, the frag-
mentary evidence we have regarding rank-and-file reactions suggests that
workers strongly support the social values underlying this change—although they have been highly critical of the implementation of some
changes. Finally, management is fully aware of work form innovations
developed in Scandinavia, Japan, and elsewhere. In fact, it appears that
just about any innovation in work forms developed anywhere has been
tried out in one or several of the ULARCO firms.

If the program has not progressed as rapidly as the leaders had hoped,
it has not been because they lacked a value and policy commitment or
information on new forms of work. Rather, the problem has been how
to put the new ideas into practice in the context of existing organizational
structures and economic pressures.

It should not be assumed, however, that market pressures in Mondragón necessarily block the implementation of new work forms. As several management people have told us, the market of the 1980s demands higher-quality products and more rapid adjustments to customer demands. These demands cannot be met by the long, rigidly controlled assembly lines typical of mass production in earlier eras. They require higher levels of quality by production and assembly workers and more flexible manufacturing systems, the details of which must be controlled by workers rather than top management.

Introducing a new form of work is a *sociotechnical* problem. Those who design the new form and those who work within it must understand the human and organizational aspects of the work, as well as the work flow, machines, and technical requirements. Students of organizational behavior are aware of many cases in which the introduction of a new technology failed to yield the expected benefits because the designers did not understand the human and organizational aspects of the work. The Lenniz case shows that a new form of work may also prove unsatisfactory when managers and workers do not adequately understand the technology and technical requirements.

Ideally, the sociotechnical design of work should be an integral part of the design and construction of a new plant—as it was in the Vergara dishwasher plant—or of a major change in technology, work flow, and utilization of physical space. Except for the Vergara plant, the introduction of major work redesign changes in Ulgor was delayed until the massive reorganization of technology in the stove and refrigerator plants, carried out from 1983 into 1987. It is too early to pass judgment on the introduction of the new forms of work in those two plants.

The potential for introducing new forms of work in an existing plant, without major investments in new technology, depends in part on the extent to which it is practical to change the existing technology. In the old Ulgor plants, the massive assembly lines left little maneuvering room for work groups. The production and assembly of small components in Copreci (and also Fagor Electrotécnica), however, offered highly favorable physical and economic conditions for change.

When beginning a program of change, it is not necessary or desirable to map out all stages of development in advance, but it is important to think in terms of stages—and to start, when possible, with simple operations. The success in Copreci built momentum to carry the program into more complex projects. Apparently Lenniz and Arrasate attempted too many complex changes at the same time. At Arrasate, there was the further problem of trying to fit together the social design of new work forms with a technology-driven shift from a function-based to a product-based organization.

New forms of work on the shop floor must be integrated with changes in the total social system of the firm, from the bottom to the top. If worker groups take over responsibilities previously held by foremen, inspectors, and other staff, then the firm will need fewer supervisors and staff. Of course, this is not simply a matter of reducing personnel. The remaining supervisors and staff need to take on quite different roles. Instead of concentrating on the details of operations and giving orders and imposing discipline, the supervisor will be expected to guide workers to build self-managing work groups, to coordinate activities, and to offer advice but not intervene in work operations unless help is needed. It is easy to describe in general the nature of this role but difficult to carry it out effectively. Furthermore, not only is it difficult for a supervisor accustomed to the conventional role of foreman to learn the new role; it is also difficult for the supervisor who comes to the job fresh from an engineering education that has provided no guidance on new forms of work or even on human elements of supervision.

Thus, what might seem like resistance to change on the part of some supervisors and higher management people may be due less to their authoritarian attitudes than to the lack of an effective program of re-education. Much can be learned on the job, but, if the organization of work changes, people need more help than their immediate experience can provide.

Personnel departments have been playing major roles in the development of new forms of work, but such programs will continue to progress only if people in personnel are part of a management planning and implementation committee strongly backed by top management. When management people become driven by other programs and priorities, work redesign efforts lose momentum.

Finally, we return to the ambiguous role of the social councils. To this writing, social councils have remained largely in a reactive stance regarding work redesign. Can they contribute more effectively if they play a more proactive role? We shall seek to answer that question in chapter 17.

PART FOUR

Coping with the Worldwide Recession

12 Sacrificing for Collective Survival

The Mondragón cooperative complex had the good fortune of developing during the 1950s and 1960s and early 1970s when the Spanish economy was expanding rapidly. Even allowing for favorable conditions, all economists who have studied Mondragón's financial history report that the cooperatives have far outpaced private Spanish firms. Henk Thomas and Chris Logan have noted (1982, 108), for example, that "a comparison with Spanish industry can only be made for 1972, in which year cooperative efficiency exceeded that of the largest enterprises by 7.5 percent and of medium and small-sized enterprises by 40 percent."

By the mid-1970s Spain had entered into what would be a long period of stagnation and increased inflation. These problems were accentuated by the worldwide recession of the 1980s, which affected Spain more severely than most other industrial nations. "Spain has performed poorly relative to other OECD countries, judging by inflation, stagnant activity, and rapidly rising unemployment. Between 1975 and 1983 output grew at only 1.6 percent per year and inflation averaged 16.8 percent, the highest in Europe" (Bradley and Gelb 1987, 83).

While the economies of other nations were reviving during the mid-1980s, Spain continued to lag behind. As late as 1986 unemployment remained around 20 percent, and it was 27 percent in the Basque country, whose "mature" industries had suffered most severely.

Beginning in the 1970s the cooperatives slowly but steadily increased their exports. In 1976 they exported about 10 percent of their total output. By 1980 that figure had risen to more than 20 percent, and by 1985 it had reached 30 percent. Nevertheless, having to sell 70 percent or more of their products in the depressed Spanish economy imposed severe handicaps.

Until 1980 the problem for economic researchers was to explain the growth of the complex and the extraordinary survival rate—almost 100 percent—of the cooperatives. In the 1980s the problem has been to explain how the cooperatives have managed to defend the gains previously made while making the sacrifices necessary for survival.

For this story, we will concentrate on ULARCO (renamed FAGOR in 1986). In 1986, nearly one-third of the total membership in the complex—approximately six thousand workers—were members of this group. In addition, the group contained Mondragón's first industrial cooperative and several of its largest, which tended to make it a pacesetter for other cooperatives and cooperative groups. Although member cooperatives did not have to follow ULARCO's example to meet their financial requirements, they tended to follow its actions closely.

Communication in any organization of ULARCO's size is complex. Management in ULARCO had the additional problem of exacting sacrifices from members who had the right to accept or reject any management proposal. Furthermore, the formulas for fixing wages (*anticipos*) and capital contributions were embedded in the governing statutes of the cooperative group, which meant that a two-thirds vote was required to make any major change.

When the first cooperative in Mondragón was created in 1956, it made sense for pay rates to be guided by prevailing rates in the Basque country and by changes in the consumer price index (CPI). Those two indexes tended to rise together, so that if Mondragón followed the regional and national pattern, the leaders could assume that the cooperatives would hold their own, and even gain ground, in competition with private firms. In those early years, exports were inconsequential and all Spanish industry was protected by high tariffs on industrial imports. As the 1980s approached, Mondragón's steady expansion in exports and the long-anticipated entry of Spain into the European Economic Community (implemented in stages, beginning in 1986) made it clear that policies oriented solely to the internal market were no longer sustainable. As Mondragón became the most important industrial complex in the Basque country, it could no longer afford to be a pattern follower. The leaders of the cooperatives had to devise new policies to ensure their survival in both national and international competition.

The story of these changes in policy is important not only because the changes were essential to the survival of ULARCO but also for what they reveal about the processes and problems of decision making in this largest and most complex cooperative group. Because the processes in ULARCO are so complex and unfamiliar to those who have background only in how decisions are made in private firms or worker cooperatives elsewhere, we asked José Luis Gonzalez (personnel director of ULARCO and chairman of the Governing Council of Fagor Electrotécnia) and Alex Goiricelaya (director of training for ULARCO and vice-chairman of the ULARCO Central Social Council) for their interpretations.

At the beginning of the 1980s, the individuals in ULARCO who played the chief leadership roles were Alfonso Gorroñogoitia, chairman of its governing council, and Javier Mongelos, general manager (CEO) of the cooperative group. As a founder of Ulgor and then chairman of its governing council as well as that of the Caja, Gorroñogoitia was widely respected for his long and continuing leadership. Mongelos also was widely respected for his executive and entrepreneurial abilities and vision. It should not be assumed, however, that the prestige of these two men was such that they could personally impose their will on ULARCO—even if they had wished to do so.

Mongelos did not act alone in shaping the plans for the future. He worked closely with his management council, supported by staff from ULARCO Central Services and in consultation with Gorroñogoitia. It was Mongelos's responsibility to prepare proposals that would win the support of the ULARCO Governing Council and that would ultimately be accepted as presented, or in modified form, by the members, following a process of information sharing, discussion, and debate within the organs of governance and participation in ULARCO and in each of the constituent cooperatives.

As Alex Goiricelaya wrote (personal communication):

> Each cooperative has an independent legal existence, and it is its own Governing Council which carries weight in its own General Assembly and which defends the positions of its cooperative. In this sense, one must not attribute to persons nor to the central organs of ULARCO more weight nor less than they really have in a *complex process* of contributions, assumptions, contrasting arguments, etc.
>
> It is important to recognize the existence of diverse organs of governance and participation, both at the level of the group and at the level of each one of the cooperatives, without falling into the temptation to oversimplify, seeing it [ULARCO] as a homogeneous whole with direct influence of certain persons in all fields of action. ULARCO is not a holding company but rather a puzzle.

We take this to mean that, although the formal structures of governance and participation and the procedures to follow are clear—at least in general—to those leading the decision-making process, the detailed actions required to reach sound decisions are by no means clear at the outset. It is, of course, unrealistic to expect such a complex and large set of organizations as ULARCO to arrive at any consensus decision. The puzzle for those leading the process is how to balance the economic and technical requirements of the business with what will be acceptable to the members—or, as in the critical cases to be described, at least two-thirds of the members.

Managing the decision-making process in ULARCO was the responsibility of Gorroñogoitia, with the support of the ULARCO Governing Council, the CEO, and the Management Council. Thus, in a general assembly meeting, it was Gorroñogoitia's responsibility to present and defend proposed changes—after they had been thoroughly discussed and debated within the constituent cooperatives.

The Permanent Central Commission (or Central Social Council) of ULARCO and the social councils of its individual cooperatives helped structure the processes of study, discussion, and debate throughout ULARCO. In the cases to follow, we will focus on the activities of these organs of participation, since their actions reveal the nature of the issues being debated and the processes for arriving at their resolution. Although the Central Social Council does not make decisions, it can exercise substantial influence. As Alex Goiricelaya explained (personal communication): "The Social Council has the power—and exercises it—to bring to the General Assembly, so that they can be debated, those questions on which it does not arrive at an agreement with the organs of governance. Sometimes it has won, and other times it has lost."

CHANGING PAY POLICIES

In a study presented to the social councils of the cooperative firms on November 20, 1978, to support the need for a changed compensation policy, the Governing Council of ULARCO cited figures to show that, from 1969 through 1977, the labor costs for ULARCO had risen 31 percent whereas increases in productivity (as measured by value added) had lagged behind at 20 percent. The governing council also pointed out that Mondragón was suffering from increasing costs in advancing credit. These costs had been 5.93 percent of sales in 1975 and were rising toward 8.90

percent in 1979. This was especially burdensome to cooperatives that depended heavily on exports because payments were not made until the purchaser received the goods.

Mondragón was also experiencing rising costs in financing its inventory. The cooperatives were committed to maintaining steady employment, even in those firms in which there was substantial fluctuation because of seasonal demand. In U.S. private firms, such seasonal fluctuations can be handled by laying off workers in slack periods. Not having this option, the Mondragón firms had been producing for inventory in slack periods and paying members overtime when more production was needed. This policy imposed heavy burdens both in inventory costs and in overtime pay.

The leaders of ULARCO decided to tackle the compensation problem first. As is typical when a change in policy is proposed, the leaders did not move directly from diagnosis of the problem to proposing the solution. Instead, they first sought to discover and articulate the basic principles that should govern compensation policy. They proposed the following three principles:

1. *Economic rationality*. Compensation should depend on the economic performance of the firm.

2. *Autonomy*. Mondragón should adopt its own independent system of compensation, severing its link to prevailing pay rates. Mondragón must also devise a system compatible with national labor legislation.

3. *Future applicability*. The new pay formula should not be simply a one-time change but should be flexible enough to permit application in the future under changing economic conditions.

The new formula did not abandon the link to the consumer price index but balanced it against the financial needs of the firm. So that the index would reflect the financial health of the cooperative group and be simple enough to be understood by the members, the governing council decided to tie the formula to cash flow. The council calculated the value of total sales for a given year and subtracted the costs of labor, materials, and services. What remained was cash flow. When the value of sales was divided into the figure for cash flow, this yielded cash flow as a percentage of sales.

In trying to establish a satisfactory base level for the percentage of cash flow, the governing council used the actual figures for 1977 (table 12.1).

If in future years the percentage of cash flow decreased from the 1977 level, pay levels would not be increased by as much as the consumer price index had increased. Conversely, if the percentage of cash flow rose above

Table 12.1.   Cash Flow of ULARCO *Firms (1977)*

	Millions of Pesetas	Percentages
Sales	14,600	100.00
Labor costs	− 4,090	− 28.00
Materials and services	− 8,650	− 59.20
Cash flow	1,860	12.80

the 1977 level, members' pay levels would be increased by more than the increase in the CPI.

This was a dual problem, involving both policy and measurement. Members might agree with the policy of factoring percentage of cash flow into the compensation formula and yet not agree with the formula proposed. Beyond the complexities involved in the new policy, there was controversy over whether changes in levels of pay should be instituted only after the end of a calendar year, based on the results for that year, or whether adjustments should also be made midyear, especially during years when the CPI was rising rapidly.

It was in the immediate interest of workers to have pay adjusted upward twice a year and to lower the base figure below which diminished cash flow would result in a reduction in pay. Naturally, the general management of ULARCO favored a more conservative financial policy whereby pay adjustments would be made annually and a higher base-line figure used to reduce pay.

In working out the proposed formula, the governing council established that fluctuations in pay would be limited to a range of 25 percent below the increase in the CPI to 25 percent above, depending on cash flow. Thus, if the CPI for the previous year rose 8 percent, the maximum increase the members could receive would be 10 percent and the minimum increase would be 6 percent. In other words, the governing council did not allow the figures of the CPI to have an unmodified effect on pay. In a period of inadequate cash flow, pay could be 25 percent below the cost-of-living increase for the previous year, and, especially in a period of rapidly rising prices, compensation would lag behind the current increase in the CPI.

To link cash flow with the CPI, it was necessary to establish a base line for cash flow, at which point increases in pay would be equal to increases in the CPI. To determine this point, management examined the financial history of the ULARCO cooperatives and concluded that a cash flow of 12 percent was the minimum needed to maintain financial health. Because the practice in the past had been to grant pay increases of 1 percent above the previous year's increase in the CPI, the governing council recommended that a cash flow of 13 percent be the base line for determining pay increases.

On receiving the report from the Governing Council of ULARCO, the Permanent Central Commission took the report and proposal to the social councils of their cooperatives for further discussion and analysis.

Five weeks later, in January 1979, the Permanent Central Commission presented its criticism of the report to the Governing Council of ULARCO and to the social councils of constituent firms. Criticism concentrated more on social process than on substance. The PCC argued that the social councils should have participated more in analyzing the problems and devising the solutions. Attention was focused on the division between the responsibilities of the governing council and the consultative responsibilities of the social councils. The PCC complained that the governing council had presented the proposals as a minor adjustment in the compensation policy, whereas it really was a major change and thus deserved more time for study and consultation. Some members also expressed suspicion of management's motives in arriving at the new formula. The PCC questioned whether the proposed formula was scientific and argued that alternative solutions should be considered.

The criticism that members had not participated in the development of the management proposal had a formal legal justification and reflected the reactions of individual members as well. By this time, the Permanent Central Commission of ULARCO had reached an agreement with the governing council that any managerial proposals that met the following criteria would involve the social councils at all stages of the decision-making process: if they affected the terms and conditions of work, were completely new or different, and had been developed exclusively at technical or managerial levels (Gutiérrez-Johnson 1982, 345).

The governing council replied forcefully to the aspersions on the motives of its members: "This Governing Council wants to make it clear that there is no other reason (beyond achieving economic rationality) of any kind behind the initiation of this proposal." The governing council agreed that the members should have the opportunity to consider other options.

To the request for "scientific justification" for the new formula, the governing council replied:

We have been asked to give "scientific" support to the figure of 13 percent. However, in spite of the fact that an elegant technical study to justify it could be produced, it would not be honest to try to do so. Our choice is based on inference from experience and on what we expect the future to be.

The exchange between the Permanent Central Commission and the governing council was heated at some points, and the governing council criticized some of the questions raised as poorly thought out. Nevertheless, the governing council took pains to answer all the questions. In the process of this interchange, the members of the PCC had convinced themselves that it was necessary to shift to a compensation formula that would reflect economic rationality, leaving to further discussion how that formula would be worked out in detail. While this discussion was going on within the PCC, its members decided to enlist maximum participation by surveying the social councils of all the ULARCO firms. The question asked simply whether members were prepared to consider a change in the existing compensation policy to reflect more closely economic performance. About 60 percent of all members returned the questionnaire, and more than 90 percent of the respondents accepted in principle the need for such a change. This vote gave the PCC a mandate to move toward a more detailed examination of the implications of the proposed new pay formula.

The Permanent Central Commission of ULARCO directed its members to return to their cooperatives to guide a process of education and discussion in their social councils and, in the largest firms, in departmental small councils. The technical nature of the problem and the magnitude of the possible sacrifices workers would have to make appeared to call for a period of extended discussion. The PCC was not simply undertaking to educate the members and sell management's proposal. The purpose was also to give members the opportunity to challenge the proposal and to present alternative ways of meeting the economic problems.

There followed a lively discussion that involved more than just the officially recognized consultative bodies. At this time, ULARCO had not yet worked out its policies regarding the roles to be played by "groups of organized opinions," but two such groups participated actively. One represented the largest Basque union, ELA (Solidarity of Basque Workers), and the other was composed of a coalition of smaller Basque political groups and unions.

Having learned from the crisis of 1974, the PCC placed special emphasis on anticipating the consequences of the proposed changes. The PCC also provided training to those members who would serve as discussion moderators and guides in the constituent social councils, to ensure that they thoroughly understood all the technical complexities of the data to be analyzed and evaluated.

Out of the discussions emerged four alternatives to the governing council's proposal. The proposals put forth by ELA and by the coalition were similar. They agreed that economic performance should be used as a criterion for compensation but urged that a lower base for the cash flow index be used to determine at what point members' pay increases would drop below the cost-of-living increase. In other words, they favored a less conservative financing policy that would give the members more immediate income. Another group challenged the need to make any change and urged that the governing council's proposal be vetoed. The Social Council of Copreci presented a minor variation on the governing council's proposal.

After a period of discussion of these options, the ULARCO PCC carried out an advisory referendum in the constituents' social councils and small councils. Because Ulgor had almost half the total membership of ULARCO, the PCC reported separately on Ulgor and pooled the returns from the other five firms. In Ulgor, the coalition's option led with 51 percent of the vote, followed by the governing council's proposal with 20 percent and the Copreci option at 19 percent. In the other five firms, the governing council's proposal fared better with 32 percent but was still only a close second to the coalition's option, which received 35 percent. ELA followed with 15 percent, and Copreci polled 11 percent.

Examining these returns, the PCC noted that the combined totals for the governing council's proposal and for the similar Copreci option fell below 50 percent. Because a change in the compensation system required a two-thirds vote, it was now apparent that the governing council could not win without modifying its original proposal. The governing council bowed to members' views by lowering the base for the cash flow index so that the point at which pay increases would exactly equal the increase in the CPI was set at 10 percent. To balance this concession to workers' interests, the governing council proposed that the 1 percent increase over the CPI should apply not only to an index of 11 percent but also to 12 and 13 percent. The 11 to 13 percent figures were then labeled the "self-required range," indicating that the governing council judged that performance within this range was acceptable but not good enough to justify higher pay increases. The governing council then circulated a revised table (12.2) for the new compensation formula.

If the revised proposal could not gain a two-thirds majority in Ulgor,

Table 12.2.   Formula for Determining Compensation

Cash Flow as Percentage of Sales for Previous Fiscal Year	Percentage Change in Pay (*anticipos*) for Current Year
6	CPI minus 4%
7	CPI minus 3%
8	CPI minus 2%
9	CPI minus 1%
10	CPI
"Self-required range" { 11	CPI plus 1%
12	CPI plus 1%
13	CPI plus 1%
14	CPI plus 2%
15	CPI plus 3%
16	CPI plus 4%

SOURCE: Gutiérrez-Johnson 1982, 387.

it was exceedingly unlikely that it would win the percentage required for ULARCO as a whole. The PCC therefore carried out a straw vote among the members of Ulgor. Because the governing council had already made some accommodation to the desire of the members to lower the base point at which their pay increases would drop below increases in the CPI, the Permanent Central Commission simply offered members of Ulgor two options: the governing council's proposal or no change at all. To the great relief of the governing council, its proposal won 1,368 to 608, polling 69 percent of the vote.

The final decision was made at a meeting of the total membership of ULARCO. At this point, only the governing council's proposal was officially presented, but the members offered three amendments. Two were voted down. The third changed the pay adjustment period for years in which there was an exceptionally high rate of inflation. Thus, when the CPI rose more than eight percentage points in the first six months of any year, members' pay for the second semester would be raised by the amount of the percentage increase in the CPI for the first semester. The amended proposal was accepted by more than the two-thirds vote required. It had taken fifteen weeks from the time the governing council presented the proposal to the Permanent Central Commission until the final decision.

Recognizing that the members and the governing and consultative bodies had gone through a very intense, new, and difficult experience, the Social Council of Ulgor devoted some time to a critical evaluation of the process. The social council noted that the members had had to decide on matters of unprecedented complexity and stated that further study was needed on the role of the Permanent Central Commission of ULARCO in the total process. The Social Council of Ulgor also expressed concern about the lack of participation by women in the process and stated that in the future more time should be given to the education, discussion, and de-cision-making process when such major changes were proposed.

INCREASING MEMBERS' CAPITAL CONTRIBUTIONS

The management of ULARCO set in motion the next major change in the financial program when it presented a report to the social councils of ULARCO on January 25, 1980. The report was accompanied by an analysis of the inadequate self-financing of ULARCO firms from 1978 to 1980. It especially mentioned the mounting costs of credit and noted that the Bank of Spain, which had regulatory powers, had been exerting pressure on the Caja Laboral Popular to tighten its credit policies.

The report proposed that total capitalization for the group be increased by 1.8 billion pesetas (approximately $12 million) and that this additional capital be provided by the members over a three-year period. Several ways to raise this money were presented. The amount needed was estimated to represent a reduction in members' incomes of approximately 11 percent, allowing for the anticipated changes in the cost of living.

The report also spelled out the differential impact of the proposal. For those at the 1.00 pay level, the additional capital contribution would amount to 56,800 pesetas ($378.66). This was a hypothetical figure, however, since no members of the ULARCO firms had indexes lower than 1.40. At the time of the report, the average member of ULARCO had an index of 1.625. Members at this index would have been required to contribute an additional 92,300 pesetas ($615.32). For those at an index of 3.00, the contribution would have been 170,400 pesetas ($1,136).

The general management also proposed two other policy changes. One was to initiate a mandatory retirement age, which might reduce labor costs somewhat since, on the average, employees with longer service would have higher pay levels. In fact, the savings would have been minor, since most members had been retiring at sixty-five.

The second proposed change was to end the privilege given older members to transfer funds from their capital accounts to sons or daughters entering a cooperative. This had made it possible for some new members to join a cooperative while bringing in little if any additional capital. Making this change would mean that more capital would be raised in the long run, but it would have no immediate effect while the cooperatives were struggling to maintain employment and were not taking in additional members. These last two proposals were to be voted on in the general assembly called to decide on the governing council's proposal to increase capital contributions.

The next steps were taken by the Permanent Central Commission. On March 10, following its own study, the PCC submitted its report to the General Management of ULARCO and to the managements and social councils of the member firms. The PCC criticized the general management for providing an inadequate explanation of the causes of the capital deficiencies. The PCC agreed that a deficiency existed but argued that it was less than 60 percent of what the general management had estimated. The PCC report estimatēd the deficiency at 1.5 billion pesetas (about $7 million) and proposed that it could be made up if members' annual capital contributions totaled about $2.33 million per year—not $4 million, as the general management had proposed.

Before submitting its alternative proposal to the general management, the PCC had consulted with the social councils of the member cooperatives and secured their support. The general manager of ULARCO, Javier Mongelos, and the chairman of the governing council, Alfonso Gorroñogoitia, rejected the counterproposal and insisted on pushing ahead with the original proposal but modifying it slightly, so that the annual contributions would be 550 billion pesetas the first year, 600 billion the second year, and 650 billion the third year.

At this time, certain members of the Governing Council of ULARCO felt so strongly about their proposal that they let it be known that they would consider resigning if the members voted it down. In other words, the vote on the proposal was becoming a vote of confidence in the existing governing council. This was interpreted as putting pressure on the members to approve the general management's proposal, although it does not appear that a threat of resignation was ever formally made. Members of the Permanent Central Commission urged that the vote on this question not be considered a vote of confidence in the governing council. The argument was that the members did have confidence in top management but that there were legitimate differences of opinion on the technical question of how much money needed to be added to capital.

Having failed to move the governing council from its initial position, the members of the PCC, meeting on February 28, 1980, had to decide whether to maintain their opposition to the governing council or abandon it. The latter option would not have involved a simple surrender but rather throwing the issues back to the social councils of the member cooperatives and inviting members of these bodies to propose their own amendments to the General Assembly of ULARCO, which would ultimately vote the initial proposal up or down.

Those in favor of maintaining the PCC's position argued that they still believed in that alternative and that it had been supported in votes of all the social councils. Furthermore, they suggested that it would be useful to maintain this position publicly so that it might become acceptable to the members and to general management as a compromise if the governing council's proposal were voted down.

Those in favor of withdrawing the PCC's proposal argued that maintaining it would put the PCC in the opposition position of pressing labor demands (*organo de contrapoder, con actitud reivindicativa*). In other words, the PCC would be acting like a union. They further argued that maintaining this position would inhibit members of the constituent social councils from expressing their own views. The PCC's proposal was withdrawn at the February 28 meeting, and the issues were passed on to the various social councils.

In the discussions of the social councils leading up to the general assembly, individual members were allowed to propose amendments to the proposal, speaking either for themselves or for a group of members. This process opened the way for participation by unions and political bodies. A member speaking for ELA presented a report and an amendment against the additional capital contributions. Based on studies by members of ELA, he stated that in fact the capital shortage did not require immediate attention. ULARCO firms had recently made major investments that would bring in additional revenue, and more time was needed for the investments to pay off. The shortage of capital could therefore be viewed as temporary and destined to be reduced or eliminated as the fruits of investments materialized.

Although ELA's position represented a marked challenge to the position of the general management, the language of ELA's report was very respectful. It complimented the general management for its good intentions and serious work and claimed simply to express a disagreement on a technical matter—the formula for estimating future capital requirements.

On matters to be decided by ULARCO, voting is based on a complex set of rules and procedures designed to balance the interests of the larger and smaller firms. On one hand, because Ulgor had nearly half the total members of all ULARCO firms, a decisive majority within Ulgor could outweigh small opposing majorities within all the other firms. Such a result would give the impression that ULARCO was dominated by Ulgor and thus produce tensions between Ulgor and the other firms. On the other hand, if each cooperative registered a single vote reflecting the majority of its members, a large majority within Ulgor could be overturned by small majorities within three or four of the other cooperatives. Such a result would appear to the members of Ulgor as a serious violation of democratic principles. The leaders of ULARCO had therefore worked out a formula so that the votes were counted two ways: one based on the unweighted totals of votes in all the firms together, the other giving the smaller firms somewhat increased weight. To achieve the final result, the sums derived from the two methods were added together and divided by two. (For further details on this formula, see Gutiérrez-Johnson 1982, 365–68.)

At the general assembly meeting in April 1980, 61.9 percent of the members voted in favor of the general management's proposal. Passage required two-thirds of the votes, so the proposal was rejected. The other proposals were approved by large majorities, but they were of lesser importance and did not require a two-thirds vote. The members voted to accept the mandatory retirement age of sixty-five and to end the right of members to transfer capital to family members who were joining a cooperative. A proposal to reduce overtime payments also was approved by 66.4 percent, slightly less than two-thirds but more than enough for the necessary majority. This change reduced the bonus for daytime overtime slightly to 10 percent and the overtime rate for the night shift from 45 to 30 percent.

The general management decided at this time to continue its study of the capital needs of the ULARCO group so that a new proposal could be submitted to the general assembly in 1981. At the same time the general management voted to strengthen the position of the PCC as an organic element in the structure of ULARCO, such that it would explicitly provide advice and consultation to the General Management and the Governing Council of ULARCO.

In 1981, the general management returned to the membership with what was basically the original proposal but supported by a different and more exhaustive financial analysis. The PCC made its own analysis and this time came out in support of the proposal. Why did the PCC change its position? Two conditions seem to have been involved. For one, an additional year had passed and Spain was still in a deep recession, so that it was harder to believe that ULARCO's financial crisis was a temporary problem that would solve itself with the revival of business activity. Two, the governing council and the PCC had consulted more than during the first effort. Members were thus more thoroughly familiar with the governing council's financial analysis.

The PCC's endorsement of the governing council's proposal was passed on to the social councils of the constituent cooperatives, where it met with a more favorable reception than in the previous year. Nevertheless, members were invited to study the proposal and to submit amendments for consideration at the general assembly in April 1981.

Of the amendments proposed, only one departed radically from the governing council's proposal, and this was voted down. The governing council had accepted three of the amendments and two of the four parts of the fourth. It is noteworthy that these amendments did not challenge the basic proposal but instead called for clarifications and changes in wording to make the proposal more understandable to the members.

The proposal and amendments were accepted by a vote of 69.6 percent of the members. Ulgor's vote was slightly less than two-thirds (64.8 percent), but the other firms were all above two-thirds, ranging from Ederlan (67.8 percent) to Copreci (81.3 percent). Almost 70 percent of the members of ULARCO voted in this referendum.

The new regulation required that the additional capital contributions be secured in equal amounts from the interest paid on each member's capital account in June and December and from payroll deductions for the next three years. Following Spanish custom, the cooperatives had been paying salaries in twelve monthly installments plus two additional payments, which were made in July and December. The plan called for half the required capital contribution to be withheld from the two extra paychecks.

In the case of recently hired members, whose interest payments would be less than half their capital obligation, the required total would be secured by withholding additional money from their two extra paychecks. Finally, general management allowed for special treatment of members who had financial difficulties. They could appeal to the governing council of their cooperative, requesting exemption from the capital contribution or for a total or partial delay in making payments.

To visualize the effects of the decision to increase capital contributions, it is important to distinguish between the transfer of cash money and paper transactions. Under the new policy, the cooperatives did not receive any cash money from their members. For three years, ULARCO reduced the cash it paid out on members' capital accounts. During the same period, it credited members' capital accounts with the sums that had been withheld from their two extra paychecks. In effect, like the members' initial capital contribution, the sums that were withheld were treated as if they were loans from members to their cooperatives. As noted before, the capital contribution policy resulted in an 11 percent reduction in the cash income (paychecks plus interest payments) of members of ULARCO.

While changing its capital contributions, ULARCO also changed its policy on working hours. The customary workday had been 8 hours and 25 minutes, and each member had been guaranteed the right to work 1,820 hours in the year. The new policy eliminated as much overtime as possible by adjusting the hours worked per day to seasonal demand. Hours worked could now be increased to ten per day for weeks at a time or reduced to six per day.

We found members of the Social Council of Ulgor in general agreement with the new policy but concerned about the way it was initially implemented. They said that some people in management were inclined to change hours worked as if pushing a button on a machine and that this posed serious problems for members. They argued that seasonal fluctuations were largely predictable and that members should be given six weeks' notice of changes in hours. Management declined to go this far but agreed to a minimum of fifteen days' notice.

We have described these changes in compensation and employment policies in considerable detail to illustrate what is involved in carrying out major shifts in policy. Changes require an extended and complex process of discussion and negotiation within each cooperative and between the cooperatives and management of the group. Major changes cannot be accomplished quickly, yet the time and money expended in the process is justified if the decisions ultimately meet the financial needs of the organizations and are reasonably satisfactory to the members. There is a further standard of judgment: Is the decision viable over a long period of time, or do the leaders and members soon have to repeat the process to find a different solution to the same problem?

In a cooperative, these apparently different standards of judgment must go together. If the decision fails to meet the financial needs of the organization and to be at least minimally acceptable to the members, leaders and members will soon have to reexamine the policy through another extended process of discussion, negotiation, and voting.

Both of the major decisions discussed in this chapter appear to have stood the test of time. The pay formula established in 1979 was not seriously questioned during the following seven years. Between 1981 and 1986 no further capital contributions were sought from the members, and by 1986 there were sufficient signs of economic recovery and increasing financial strength to provide hope that ULARCO had moved beyond the period of financial sacrifices.

In these two changes, the decision-making process differed in one important respect. At the end of the discussion process, the members agreed to shift the basis of compensation to economic performance, thereby introducing only a minor adjustment in the formula proposed by the management and governing council. In the first vote on capital contributions, less than the necessary two-thirds of the members endorsed it. They then had to spend another year in study, discussion, and negotiation before the final vote of approval.

Why did the capital contribution issue prove to be so much more difficult to resolve? In the case of the pay formula, the members were not being called upon to make any immediate financial sacrifice. They probably recognized that, for the next few years, their pay might be lower than they would have received under the old policy. Still, there was a chance of avoiding any sacrifice if the performance of ULARCO improved, the national and world economy revived, and inflation did not increase. With the capital contribution, the situation was quite different. The proposed contribution meant a decline in annual income of about 11 percent for three years.

Even in facing these most difficult and complex decisions, characteristically, the leaders of ULARCO were unwilling to push for solutions that would simply address immediate problems. Before deciding on any compensation formula, they had to agree on a set of guiding principles. This was not only a reflection of the values of the decision makers. They recognized that they had to provide an understandable rationale grounded in basic principles before the members would accept any formula.

The process involved in bringing about this major change required that extended time be devoted to education, discussion, and decision making and that a large number of members be actively involved. If the governing council's proposal had simply been announced to the members before the membership meeting and a vote called for, it is likely that the proposal would have been rejected. Out of this participation process arose a consensus on the need to abandon the status quo and to adopt a new pay formula that would more adequately represent economic performance. Yet, the final result did not just reflect the ability of management to get the members to accept its decision. To gain acceptance for the basic principles of its proposal, management had to modify the formula in response to members' expressed desires.

This case provides an impressive testament to the need for dual representation in large worker cooperatives or cooperative groups. In Mondragón, the governing council represents the interests of members as co-owners, whereas the social councils represent the interests of members as workers. In the long and painful process of working out the financial sacrifices necessary for the economic health of the ULARCO firms, the social councils played the essential role of organizing and guiding the education, discussion, and decision making.

How did the members view the basic decisions and the process of arriving at them? We have no idea about rank-and-file members, but managers we talked to believed that they had gone through a very difficult period of readjustment and had emerged from the struggle with a membership that was more mature and understanding of its financial needs. Those in leadership positions also had learned how to improve the consultation and participation process in working through highly technical matters.

We were particularly interested in Alfonso Gorroñogoitia's evaluation. A man of enormous prestige who was one of the five Ulgor pioneers, Gorroñogoitia still held two key positions as chairman of the governing councils of ULARCO and of the Caja. Initially, Gorroñogoitia had been very disappointed with the 1980 rejection. He pointed out that the general management faced two major difficulties. For years, members had been accustomed to increasing their incomes every year, and suddenly they had to face the trauma of making sacrifices. He also objected to the requirement that a major change required a two-thirds vote and thus that just over one-third of the members could block necessary changes.

Did general management make mistakes in handling the process of decision making? He did not think that management's mistakes were important but added that having only two months to act on such a major matter did present problems. Furthermore, the data required for an informed decision were highly technical, so that it was impossible for most members really to understand the figures. He acknowledged that honest and intelligent individuals could examine the same figures and come to different conclusions. He pointed out that those who had opposed the initial proposal had not only stated their position but had backed it up with their own technical analysis. Finally, although he was upset that the proposal was initially rejected, he insisted that he was now encouraged by the interest members showed and by their recognition of the necessities of business operations.

The way this issue was handled provides an interesting illustration of the problems of defining the role of the social councils. If the same individuals in the PCC had been representing a union in a private firm and had been at an impasse with the management on wage issues, the union would have had to accept management's position or express its opposition by calling a strike. Within ULARCO, there was another alternative: Because members ultimately had the right and the power to make decisions, the PCC could refer the question back to the social councils in preparation for the vote. In the case of these major policy questions, ultimate power rested in the hands of the total membership.

On the one hand, if power means the capacity to make a decision and impose it on others, then the PCC and the social councils were powerless. On the other hand, in clarifying technical aspects of management proposals and building an educational process to make management more aware of and concerned with the views of workers, and in helping workers understand the rationale behind management's recommendations, the advisory organs played indispensable intermediary roles.

This chapter has focused exclusively on ULARCO. Although the experience of ULARCO must have been followed with interest by leaders in other cooperatives, they had to adjust to the recession in their own ways, within their own groups. In the next chapter, we turn to a problem that could not be handled completely within any cooperative group and that required a systemwide program.

13 Providing for Unemployment Compensation and Support

During the years of expansion, unemployment in Mondragón was a minor problem. Displaced workers generally could be temporarily transferred to cooperatives that were expanding, and even if there were no immediate openings, unemployed members rarely had to wait longer than a few weeks.

The recession required the leaders of the complex to make major changes to support unemployed workers. These changes were made in several stages, but to simplify a complicated story, we will limit ourselves to an examination of the system prevailing in 1985. The policies and procedures we describe provide further evidence of the ways in which leaders and members support the principle of solidarity throughout the complex.

By the beginning of the 1980s, approximately two-thirds of the industrial and agribusiness cooperatives had been formed into groups, and the Caja was continuing to promote the formation of such groups by offering to contribute half the salaries of the members of the general management for the first three years. Although none of the other groups had as tightly integrated a structure as ULARCO, the general managements were being called on by the Caja, Lagun-Aro (the social security cooperative), and their own cooperatives to assume increasing responsibilities in adjusting to the conditions of the recession.

In the discussion that follows, we will focus particularly on the ways in which Lagun-Aro worked with and through the cooperative groups. To deal with the cooperatives that were linked with Lagun-Aro but that did not belong to any group, Lagun-Aro worked out somewhat modified policies and procedures (not described here).

BALANCING RIGHTS AND OBLIGATIONS

The cooperative group assumes primary responsibility for finding jobs for surplus members of its constituent cooperatives. When the group is unable to absorb these members, as was often the case during the recession, major responsibility shifts to Lagun-Aro. But this does not mean that the cooperative group has no future responsibilities. According to policies to be described, the individual cooperative and the group of cooperatives share the expenses of the relocation and unemployment-support program.

On the twelve-member Governing Council of Lagun-Aro, only one member, Chairman Román Balanzategui, works full time for Lagun-Aro, where he is director of the medical program. One member represents the Caja Laboral Popular, and the others each represent a cooperative group. Thus the governing council provides representation both for Lagun-Aro and for the cooperatives and cooperative groups it serves. To be sure, the numbers are heavily weighted in favor of the organizations served, but this does not mean that it is in the interests of those organizations to extract the maximum possible financial benefits out of Lagun-Aro. The social security cooperative is financed largely by payroll charges levied on the members of the cooperatives linked with it. These charges are discussed and negotiated between Lagun-Aro and the cooperatives and are discussed and finally determined within the Governing Council of Lagun-Aro. Decisions do not reflect the bargaining power of the parties in these discussions but rather their commitment both to aiding laid-off fellow workers and to maintaining a financially sound support organization.

In 1980, Lagun-Aro established the payroll tax at 0.50 percent so that a fund could be built up to support the costs of unemployment and relocation of members. By 1985, the tax had risen to 2.35 percent. This does not mean, however, that the fund supported the entire costs of relocation and unemployment. Major costs were shared by the cooperatives and Lagun-Aro, as we will see in the following account of policies and procedures.

POLICIES AND PROCEDURES FOR
PROGRAM IMPLEMENTATION

Lagun-Aro distinguishes between transitory unemployment, caused by seasonal or short-term fluctuations in the product market, and structural unemployment, a condition in which previous levels of employment seem impossible to maintain. In the latter case, the affected cooperative reports to Lagun-Aro that it is in a situation of "structural unemployment."

Lagun-Aro has two commissions to deal with such cases. The Support Commission (*Comisión de Prestaciones*) evaluates the cooperative's report that it is experiencing structural unemployment and, if it accepts the designation, works out with the cooperative the kinds and levels of support it will get. The Relocations Commission (*Comisión de Reubicaciones*) works with the cooperative and its cooperative group and beyond that group, if necessary, to transfer surplus people to cooperatives that need new members. Both commissions are chosen by the Governing Council of Lagun-Aro.

Lagun-Aro provides financial support for relocation, unemployment, early retirement, indemnities, and retraining.

Relocation

If the cooperative group is unable to transfer displaced members to a firm in its own group, Lagun-Aro assumes responsibility for trying to find a job for the displaced member in one of the other Mondragón cooperatives. If a job is found in a cooperative no more than fifty kilometers from the member's home or previous place of employment (whichever is shorter), the member is required to accept it—the alternative being to give up the unemployment support. At the same time, these cooperatives agree not to hire new people without the approval of Lagun-Aro.

If it is necessary for a member to relocate, Lagun-Ago covers the costs involved. A distinction is made between temporary relocation and permanent relocation. In the former case, the displaced worker retains membership in his original cooperative for a period of time, on the assumption that he or she will return to it. Lagun-Aro covers the costs of the worker's travel, per-diem costs, and the difference between the pay the member is now receiving and what he or she received before being displaced. If a worker is permanently relocated, Lagun-Aro pays only "extraordinary expenses," the determination of their nature and justification being in the hands of the Governing Council of Lagun-Aro, in consultation with the Relocations Commission.

Unemployment

While members are unemployed, they receive 80 percent of their basic take-home pay (*anticipo de consumo mensual*) plus 100 percent of what they would be paying to the social security fund if they were still employed. These combined amounts are paid fourteen times over a twelve-month period, in conformity with the Spanish practice of having two extra pay periods.

Unemployed members are allowed to receive up to twelve months of unemployment compensation in any two-year period. If more than 25 percent of the members of a given cooperative are out of work, support can be continued for a longer period if the Governing Council of Lagun-Aro so decides. If a cooperative is shut down and abandoned, displaced members are entitled to twenty-four months of unemployment compensation. If a member becomes self-employed or takes a job outside the complex, unemployment support is discontinued—unless Lagun-Aro authorizes continuing payments. (This exception allows for cases in which someone who is self-employed is struggling on far less income than he or she received from the cooperative.)

Early Retirement

A member is entitled to early retirement if the cooperative has been declared in a state of structural unemployment and if he or she is fifty-eight years old (and less than sixty-five), is difficult to relocate, and has already received twelve months of unemployment compensation. On retirement and until he or she is sixty-five, the member gets 60 percent of his or her regular take-home pay and 100 percent of what would have been paid for social security coverage, but only twelve monthly payments. At sixty-five, this support is canceled and the member begins receiving a regular pension. The early retirement support is also canceled if the member becomes self-employed or gets another job, unless continued support is approved by Lagun-Aro.

Indemnities

Members are also eligible for a lump-sum payment, or indemnification, if the cooperative for which they worked has been declared in structural unemployment and they are under fifty-eight years of age, have already contributed for at least two years to Lagun-Aro, and are hard to relocate—as judged by the Relocations Commission.

The lump-sum payment varies depending on the number of years that the member has contributed to Lagun-Aro. A member who has been in the social security system for two to five years receives the equivalent of twelve monthly payments. For each additional year, the lump sum is increased by one monthly payment. In accepting this indemnification, the member relieves Lagun-Aro of any further financial obligation. If the member gets a job within the cooperative complex in less than a year, he or she is obligated to repay all the support. If the member gets a job after receiving payments for a full year, he or she is required to pay back 75 percent. If the job is secured after two full years, the repayment is 50 percent; after three full years, 25 percent; and after four full years the member has no obligation to repay. A cooperative can agree to supplement what the laid-off member receives from Lagun-Aro.

Retraining

The cooperatives assume responsibility for retraining members moved from one cooperative to another. To receive support from Lagun-Aro, the cooperative must first apply to the government for as much assistance as can be granted. Lagun-Aro helps secure this state support.

Eligibility Requirements

There is a waiting period of eighteen months from the time a cooperative is started until its members are eligible for support from Lagun-Aro. There is no waiting period, however, if the cooperative is a spinoff of a preexisting cooperative.

To be eligible for support from Lagun-Aro for its laid-off members, a cooperative has to meet certain financial and other requirements. It must be up-to-date in meeting its financial requirements to Lagun-Aro. The cooperative must not pay any overtime, hire any new workers, or increase the pay of its members unless specifically authorized to do so by Lagun-Aro.

COST SHARING

A cooperative also is heavily obligated to share in financing unemployment support. The formula in effect in the spring of 1985 linked the percentages contributed by the members of the firm affected and Lagun-Aro according to the extent to which the cooperative had reduced its rates of pay to help cover unemployment expenses.

Table 13.1. Formula for Determining Responsibility in Sharing Unemployment Costs

Level of Pay	Maximum Reduction of Pay	Percentage Paid by Employed Members	Percentage Paid by Lagun-Aro
100%	16%	70	30
100	15	50	50
99	14	47	53
98	13	44	56
97	12	41	59
96	11	38	62
95	10	35	65
94	9	32	68
93	8	29	71
92	7	26	74
91	6	23	77
90	5	20	80
89	4	16	84
88	3	12	88
87	2	8	92
86	1	6	96
85	0	0	100

To figure the obligations of the affected cooperative, its current pay level is compared with the weighted average pay of the other cooperatives in its group. The higher the pay level of the affected cooperative, the larger the share of support to unemployed members it is obligated to cover. The higher the pay deductions the employed members of the cooperative are willing to accept, the greater the proportion covered by Lagun-Aro. In table 13.1, the 100 percent level of pay is that prevailing in the cooperative group before the recession forced the members to take cuts.

Mondragón has been able to provide displaced members with far more employment and financial assistance than is available from private Spanish enterprises. This level of support would have not been possible had Mondragón not had far lower unemployment rates than private firms. A June 1985 survey (Trabajo y Unión, November 1985) reported that 1,197 members of Mondragón cooperatives—6.9 percent of the total membership—were unemployed. The rate was three times higher in the Basque country. If we look at how Mondragón defines unemployment, the figures are even more impressive. Of the 1,197 members who were unemployed, 792 were temporarily relocated in other Mondragón cooperatives (classified as "underemployed"), and 301 were still on the payrolls of their own cooperatives although their work was not needed (classified as "hidden unemployment"). Only 104, 0.6 percent, were receiving support payments from Lagun-Aro and would therefore be classified as unemployed according to customary definitions in the United States.

14 From ULARCO to FAGOR

To understand how ULARCO coped with economic adversity, adopted a new development strategy, and became FAGOR, we need to review the earlier years of the cooperative group.

FROM A LOOSE FEDERATION TO AN INTEGRATED MANAGEMENT: 1964–75

During the first five years of ULARCO, from 1965 to 1970, the general management of the group consisted of the coequal managers of the constituent cooperatives, plus some support personnel. This structure provided freedom to develop some exchange of services and information but lacked the capacity for leadership in strategic planning for the group as a whole.

The appointment in 1970 of Javier Mongelos to the newly created position of general manager of ULARCO was important in that it opened the way to strategic planning for the group. It also marked an important stage in managerial succession. Up to this point the key leadership positions both in the Caja and in Ulgor had been held by the Ulgor pioneers. Mongelos was not part of this founding group; nor had he grown up in the city of Mondragón. His educational background was also somewhat different from that of the founding group in that his major field in the university was not engineering but physics.

In 1986 we had a long talk with Mongelos about his views on the problems facing him in his new position and his general strategies and philosophy. Moving from manager of a single cooperative (Fagor Electrotécnica), Mongelos spent the first months as general manager studying the financial aspects of each firm. When his personnel director left ULARCO, Mongelos concentrated on studying the personnel field.

I got myself a bibliography and began reading. As I studied the writings of several people who were supposed to be experts in the field, I realized that our personnel people were not performing the right functions for management. They were being sort of confessors (*confesionarios*) for individual workers. It was all on an individual basis. Some individual would come in to talk about his problems. With this orientation, some small individual problems might be solved, but that did not deal with major structural problems.

With Mongelos's encouragement, the personnel department began to play a major role in leadership training for participatory management by objectives. Personnel people also began working closely with management in analyzing organizational problems and working out changes in structure and in appointments to managerial positions. And, as we have already discussed, personnel people played leading roles in designing and implementing changes in the forms of work.

INTERVENTIONS AND REORGANIZATIONS: 1976–83

Beginning in the 1970s, the general management became involved in the first of a series of emergency interventions to reorganize Fagor Electrotécnica, which was in serious financial difficulties.

Fagor Electrotécnica

The crisis threatening Fagor Electrotécnica (manufacturer of electronic components and products) had been building well before the end of the 1970s, as reflected in the record of pooled profits and losses among all the ULARCO firms. Through 1974, the firm had received 17.5 million pesetas more than it had contributed to that pool. In a single year (1975) the firm's drain on the pool jumped to 60 million pesetas, and a year later the deficit had increased to 85.4 million. Because Fagor Electrotécnica was becoming such a heavy drain on the resources of the total group, attention had shifted to whether it should be sharply reduced in size or abandoned. Seeing no way to save the firm, members of the cooperative's top management had become demoralized. The head of marketing, who could not in good conscience claim that his firm's products were superior to those of the competition, had asked to be reassigned. At the same time, the whole management team had appealed to ULARCO for help in reorganizing the firm.

The reorganization of Fagor Electrotécnica took five to six years, beginning in 1976, and there was much to be done. One might therefore assume that it took a major portion of Mongelos's time. On the contrary, he told us, "I only dedicated about three or four mornings a month to Fagor Electrotécnica." Those mornings, though few, were clearly vital to turning the firm around. In addition to the workers still with the firm, Mongelos depended on the full-time support of José Luis Gonzalez, whom he shifted from a position as head of ULARCO's Organizational and Evaluation Services.

Mongelos and Gonzalez worked with Fagor Electrotécnica committees in carrying out the following changes:

1. The number of items in the catalog was reduced by discontinuing production of some items generating high costs and little revenue. This reduction was complemented by intensified efforts in export marketing.

2. New products were developed and introduced.

3. Personnel was reduced from 500 to about 425—affecting direct and indirect labor, middle and top management, and engineers. This was the largest reduction yet within ULARCO, and it involved transferring the surplus people to other cooperatives.

4. A new chief executive was appointed.

5. One electronics section of Fagor Electrotécnia and a section of Copreci were added to Aurki, which then expanded rapidly in the production of machines for automated assembly processes.

6. Low-interest loans were secured through a national government program aimed at strengthening firms with a record of exporting and prospects for increasing their exports. (According to a later report of the minister of industry to a commission of the national legislature, Fagor Electrotécnica became a model of how a firm should use such government assistance.

Ulgor

The next intervention, in Ulgor, presented a much more difficult challenge to ULARCO. Not only was Ulgor the first and largest firm in the complex, but over the years it had been by far the most profitable. The figures show (Gutiérrez-Johnson 1982) that from 1964 to 1974 only two of the six ULARCO firms had contributed more to the common pool than they had received. The machine tool firm, Arrasate, had contributed a net amount of 4.5 million pesetas, whereas Ulgor had contributed 67.9 million. In 1975, Ulgor was the only contributor to the common pool, and it contributed 133.6 million pesetas. In 1976, it contributed 133.1 million pesetas, dwarfing the contributions of Arrasate (11.5 million) and Fagor Industrial (6.1 million).

Suddenly, in 1979, Ulgor's earnings dropped precipitously to the break-even point. In 1981 and 1982, the firm suffered serious losses for the first time.

The losses sent shock waves throughout ULARCO and were a matter of serious concern to the supporting organizations, particularly the Caja. Because the other firms in ULARCO were struggling to hold their ground and could not possibly make up for Ulgor's deficits out of current earnings, Ulgor's losses threatened to decapitalize the whole cooperative group.

During the intervention, Mongelos worked closely with the Governing Council of Ulgor and with Ulgor committees to carry out a study of the firm's problems and of management's performance. The study concluded that Ulgor had become a victim of its own success. With a rapidly expanding market, Ulgor had grown without a long-term strategic plan. In the process of growth, the firm had also become rather rigid, so that people tended to remain in the same department or plant and to develop strong attachments to their particular turf. Rapid growth had been accompanied by rapid internal promotion, which had raised to middle- or higher-level positions individuals who seemed lacking in the perspective and vision needed for future operations.

The reorganization plan called for changing three of the four men in the top positions and all the plant managers. The plan also called for a reduction in total employment, by about 120 the first year and another 100 in the second. No one was laid off, but some workers had to move from white- to blue-collar jobs within Ulgor or in another cooperative in the group.

Management made the initial judgments on which workers should stay and which should move, but these decisions were reviewed by the Central Social Council, which established a committee of white-collar workers to consider any appeals. Displaced members could also appeal to the Governing Council of Ulgor. During this reduction in personnel, management refrained from bringing in new people unless they had abilities essential to the cooperative.

The reorganization also involved major structural changes. Previously, responsibilities for quality, manufacturing processes (industrial engineering), and production had been separate. Now each plant manager (*jefe de planta*) assumed overall responsibility for approximately six hundred workers. Reflecting this enlargement of their responsibilities, the plant managers became members of the Management Council of Ulgor.

The reorganization of Ulgor got under way at the time the Spanish government was intensifying its program to assist companies that had performed well in the past and that appeared to have good prospects for expanding their exports. For guidance on which firms in "white goods" (kitchen and household equipment) to support, the government had contracted with the Spanish branch of the U.S. firm of McKinsey and Company.

McKinsey reported that the inherent strengths of Ulgor and its future prospects justified support. Ulgor indeed had major financial problems, but it remained in sounder condition than most of its competitors. For example, Fernando Gomez Acedo, the new manager of the refrigerator plant, told us in 1983 that, although Ulgor was producing 22 percent of the refrigerators in the Spanish market, it had only 4 percent of the total losses of all the Spanish refrigerator manufacturers.

The Spanish government loaned Ulgor $12 million based not only on the McKinsey feasibility study but on the reorganization plan worked out within Ulgor and ULARCO. The plan had demonstrated to the government that the cooperatives were taking major measures to strengthen their organizations.

In consultation with Mongelos, the Governing Council of Ulgor decided to offer the position of CEO of Ulgor to Jesús Catania, who was then the CEO of Copreci, the electromechanical components firm which, with about eight hundred members, was second in size to Ulgor. A decade earlier, when he had been plant manager, Catania had played a major role in the job-redesign program at Copreci. He was looked on not only as an administrator who was skilled in handling human resources but as a creative, imaginative individual. As an indication of his reputation in and commitment to the field of technological research, Catania was also chairman of the Governing Council of Ikerlan.

At first Catania declined the position in Ulgor. He explained that he was happy in his position at Copreci and was reluctant to move.

Several weeks later, Mongelos made the offer again and urged Catania to change his mind. The message was that the fate of Ulgor was crucial to the ULARCO group and that Catania was the only man who could assure Ulgor's success. Catania explained his decision to accept by saying that he weighed his personal preferences against his obligations to the Mondragón movement. When we talked with him in October 1983 he was in the middle of the reorganization of Ulgor and seemed to be enjoying the challenge. By 1985 Ulgor was making modest profits, and in late 1986 the demand for its products was expanding so rapidly that production was hard-pressed to keep up with orders.

RESTRUCTURING THE COOPERATIVE GROUP: 1985–86

In the 1970s and 1980s, the management of ULARCO concentrated its efforts on the rescue and revival of individual cooperatives, especially Fagor Electrotécnia and Ulgor. Management continues to devote some of its resources to interventions. In fact, during our visits from 1984 to 1986, major efforts were under way to return Arrasate to a sound financial base. The machine tool firm had been suffering from the same sharp drop in the world market that had affected companies in the United States.

Having resolved the severe crises in Fagor Electrotécnica and Ulgor, ULARCO's management concentrated on developing a basic strategy for the next ten years. The new strategy, approved by the members in June 1986, involved a restructuring of the cooperative group. The reorganization was based on plans initially presented by the general manager to the Governing Council of ULARCO and then discussed extensively by that council, the Central Social Council, and the governing councils and social councils of the various member cooperatives. This process led to some modifications of the original plans. The restructuring of the central cooperative group was considered of such importance that three consecutive issues of *Trabajo y Unión* (Nos. 293–295, June, July-August, and September 1986) were devoted largely to describing and discussing the changes.

The rationale for management's proposals was laid out at length by General Manager Mongelos (No. 293) and by Alfonso Gorroñogoitia, chairman of the Governing Council of ULARCO (No. 295). Both Mongelos and Gorroñogoitia emphasized the importance of marketing as the driving force behind the restructuring. Mongelos pointed out that, in that the Spanish market for consumer products in 1986 was only 70 percent of what it had been in 1979, it was more vital than ever that the cooperative group orient its strategies and plans toward exports. Since the entry of Spain into the European Common Market, in 1986, the marketing challenge has been even more serious. Before this, the tariff barriers against Spanish industrial exports to the rest of Europe were small compared to those Spain imposed on industrial imports from Common Market countries. The entry of Spain into the Common Market has accentuated the drive of Common Market countries to Spain, whereas the reduction in the tariffs on Spanish exports has yielded little advantage to Spanish industry.

To ensure the survival of its consumer products companies, the cooperative group must continue to invest heavily in technological modernization. Only then will output per worker continue to increase as the work force steadily decreases. To increase or even maintain overall employment, the group must give special emphasis to the development of technologically advanced firms and the creation of new cooperatives.

Mongelos indicated that, although the group had invested a total of 3 billion pesetas in development during the three years 1981–83, the figure had jumped to 7.5 billion for 1984 and 1985, and for one year, 1986, the group was committed to investing 6 billion. This investment program was worked out jointly with Ikerlan so that its contribution to the technological progress of the various firms of the group could be guided by the strategic plan. Mongelos also stressed the importance of developing relations with other research and educational institutions.

The strategy now being implemented depends on restructuring the group's management and strengthening the marketing appeal of the group's products. This program represents a greater unity of purpose than in the past.

Another major change during this period was in the name of the group. Ulgor had been producing products under the trademark of FAGOR, and some, but not all, of the other firms in the group also had. Because the FAGOR trademark was by far the best known internationally, management proposed that all future products of firms in the group bear the FAGOR trademark. Although the logic of this change was well recognized, the proposal provoked a vigorous debate and resistance from those who felt that the change would reduce the autonomy of the individual cooperatives. The proposal was finally adopted, but with the understanding that Copreci, which sold some of its products to companies in competition with Ulgor, could continue for a time with its own trademark.

The symbolic change in name was accompanied by a shift to a divisional organization. Formerly, there had been no position in the hierarchy between the individual cooperative and the management of the group. With

Table 14.1. *Divisional Organization of* FAGOR *(1986) (estimates for sales and investments in billions of pesetas)*

	Sales			Investments Committed	Employment
	Spain	Exports	Total		
Consumer Products					
Ulgor	16,248	6,069	22,317	4,316	2,189
Lenniz	662	171	833	30	123
Radar	1,401	57	1,458	63	118
Fagor Clima	1,489	221	1,710	168	204
Fagor Industrial	1,856	892	2,748	174	320
Total Division	21,656	7,410	29,066	4,791	2,954
Industrial Components					
Copreci	2,101	2,928	5,029	485	958
Ederlan	2,367	2,286	4,653	486	640
Fagor Electrotécnica	791	1,944	2,735	343	538
Leunkor	289	—	289	62	74
Total Division	5,548	7,158	12,706	1,376	2,210
Engineering and Capital Goods					
Arrasate	1,054	632	1,686	48	305
Aurki	1,102	806	1,908	111	251
Uldata	726	—	726	29	81
Ulmatik	274	404	688	34	71
Total Division	3,156	1,842	4,998	222	708
FAGOR Totals	30,360	16,410	46,770	6,389	5,878

SOURCE: *Trabajo y Unión*, No. 294 (July-August 1986)

the approval of the restructuring in June 1986, the group now called FAGOR was organized in three divisions: consumer products, industrial components, and engineering and capital equipment.

Table 14.1 provides a list of the firms in each division and projected 1986 figures for sales (Spain and exports), investments, and employment.

Although Ulgor had been reduced in size between 1974 and 1986 from approximately 3,500 members to 2,189, as the table indicates, it still produced almost as much income as all the other FAGOR cooperatives together. Over the years, this heavy financial dependence on Ulgor is expected to decline, but clearly the success of the total cooperative group still depends in large measure on the performance of Mondragón's first cooperative.

The cooperative group also made enormous gains in exports from 1976 to 1986. In 1976, exports totaled little more than 10 percent of total sales. In 1986, FAGOR's total exports were estimated at 35 percent. The industrial components firms led with 56 percent, followed by engineering and capital equipment (37 percent) and consumer products (25 percent).

Also included are a chart indicating the products of each cooperative (table 14.2) and a chart representing the evolution of the cooperative group (fig. 14.1). Note the leading role of Ulgor in this evolution. Of the thirteen cooperatives in FAGOR, four were spun off from Ulgor. Ulgor played a leading role in converting a private firm to Ederlan by spinning off its own foundry to join it, and Ulgor cooperated with Ederlan, Arrasate, and Copreci in creating Leunkor.

The new organizational plan involved the selection of three division managers. The selection of a woman to head one of these divisions represented a dramatic advance for women into top-management positions. Through most of the 1970s, high-ranking women were found only in advisory positions. By the 1980s, several women had moved up to positions as plant managers in FAGOR. The plan also called for changes in the management council, which previously had been composed of the directors of the various services of each of the individual cooperatives— a total of twenty members. The new structure reduced the management council to the three directors of the divisions, the directors of the five central services units, the chairperson of the Governing Council of FAGOR, and the general manager. The new structure established a management council for each division, presided over by its manager and composed of the managers of each cooperative in the division.

The governing council recommended a change in its own composition

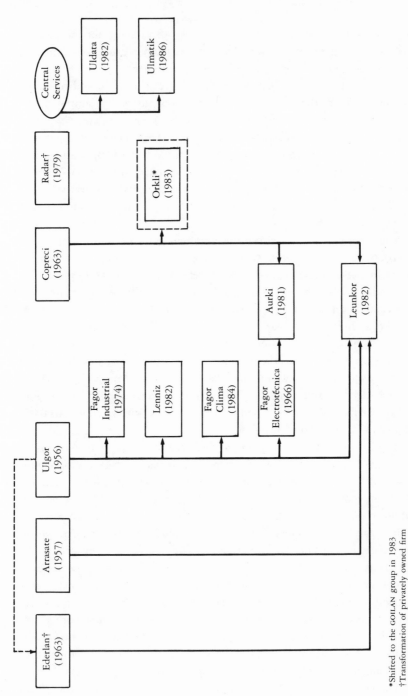

*Shifted to the GOILAN group in 1983
†Transformation of privately owned firm

Figure 14.1. *Evolution of ULARCO/FAGOR Cooperatives*

Table 14.2.   *Products and Processes in* ULARCO/FAGOR *(1986–87)*

Consumer Products	Industrial Components	Engineering and Capital Equipment
Ulgor Refrigerators, gas and electric stoves, automatic washing machines, and dishwashers	**Copreci** Components for electric household appliances	**Arrasate** Machine tools
Lenniz Kitchen cabinets and equipment	**Ederlan** Foundry for shaping and finishing iron and aluminum castings	**Aurki** Numerical controls and digital readouts
Radar Cookware (stainless steel and aluminum)	**Fagor Electrotécnica** Electronic components for transisters, telephones, and televisions	**Uldata** Mini-computer software for management and production
Fagor Clima Gas and electric water heaters	**Leunkor** Light machining and assembly; index drives	**Ulmatik** Engineering production organization and management. Production-problem diagnosis. Feasibility studies.
Fagor Industrial Commmerical equipment for laundry and food services		

SOURCE: FAGOR Central Services

to include balanced representation of chairpersons of the governing councils and of managers of the individual cooperatives. The Central Social Council argued that this involved a confusion of the functions of governance with those of management. In response, management changed the plan to provide for direct election of all the members of the governing council by the General Assembly of FAGOR. The general assembly is a representative body whose members are elected by the six thousand members of the firms in the cooperative group, roughly in proportion to the total membership in each cooperative but modified so as to ensure representation even to the smallest cooperatives.

The new program reflected two major changes in the role of the Central Social Council. Probably the most important was that, for the first time, it elected its own chairperson, thereby strengthening its influence. Complementing this structural change, a new clause granted the Central Social Council the right to negotiate with management and the governing council on matters of interest to the members of the social council. In effect, negotiations had been taking place, particularly during the reorganizations and restructurings of the 1980s, but now for the first time this function was legitimated.

From 1965 to 1975, ULARCO evolved from a loose federation of cooperatives toward a unified group, but one that strived to balance the desire of the cooperatives for autonomy with the need for an integrated business and organizational development strategy. The period was marked by the growth and increasing importance of the Department of Central Services and by the leadership role played by the Department of Personnel in taking on major responsibilities for introducing new forms of work and, by transferring members from one firm to another, in adjusting to changing economic and technological conditions.

Fortunately, the process of consolidation of the general management of the cooperative group was well advanced by the time management was called on to intervene in major reorganizations, first in Fagor Electrotécnica and then in Ulgor and Arrasate. Experience with the reorganization process in those firms convinced management of the need to carry out a major restructuring of the group so as to strengthen its position in the market. Management then supported these structural changes with the adoption of the name FAGOR for the group. The implications of these changes will be further explored in chapter 17, "Mondragón in the 1980s."

15 The Changing Role of the Caja Laboral Popular

The recession of the 1980s had two major effects on the Caja. The Entrepreneurial Division had to shift its emphasis from the creation of new cooperatives to emergency intervention to help reorganize and revitalize cooperatives that were in serious financial difficulties, and the Financial Division had to work out new programs and policies to refinance those cooperatives that were failing. Because of their financial weakness, many cooperatives had become increasingly dependent on the Caja—a change neither side considered healthy. Leaders of the Caja responded by making internal structural changes and by proposing that two new organizations be established: the Congress of Mondragón Cooperatives and the Council of Cooperative Groups. We see this process of change as progressing from defense and rescue to strategic organizational restructuring.

DEFENSE AND RESCUE

At the time of our 1975 visit, the emphasis of the Caja's Entrepreneurial Division was on the problems and processes of creating new firms. By the time of our 1983 visit, the emphasis had shifted to intervention to save threatened cooperatives. The promotion department was facing abruptly rising costs in the investment required for each job created and decreasing market opportunities. Only two new cooperatives were created in 1982 and only one in 1983 (ICA 1984). Those promoting the development of new firms were expecting to increase their efforts from 1984 on, but clearly more severe economic challenges lay ahead. Alfonso Gorroñogoitia, chairman of the Governing Council of the Caja, told us that of all the cooperatives created from 1977 to 1982, only 20 percent had

169

become profitable within two years, and some were still incurring losses in their fifth year.

Until 1982, the needs for intervention were met by staff in the promotion department, with some assistance from the consulting department. In response to the growing need for intervention, the division established an independent intervention department, staffed by seven professionals. The plan was that each professional would work on three to four cases at the same time but no more than one case that needed urgent, almost full-time attention. During 1983, thirty-four of the one hundred worker cooperatives required help from the intervention department.

Caja staff members assigned to the interventions do not start from scratch. Some have experience in creating the cooperative where they are now intervening. In all cases, the professionals are thoroughly versed in the structures, policies, and social processes involved in managing the cooperatives. Finally, they can draw on the Entrepreneurial Division's computerized data bank, which stores month-by-month operating and financial statements of each cooperative on a standard form worked out by the bank. In a few minutes the professional can put together a financial and operating profile of the company, using not only the most up-to-date figures but also data needed to plot trends. The data bank also enables the intervenors to spot emerging problems in a cooperative—sometimes before its management recognizes the seriousness of a situation.

If intervention is required in a company and an industry with which the professional has no experience, he or she can nearly always find an individual in the bank who has such experience and background and can direct the intervenor to materials he or she needs.

The data and human resources available within the Entrepreneurial Division give the intervenor a running start in dealing with any new case. Before meeting with people in management and looking over the plant and offices, he has a systematic record of the operating and financial performance of the firm throughout its existence. Substantial information from the division about the industry in question and the national and international markets for its products is used to put the record in context. While in the field, observing and interviewing, he can focus his attention on those aspects of the problem not reflected in the data bank: human resources, organizational structure, coordination among departments, and managerial leadership.

The intervention department established three levels of risk, which determined the intensity of each intervention (ICA 1984). Classification was based on an index number reflecting the firm's current and recent financial and operating performance.

1. *High risk.* The life of the cooperative is threatened. The intervenor reviews every aspect of operations and in effect takes over management on a full-time basis until a reorganization plan is approved or the cooperative must be closed.

2. *Medium risk.* Bankruptcy is not imminent but could occur in the near future. In such cases the intervenor spends at least one day each week at the cooperative during the reorganization but does not take over management of the firm.

3. *Warning or alert level.* Here the threat of failure is not imminent but current trends are negative, suggesting a need for remedial action that may be beyond the capacity of the cooperative.

The bank's interest rates on loans to cooperatives undergoing intervention are keyed to the levels of intervention required. Interest payments on outstanding loans are suspended entirely for cooperatives at the first or high-risk level until the reorganization plan is in place. The expectation is that reorganization will enable the cooperative to resume interest payments at 8 percent in the third year and at 14 or 15 percent by the fifth year. The interest rate for cooperatives at the second level is reduced temporarily to 8 percent, but the cooperative is committed to paying 14 to 15 percent as the reorganization takes effect. The interest rate for cooperatives at the third level remains at 14 to 15 percent, but the expectation is that the intervention will improve performance enough to make this burden manageable. (It should be noted that even the Caja's maximum rate of interest has regularly been 3 to 4 percentage points below the national market. Furthermore, as in the United States, private firms in Spain that are in financial difficulties have to pay higher interest rates than financially successful firms.)

Except for those emergency situations in which a cooperative is flatly unable to pay the interest on its loans, the Caja makes no concessions on the interest rates on outstanding loans until it has approved a five-year business and reorganization plan prepared by the firm with the assistance of the intervenor. If additional financing is needed, as is usually the case, the Caja decides how much to loan, based on the reorganization and business plan.

The first step in intervention is a feasibility study conducted by the intervenor, in consultation with the firm's management and the governing council, to determine whether there is a reasonable possibility that the cooperative can be saved and set on a course of increasing economic and social strength. In most cases the conclusion is that success is possible but only under the conditions specified by the Caja. The new business plan may call for changes in products, manufacturing methods, and marketing strategies. It is likely to call for reductions in members' pay and, in extreme cases, for additional capital contributions by members. The plan may involve changes in the organizational structure of the firm and personnel changes in key management positions. The policy is to determine first whether the cooperative is likely to succeed without personnel changes. Only if the answer is negative does the reorganization plan call for such changes. During the thirty-four interventions in 1983, only two chief executive officers, six department managers, and three chairpersons of governing councils were replaced (ICA 1984).

The reorganization plan may indicate that the cooperative could be successful but only with a reduced labor force. In this case, it is the responsibility of management, working with its social council, to determine who continues in their present job, who stays but is assigned to a different position, and who must leave. The leaders of the firm must work with the people affected to make the changes as painless as possible.

To avoid cooptation of the intervenor by the cooperative being assisted, the intervention department now requires that the management of the cooperative be responsible not only for developing the reorganization and business plan, with the assistance of the intervenor, but for making its own case to the Caja for refinancing. Furthermore, in applying for refinancing, the management of the cooperative presents its proposal to the Financial Division, rather than to the intervention department. The planners of these policies and procedures are not assuming that there will be no contact between the intervenor and the officials who are to decide on the refinancing but, rather, that it is essential to protect the objectivity of those making the final decision.

By the end of 1983, the intervention department had abandoned rescue efforts for two cooperatives and was proceeding to liquidate them. Both were very small, recently created cooperatives that had never been able to establish a market.

Mondragón's record from 1956 through 1983—of 103 cooperatives that were created, only three have had to go out of business—is unparalleled. Furthermore, in all three cases very small numbers of worker-members were involved. So far, every intervention in larger firms has been successful.

The costs of intervention are high, but they are shared by the Caja and the firms being assisted. As part of the total reorganization process, cooperatives receiving assistance are expected to cover the direct costs of personnel and services from the intervention department. They are not expected to cover the indirect costs of maintaining the intervention department. Indirect costs, which amount to about 40 percent of the total costs of operating the department, are covered by the Caja itself. Although the program is costly to the bank, it has financial advantages. In all cases, firms in the cooperative complex do all their banking with the Caja. From this standpoint, the intervention program can be seen as a means of protecting and extending the business operations of the bank, in that the Caja continues to profit from the regular banking operations and from the credit programs arranged with the firms in which intervention is taking place.

SAVING ZUBIOLA

The First Reorganization

The Zubiola case provides us with an opportunity to follow in some detail one of the most difficult rescue operations carried out in the Mondragón complex. It was not a single operation; Zubiola struggled through a reorganization in 1983 and then, when that failed, underwent a much more drastic reorganization in 1985. The case illustrates the lengths to which the members and leaders of the complex will go to rescue failing cooperatives and save jobs.

We visited Zubiola in October 1983, shortly after the first reorganization. At that time we had a long discussion with the chairman of the Governing Council of Zubiola and with María Angeles Amenabar, its administrative secretary. We also interviewed several members of URKIDE, the group of cooperatives that included Zubiola. In October 1985, Amenabar told us the story of the second reorganization and gave us a copy of a report entitled "Zubiola: 2° Reconversión," which she had prepared for the managements of Zubiola and URKIDE. The report provides not only a detailed account of the major events and decisions of the second rescue effort but also an interpretation of the underlying issues involved.

Zubiola is located in the small industrial city of Azpeitia, about an hour's drive east of Mondragón. The city is best known as the birthplace of St. Ignatius of Loyola, the founder of the Jesuit Order. At the time of our 1983 visit, Zubiola was one of six cooperatives that had recently formed the URKIDE group. Four of the firms manufactured furniture. Egurko, located in Zumaya, on the coast about fifteen miles from Azpeitia, manufactured woodworking machines. At the time of our visit, Zubiola was producing both woodworking machines and tools.

Zubiola was created in 1966 from a private firm. At that time, the owner, a self-taught craftsman, was working with fifteen employees. He was aware of the Mondragón cooperative movement and began talking with his workers about the possibility of converting his firm to a cooperative.

He did not own the building, so the purchase price reflected primarily the value of his machines. These were acquired by the fifteen employees, who became worker-owners by paying 50,000 pesetas each (then about $1,000). One of the fifteen members became technical director. Because the members of the new cooperative wanted to prove they could "stand on their own feet," they did not ask the Caja for financial or technical help.

In January 1970, Zubiola joined Lagun-Aro, so that its members would have social security coverage and unemployment insurance. In February of that same year, Zubiola signed a contract of association with the Caja, opening the way for technical assistance in planning and financing its expansion. Growth came rapidly, and Zubiola had to move to new buildings twice from 1977 to 1983. Along with this physical and operational expansion, the number of members grew rapidly to a high of 144.

At the height of its operations, Zubiola was a firm of young members, whose average age was twenty-seven. In the contraction process necessary up to 1983, the average age rose to thirty-six.

Through 1978, Zubiola was yielding high profits. In 1979 profits fell sharply, and in 1980 income just balanced expenses. In the prosperous years, Zubiola had gained 70 percent of the Spanish market for its type of machines and 10 percent for its line of tools.

As sales dropped in 1979 and remained much lower than before, Zubiola also had an acute problem in collecting payments for its exports. For three years in a row, the firm had been exporting more than 20 percent of its production. The recession reduced exports and at the same time made collecting payments for exports increasingly difficult. Because the machines Zubiola produced were expensive, the firm had been allowing buyers to pay on time and had retained title to the machines until the final payment was made. This meant that the firm had to maintain substantial customer credit even in good times, and Zubiola had about

15 million pesetas of past-due debts in each year up to 1978. By 1980, the customer debt had risen to 60 million pesetas. It continued increasing up to 100 million in 1981 and 150 million in 1982, or approximately $1 million. The figure was reduced to 125 million pesetas in 1983, as management began to pursue more aggressive credit policies.

Zubiola had the right to respossess the machines from customers behind in their payments, but this was very costly , especially in foreign countries. For some months, especially on sales to developing countries, the credit problems were not caused by the inability of the customers to pay but by government actions that had frozen foreign exchange.

By this time, Zubiola was getting some assistance from the Spanish government, which had special programs to aid any firm that exported more than 15 percent of its production, provided that the export was equal to at least 10 percent of the production of this type of product manufactured in Spain. The government provided subsidized credit and paid travel expenses for officials from these firms to visit international exhibitions.

Looking back on their experience, people at Zubiola recognized that they should have undertaken a reorganization no later than early 1980, but at the time they assumed that the downturn in their business was a cyclical phenomenon and thus continued at previous levels of production until their warehouse was full. In addition to the cash tied up in inventory, storing such large machines presented major problems. At the same time, Zubiola had been forced to borrow increasingly heavily to compensate for slow payments.

In early 1981, Zubiola called on the Caja for an "urgent diagnosis" (*diagnóstico de urgencia*) to determine whether the problems were primarily the quality of Zubiola's products, the efficiency of its sales network, or general market conditions. The intervenor's study indicated that Zubiola's products enjoyed a very good reputation in the market. The products lasted a long time, however, and sales of new models of the same machine to previous buyers did not support an active market. The marketing evaluation indicated that there was some room for improvement in the sales organization but that the problem could not be attributed to an incompetent sales force. This reduced the basic explanation to a single cause: overproduction.

The five-year plan (1983–88) that was worked out with the management of Zubiola indicated that about seventy-six worker-members could supply its anticipated market. This meant that 50 of its 126 people were surplus.

Major reorganization could not be delayed until 1983. To get its inventory down to acceptable levels, Zubiola could produce no new machines during all of 1982 and simply had to maintain the production of replacement parts and the sales and administrative organization. Thus the number of excess people in 1982 was not fifty but sometimes as many as eighty.

Zubiola carried out this painful reduction of the work force in six months of 1982. At this time, unemployment coverage for workers who were temporarily unemployed was the responsibility of their cooperative, which covered 80 percent of their regular pay until they returned to work or were placed elsewhere. If more than 10 percent of the members of a cooperative were out of work, however, as in Zubiola, Lagun-Aro assumed responsibility for covering these members for up to eighteen months. At the same time, the cooperative was responsible for transferring, temporarily or permanently, as many of its laid-off members as possible. Thus Zubiola faced a paradoxical situation: If it was successful in locating a large percentage of its members in other cooperatives, it would receive no aid from Lagun-Aro. In response to this problem not only at Zubiola but at other cooperatives, Lagun-Aro changed its policies in April 1983 so that it covered unemployed members even when less than 10 percent of the work force was laid off. At the same time, to cover these increased costs, Lagun-Aro raised the payments due it from the member cooperatives. This new policy was negotiated between the managements of the cooperatives and cooperative groups and the management of Lagun-Aro and was finally ratified by the General Assembly of Lagun-Aro, where the member cooperatives have representation.

By the time of our October 1983 visit, Zubiola had successfully placed twenty-three of its fifty unemployed members in permanent jobs in other cooperatives. The other twenty-seven had been placed but expected to return to Zubiola. The reductions did not end Zubiola's financial obligations to its people. If their pay in their permanent positions was lower than in Zubiola, Zubiola had to make up the difference. This was a continuing drain on Zubiola's funds since its workers had been highly skilled and relatively well paid and the jobs offered them in other cooperatives were generally at lower pay levels.

According to a 1983 policy, workers temporarily relocated to positions that paid less than they had made in Zubiola also continued to receive the pay they had been earning, but in this case the difference was made up by Lagun-Aro. The Social Council of Zubiola had the right to participate in decisions regarding which workers should be retained and which should go but decided to leave the initial decisions in the hands of a management committee. The social council and the governing council established a joint committee to work with the manager and the workers to carry out the change. The chairman of the governing council was responsible for working with workers permanently or temporarily placed in other cooperatives.

In establishing criteria for these decisions, the management committee emphasized productivity, which in general would have favored the retention of younger and more highly skilled people. After many discussions, the Governing Council of Zubiola decided to broaden the criteria. Decisions were now based also on seniority—the right of people with longer service to be retained—plus age and health. It was obviously to the advantage of Zubiola to keep the healthiest members but inhumane to put the burden of moving on those in less than good health. Thus health cut both ways in the evaluation, as did age. Although it might have been to the advantage of the firm to keep the younger and more vigorous people, many of whom also had a higher level of education, these people were likely to have fewer family responsibilities and could more readily move.

It is important to note that management refrained from establishing as controlling any single criterion such as seniority, which, because it was entirely objective, would have made decisions in individual cases almost automatic. Instead, the governing council decided to weigh several criteria in an effort to arrive at what they called an *equilibrio*—a term frequently used when Mondragón people explain their decisions. The idea is that basic decisions should be made by *balancing* the interests and values of the members against the interests and needs of the firm.

After general assembly meetings to present, explain, and discuss the business plan, the Governing Council of Zubiola began the relocation process by calling for volunteers to leave the cooperative. Six members who had been thinking of starting their own cooperative responded.

The severe losses experienced by Zubiola over several years had wiped out its reserve fund, and contributions to try to save the firm had drained the capital accounts of members to the point where some workers with low seniority had negative capital balances—in other words, they owed money to the firm. Because those leaving the firm with positive capital balances could take their remaining funds with them and the governing council had decided that those leaving with negative capital balances would have those debts canceled, those remaining with Zubiola did not have all the financial advantages.

At the time of the first restructuring of Zubiola, the five-year plan called for each remaining member to put up 480,000 pesetas in additional capital (about $3,200). The Caja loaned each member this money, and each had to sign for it personally. The member then had five years to repay. During this period, the member's pay was reduced to 80 percent of what it had been. Ten percent of the previous rate was to be used to replenish the member's capital account with the firm, and the other 10 percent was to go to the Caja to repay the loan. Members leaving the firm temporarily had no obligation to put up the 480,000 pesetas of additional capital until and if they returned to Zubiola, but their capital remained with Zubiola.

The chairman of the governing council had primary responsibility for working out with members who were leaving whether they would go to permanent or temporary jobs. We were impressed with the personal interest the chairman displayed. Infinite pains were taken to work out decisions that were acceptable to both the individuals and the firm. We were also impressed with the willingness of workers to consider seriously the interests of their fellows, as well as their own.

Late in the process, six or seven members were undecided about what they wanted to do, and only three jobs remained within Zubiola. At this point, the younger workers voluntarily gave up their claims, saying it was fairer for the older members to remain. This placed two of the older men but left two individuals in competition for the remaining job. They told the chairman that they would decide between them who should have it. The next day they came back to inform him of their decision. They had made it by flipping a coin. Both the chairman and the secretary of the governing council expressed satisfaction that, although the process was necessarily difficult and painful, the people affected had been very fair and reasonable, giving full weight to the needs and interests of the firm and other workers, even when they were faced with substantial sacrifices.

In this restructuring process, the management and the Governing Council of Zubiola worked closely with the management of the cooperative group, URKIDE, and with the intervenor from the Entrepreneurial Division of the Caja. Furthermore, on three occasions the chief executive of the Caja, José María Ormaechea, drove to Azpeitia to meet with people struggling to work out the reorganization or with the membership as a whole. Each visit must have taken at least half a day of Ormaechea's time.

It is hard to imagine the top executive of a major bank in the United States giving such attention to a small private firm.

Zubiola's Second Reorganization

Painful as the intervention was, the problems in Zubiola unfortunately did not end with the changes carried out through 1983. The financial difficulties became increasingly severe.

In April 1983, shortly after the Caja had approved the reorganization plan, key management people who had been expected to carry it out left Zubiola to take jobs in the private sector. This created a leadership crisis. At the request of the Governing Council of Zubiola, the general manager of the URKIDE group temporarily assumed the role of manager of Zubiola.

With the help of the Caja in recruiting and selection, the governing council appointed as manager an industrial engineer who had held the position of commercial director in another Mondragón cooperative. This appointment posed difficulties both for the executive and for the members. The new manager was unfamiliar with woodworking machines and had never managed production. These disadvantages were compounded by the critical situation in Zubiola.

The URKIDE group made substantial efforts to help Zubiola solve its problems, but one of its main hopes was vetoed by the Caja. URKIDE had presented a feasibility study to the Caja for the production of machines to manufacture chairs. This venture would have provided important support to other cooperatives in the URKIDE group and would have employed many of the people being laid off from Zubiola. The Caja declined to provide financing because the proposed product would have been in direct competition with products made at other Mondragón cooperatives. In the fall of 1983, we found the URKIDE group, blocked on this plan, pushing research and development on another product.

Following a review of the figures for the first three months of 1983, which revealed that Zubiola was still losing money and showing no signs of recovery, a member of the management of URKIDE presented a report to the governing council of the group suggesting that production of all the woodworking machines of Zubiola and Egurko be consolidated at one location. The management of the group and of the Caja were concerned about the precarious state of Egurko, and it seemed possible that this consolidation could improve the situation for both cooperatives.

This idea was not a new one. Ten years earlier, the Entrepreneurial

Division of the Caja had suggested that the two cooperatives merge their machine manufacturing divisions. Both the technical considerations and social concerns of this idea had been intensely debated in both firms. At that time, it had been voted down in the General Assembly of Zubiola.

Over the years there had been considerable friction between Zubiola and Egurko, both at the management levels and in their social councils. The two cooperatives had been sharing the costs of marketing on a fifty-fifty basis, although Egurko's machine manufacturing division produced twice what Zubiola's did, and a split based on volume of sales would have reduced Zubiola's costs. Furthermore, because Egurko's machine manu-facturing division was twice as large as Zubiola's, any consolidation would have involved moving Zubiola's operations to Egurko in Zumaya, a town that was culturally different from Azpeitia, where Zubiola was located, and about twelve miles away.

On June 28, 1984, the Governing Council of Zubiola formed a com-mittee composed of its chairman and two of its members to study the possibility of combining the machinery divisions of the two cooperatives. At the same time, the Social Council of Zubiola, which had begun to question the abilities of its management, began an analysis of various alternatives. The general point of the analysis was to question any proposal for a merger. Nevertheless, the leaders of Zubiola and the majority of the members were beginning to recognize that there were few alternatives. Furthermore, the Entrepreneurial Division of the Caja was convinced that only by unifying machinery production could the survival of both Egurko and Zubiola be ensured.

There followed a long and heated process of discussion of the proposals of the Zubiola committee and of the modifications and various counter-proposals of its governing council. Finally, on January 3, 1985, the governing councils of the two cooperatives presented to their general assemblies a proposal to combine the machinery divisions of the two cooperatives by centralizing their production in Egurko. The proposal was approved by the members of Egurko but voted down by the members of Zubiola, who were still desperately seeking another alternative.

In response to this rejection of the proposal, the Governing Council of Zubiola resigned. Members of a new governing council were elected from among those who had been most critical of the rejected proposal. Never-theless, they could find no alternative to the basic decision to move the machinery division of Zubiola to Egurko and only concentrated on trying to work out more favorable terms for Zubiola.

To protect the rights and interests of its members, Zubiola proposed that thirty-six of its members be incorporated into Egurko in the course of five years: twenty-five in 1985 and the remaining eleven in the next four years. Furthermore, Zubiola proposed that during eighteen months in 1985 and 1986 members eligible to transfer to Egurko would have the choice of accepting this option or going elsewhere. The proposal also called for Egurko to cover the costs of moving Zubiola's members to Egurko. From its capital accounts, Zubiola agreed to pay members' entry fees to Egurko. Members would take any money remaining with them. If a capital account was below zero, no funds would be transferred. Zubiola would have no further obligation to the member, and the member would have no obligation to Zubiola. Egurko would let such a member join the cooperative without a capital contribution. In those cases in which members were offered positions in Egurko but chose to become members of another cooperative, Egurko would pay 50 percent of the obligatory capital contribution due from those members when they joined the new firm.

The transfer of the machines to Egurko would not be completed for eighteen months, and not until Egurko was ready to put them into production. Finally, the Governing Council of URKIDE would be responsible for resolving any conflicts over interpretation of this agreement between the two cooperatives and would see to it that the proposed plan was carried out faithfully. This proposal received the necessary two-thirds majority from the members of both cooperatives.

In the course of 1984 it had become evident that the manager of Zubiola had lost the confidence of both the Governing Council of URKIDE and the Entrepreneurial Division of the Caja. It was replaced on January 3, 1985, by a man who had earlier been chairman of the Governing Council of Zubiola. This appointment was proposed by URKIDE and accepted by both the Governing Council and the Social Council of Zubiola.

Because Zubiola's 1983–88 plan was now invalidated by these changes, the Entrepreneurial Division called upon Zubiola to present a new five-year plan for 1985–89 that would focus solely on the production and sale of woodworking tools. This plan was developed by Zubiola's management and approved by its governing council. The Entrepreneurial Division and the Financial Division of the Caja also approved it. The Caja agreed to write off a portion of Zubiola's debt and supported further investments with a substantial new loan, leaving Zubiola's management free to study potential new products.

At the start of 1985, Zubiola had eighty-six members, of whom only thirty had secure positions in the manufacture of tools. By the end of 1985, all the members who had to leave had been relocated: Twenty were placed in twelve different cooperatives as temporary members; thirty-six were promised permanent positions in Egurko in the course of five years, and of these, twenty-five were placed in the first year.

During 1986, some of the displaced members of Zubiola became members of Leroa, a pine furniture cooperative created out of URKIDE's applied research project (described in Chapter 8). By the end of that year, Leroa's total employment had risen to twenty-four.

In spite of the guarantee of employment in Egurko, the eleven employees remaining in Zubiola who were eligible to transfer continued to resist making that move, and it remained to be seen whether they would comply when that option was due to expire, eighteen months after it had been offered. The reluctance of these members to transfer to Egurko focused attention on conflicting interpretations of the rights and obligations of members. There was a difference of interpretation between Zubiola's management group and its governing council. The governing council adhered to the principle that relocation of members into permanent positions in other cooperatives should be voluntary, whereas the manager, while agreeing with this principle in ordinary situations, argued that unless the members were obliged to take permanent positions in other cooperatives, the costs of covering their expenses would be too heavy for Zubiola to bear. The governing council had the last word, insisting that permanent relocations remain voluntary.

For some time the interpretation of various clauses of the agreement regarding the shift of machinery from Zubiola to Egurko continued to cause considerable conflict between the two cooperatives. Following unsuccessful efforts of the two managements to resolve their differences and similarly unsuccessful interventions by URKIDE, in September 1985, the parties invited the Caja to arbitrate.

As we were leaving Spain from the Bilbao Airport in May 1986, we met the manager of Zubiola, who was flying to Milan to work out a licensing arrangement for a product controlled by an Italian firm. He commented that Zubiola had gone through a very difficult period but that he was confident the worst was over and optimistic about the future of his cooperative.

As this story makes evident, the process of intervention at Zubiola was painful for everyone involved. Although it was full of conflict, the leaders and the members were able to work their way through the most severe differences in their dedicated efforts to find solutions that would provide some balance between economic necessities on the one hand and their social values on the other.

STRATEGIC ORGANIZATIONAL
RESTRUCTURING

While the Caja continued to grow and gain financial strength year after year, increasing numbers of cooperatives were struggling to survive. This unhealthy situation had caused growing concern within the management of the Caja years before the problems became critical. Figure 15.1 illustrates the trend over the ten-year period from 1973 to 1982. Charting the percentage of net profits by volume of sales, we see that the cooperative complex began this period with the exceptionally high net profit of 10 percent and that, except for a small gain in 1976, profits fell steadily, putting the complex in the red in 1980 and deeper in the red in 1981. In 1982 it appeared that the complex would recover to the breakeven point, but the leaders of the Caja could not assume that the crisis was over.

The managers of the Caja probably recognized the need for major changes before the leaders of the individual cooperatives did. In February 1981 they decided to undertake an intensive study of problems and options for change, and in April of that year, they circulated a draft report to the general managers of all the cooperative groups. During the rest of that year and the first half 1982, the managers of the Caja held several meetings with leaders of the cooperative groups, and the proposed changes were widely discussed within the cooperatives. Leaders of FAGOR strongly supported the proposals for change.

In August 1982, under the title of "Reflections Regarding Change Concerning the 'Cooperative Experience'," the management of the Caja circulated to the cooperative groups and the supporting organizations a 112-page report analyzing the problems of the Mondragón complex and outlining the measures for change tentatively agreed upon in fifteen months of discussion. This report has become one of the most important documents issued by any unit of the complex in recent years. It demonstrated that, in spite of the increasing burdens borne by the Caja in supporting job creation and maintenance, the bank was growing faster than any other bank in the Basque country and was also more prosperous. At the same time, this growth and financial strength posed serious prob-

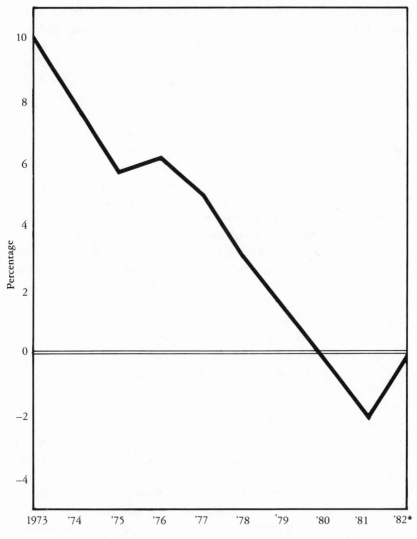

*Estimated July 1982
SOURCE: *Reflexiones para el Cambio en Torno a la "Experiencia Cooperativa,"* Caja Laboral Popular, 1982

Figure 15.1.   Net Surplus (Profits) as Percentage of Sales (1973–82)

lems regarding the placement of the Caja's funds. Created mainly to provide loans for the creation and expansion of Mondragón cooperatives, the Caja had been devoting less than 40 percent of its funds to these purposes. Under existing conditions, the Caja could not substantially increase its loans to cooperatives without jeopardizing its financial stability. The Caja had to consider broadening its loan policies (credits to public agencies, to private firms, and for joint ventures), but also, remaining true to its original mission, had to take steps to strengthen the ability of the complex to create and maintain jobs in line with the Caja's original purpose.

The report basically proposed two initiatives: one to strengthen emergency financing and one to establish new structures designed to decentralize financial control and strengthen the responsibilities and capacities of the cooperative group. Financial emergencies would be met more effectively through the creation of an Intercooperative Solidarity Fund (Fondo Intercooperativo de Solidaridad). This fund would be built up from contributions from each cooperative on the basis of 70 pesetas per member, with the aim to have a fund of 1 billion pesetas by the end of 1985. Cooperatives in financial difficulties would have up to five years to pay. The fund would be administered by one of the two organizations to be created, the Council of Cooperative Groups.

In addition to the Council of Cooperative Groups, a cooperative congress was to be created, to which every Mondragón cooperative would elect at least one representative. Larger cooperatives would have additional representatives, but, to limit the total membership to between 200 and 250 representatives, they would not be in direct ratio to the size of the cooperative. The congress would meet once a year or every two years and would provide a forum for discussion and debate on major issues of policy. Membership in the congress would be voluntary, to be determined by a vote of the membership of each cooperative.

The Council of Cooperative Groups was designed to be the executive arm of the congress. It would be made up initially of the general managers of the ten cooperative groups and of Eroski, the Caja and its Entrepreneurial Division, Lagun-Aro, and Ikerlan. The council would have a small secretariat with full-time responsibility for developing the council's program. The report proposed that the council have main responsibility for working out the constitution and bylaws of the congress and the council, and its proposals were to be ratified, modified, or rejected by the congress.

At the first meeting of the cooperative congress, in October 1987,

Alfonso Gorroñogoitia, chairman of the governing councils of the Caja and of FAGOR, was elected chairman of the congress. Another Ulgor pioneer, José María Ormaechea, general manager of the Caja, became chairman of the Council of Cooperative Groups. Ormaechea left his executive position with the Caja to assume these new responsibilities.

The 1982 report also proposed that the Entrepreneurial Division be established as an autonomous second-level (support) cooperative separate from the Caja, with the aim of increasing the independence and strength of entrepreneurial activities. Because fees and contracts with the cooperatives covered only about 60 percent of the annual expenses of the division, the Caja agreed to turn over approximately 60 percent of its own capital to the division. From the interest on this capital, plus its fees for services to outside organizations, the new cooperative could then subsidize its services to cooperatives, as the Caja had done. For example, the division has been publishing an annual report on the Basque economy based on the research of its own economists. This volume has become a basic document for the Basque regional government and for public and private economic planners, as well as for the Mondragón complex. Its publication each year has provided the occasion for a press conference, widely reported in the regional and national press. The responsibility for financing such research and publications would normally fall on a government agency, but, because Mondragón's economic reports have gained the confidence and respect of leaders in the government and private sector, there is no reason for the Basque government to duplicate Mondragón's efforts. It is hoped that instead the Basque government will help finance this project.

The proposal to establish the Entrepreneurial Division as an autonomous cooperative was accepted in 1984. The new cooperative, named Lankide Suztaketa (LKS), moved into a new building in late 1986 but will not become officially independent until the end of 1990.

When Iñaki Gorroño, the technical secretary of the Caja, described the structural changes in progress in 1985, it seemed to us that they were designed to decrease the power of the Caja. It was hard to imagine the management of any private bank proposing such changes. Gorroño agreed but pointed out that the leaders of the Caja were not motivated simply by altruism or by their own social values. When a company is unable to keep up payments on principal and interest to a private bank, the banker in charge is obligated to act primarily in the interests of the bank. He can negotiate to ease the terms of the loan if such changes will be more advantageous to the bank than foreclosing on the collateral, which would force the company to close or sell out to other investors. If foreclosing seems substantially more advantageous to the bank, he is expected to overcome whatever personal concerns he has for the debtor company and call the loan. Furthermore, unlike the Caja, no private bank makes loans at zero percent for the first year to a company in desperate financial straits, whatever the plans for a brighter future. Any such company is classified as a poor risk and must pay substantially above market rates to borrow from any lender.

In other words, the great power of the Caja had to be weighed against its great obligations. The Caja has a mandate to support the creation and maintenance of jobs. It has a right to withhold financial support from a failing cooperative only if the Entrepreneurial Division, the management of the cooperative group, and the members of the cooperative have done everything possible to devise a new business plan that offers reasonable promise of success and have been unable to do so. The Caja will continue to carry heavy burdens to support its weaker cooperatives, but Gorroño believed that it would be better for all concerned if the responsibilities and sacrifices could be shared more broadly with the cooperative groups.

Will these structural changes decrease the power of the Caja and reduce the dependence of the cooperatives? That remains to be seen. In the initial stages of reorganization, the key positions in the congress and in the Council of Cooperative Groups have been held by two men who played leading roles in the Caja. The domination of these new structures by the Caja can be avoided only to the extent that the general managers of the cooperative groups are able to take the initiative and demonstrate leadership ability.

16 Expanding Service and Agribusiness Cooperatives

The founders of the Mondragón movement were dedicated to building industrial worker cooperatives with the infrastructure to support their development and growth. In the early years, Mondragón's leaders reacted with only minor interest to requests for assistance in creating enterprises such as services and agribusiness cooperatives. In the 1980s we see a shift toward a more proactive role, brought about in part by the recession, which had a serious impact on industrial production and employment, and by the interest of the autonomous Basque government in the growth of agriculture and agribusiness. Since 1980, growth in employment in the complex has been limited to services and agribusiness, and it is expected to progress more rapidly in these sectors than in industry in the coming years.

Spain has long been a land of small merchants and small stores. It has lagged far behind France and the United States in the volume of sales per establishment and has had far more stores in relation to the population. The field was thus open for the rapid expansion of supermarkets when the consumer cooperative Eroski opened its doors.

In agricultural development, the problem has been a trend among young Basques to choose part-time over full-time farming (Greenwood 1976). The Basque government is now making serious efforts to reverse this trend, but so far educational institutions in the Basque country have provided practically no support for this effort. At this writing, no university in the Basque country provides a college education in agricultural sciences, and there is only one technical high school of agriculture, in the province of Navarre, which is only partly Basque and not within the jurisdiction of the Basque regional government. This weakness of Basque agricultural education is a serious handicap to the growth of agribusiness.

THE GROWTH OF THE EROSKI
SUPERMARKETS

The founders of the first worker cooperatives had no interest in consumer cooperatives, but the growth of Eroski and the slowdown in the growth of industrial cooperatives by the late 1980s gave Eroski a more central role in development strategies. From 1979 to 1984, Eroski expanded from 76 stores and supermarkets to 225 and more than tripled its volume of business. By 1984, Eroski was serving 130,702 consumer-members and providing employment for 1,228 worker-members. By this time Eroski had become the eighth largest merchandising firm in Spain and the sixth largest among food-marketing firms.

During Eroski's growth in recent years, its leaders have been contracting with producers for items to be sold under the Eroski label and produced according to Eroski's standards. This expansion has also stimulated the growth of other cooperatives in the agribusiness sector.

EVOLUTION OF THE AGRIBUSINESS SECTOR

As described in chapter 5, the first agricultural cooperative at Mondragón, Lana, was created in 1960. Although farm cooperatives elsewhere generally limit membership to farmers, Don José María persuaded them to admit as equal members workers who were engaged in processing and selling farm products. We wondered whether including such people with some-what different interests might have led to friction. According to the director of the agribusiness department of the Entrepreneurial Division, Txomin Otamendi, who was the manager of Lana for ten years, problems occasionally arose but were not serious. He explained that most of the workers who produced milk (and later forest products) were not full-time farmers, and most of those in processing and sales were part-time farmers, so that the differences in culture and economic interests between the farmers and the workers were not great. From the beginning, Lana es-tablished a policy of distributing income according to market principles. That is, the farmers were paid what they would get for milk or forest products on the market, and the workers in processing and sales were paid according to what their work added to the value of the final product. Lana later signed a contract of association with the Caja Laboral Popular which provided limits and guidelines on what was paid to workers, so that the workers and the farmers did not need to negotiate the distribution of income.

From the beginning, Lana expanded slowly but steadily. It also assumed the same creative role as Ulgor in the creation of other cooperatives, although on a much smaller scale.

Lana began by producing only milk but soon added a warehouse for the storage and sale of inputs required by the farmer-members. In 1964, Lana began to sell forest products, capitalizing on the fact that most of the milk producers also had woodlots. In 1965, it took over a private sawmill.

Along with the expansion and diversification in production, Lana developed services for its members and, in some cases, for nonmembers. A veterinary service was established in 1963. Lana then negotiated with Lagun-Aro to provide health coverage for its members, like that available to members of worker cooperatives. In the 1970s, Lana began investing in woodworking machines, to add value to its wood operations, and in 1976, it began developing a cattle division.

Miba was created as an independent cooperative in 1963 as a spinoff of the Lana warehouse. By the 1980s, Miba had gone beyond simply selling agricultural inputs and had extended its activities to producing fertilizers.

No more new agribusiness cooperatives were created from the early 1960s until the 1980s. Around 1980, the Entrepreneurial Division of the Caja began devoting more attention to the development of these cooperatives. This led to the creation in 1980 of Barrenetxe, which brought together thirty workers involved in the distribution and sale of fruits and vegetables. In 1982, Cosecheros Alaveses, a tiny cooperative of seven farmers and one worker, was formed to produce and market wine.

In 1983, the cattle division in Lana became an independent cooperative, Behi-Alde, in which twenty-seven worker-members and two associated farmers managed more than 1,500 cows on 405 hectares of pasture. Behi-Alde produced milk and meat, while Lana continued to concentrate on milk.

In 1984, Etorki, a cooperative sawmill, and Artxa, a pig-raising cooperative, began operations. Preceded by several months of preparatory work, these developments marked the beginning of a new stage in the growth of the agribusiness sector. This stage has been marked by two organizational innovations: the establishment of an agribusiness department in the Entrepreneurial Division and the major involvement of Eroski in agribusiness. We will follow these developments as they were described to us by Txomin Otamendi, who was the first director of the agribusiness department and a leader in the creation of Artxa. We begin with a brief account of the personal history of Otamendi to illustrate the gradual shift within the Caja from a rather casual approach to agribusiness development toward a more systematic emphasis.

Otamendi was born and grew up on a farm in a village near San Sebastían. As the oldest son, he was expected to take over the farm. At the age of fourteen he left school to work on the farm for two years, always hoping to go back. His grandparents were very much opposed to his abandoning his family responsibility, but his father helped him to make the change. Further education led to the engineering degrees of *perito industrial* and then *ingeniero técnico*, which involved a good deal of physics and mathematics. After coming to Mondragón, he studied for three years for a master's degree in business administration.

Otamendi had worked for a year in the Caja when Director General José María Ormaechea called him in and said, "You came from a farm and must know something about that kind of work. We want you to take over the management of Lana."

Otamendi served as director of Lana for ten years, during which the membership rose from 40 to 379. It was this record that led to his appointment as the first director of the agribusiness department.

The mission of this department is to expand existing agribusiness cooperatives and to promote the development of new ones. As one means of accelerating such development, the Caja decided to raise the amount of investment permissible per job created. Job creation was becoming increasingly expensive in industry, and the Caja was no longer financing any industrial project in which the feasibility study indicated that the cost per job would be more than 5 million pesetas (about $33,000). In 1983 the Caja removed this restriction on agribusiness projects. Although such projects may require a larger investment per job, they often need a variety of organizations to form them, and investing jointly eases the burden. Furthermore, by this time the Basque government was taking a special interest in agribusinesses and liberalizing loan policies.

The creation of the pig-raising cooperative, Artxa, illustrates the new strategy. This was the first project carried out with the stimulus and guidance of the agribusiness department. Director Otamendi established a project team with representatives of Eroski, which was going to buy pigs produced by Artxa, and Miba, which produces and sells animal feed and fertilizer, sells insecticides and farm implements, and provides veterinary services to cooperative members. A member of the Financial Division of the Caja, which was to provide the major financing, also participated in the planning process. The team went outside the cooperatives to include in its membership a representative of Anoga (Asociación Norte de Ganaderos, Northern Livestock Farmers Association), which had two hundred members, eighty of whom raised pigs.

According to Otamendi, the eight worker-members in the pig-raising operation put up about 3 percent of the total capital requirement of 120 million pesetas. The members of Anoga invested 10 percent. Twenty-five percent was from a low-interest loan from the Basque government. The remainder was divided equally among the three cooperatives, Eroski, Miba, and the Caja.

The planning team also worked out a formula for the control of Artxa. Decision-making power was allocated in proportion to the *value added* by each of the participating groups: Eroski, Miba, Anoga, and the Artxa workers.

Artxa began operating in June 1984. The cooperative first purchased forty genetically improved breeding sows. The plan was to expand to about 130 within six months. Artxa sells the offspring to the Anoga pig farmers, who breed the sows and sell the piglets back to Artxa, which fattens them for sale to Eroski. Miba sells fodder and other products to Artxa and to the Anoga farmers. To support its production and development operations, Artxa also has an extension consulting service for the swine farmers of Anoga to help them improve the productivity of their livestock operations.

In 1986 (*Trabajo y Unión*, July-August 1985), Artxa was expected to reach an annual production of 6,000 pigs. Of these, 5,400 were to be sold directly by Artxa. The balance was to be marketed by Artxa for the Anoga members.

The 120 sows of the pig-breeding unit of Artxa are expected to produce sixteen piglets per sow per year. The boars are eventually slaughtered, whereas the best of the sows are retained to expand the breeding operation or to sell to the livestock producers of Anoga. The sales volume is expected to be well over a million dollars per year.

In 1985, Artxa sought support from the Basque government for help in financing a biogas plant that would process the excrement from the pigs into several valuable outputs. The organic material remaining after the fermentation process can be converted into fertilizer and sold to Miba. The biogas operation will provide light and heat for the pig-raising operation and some for the neighboring cattle-raising cooperative, Behi-Alde.

According to Mario Zubía, who was directing the agribusiness department of the Entrepreneurial Division in 1986, Artxa at this time was selling its pigs to Eroski, which arranged for their slaughter with private firms. Artxa was working on plans to establish its own cooperative slaughterhouse, which would also market the fresh pork. The next steps are obvious: future projects for the processing and production of ham, bacon, and sausage. For each element of the plan, however, systematic feasibility studies need to be done to determine the state of the market and the technical and financial requirements of each new activity. Beyond that, the leaders have to work out organizational structures to determine whether the new operations will be included in Artxa or whether one or more will be spun off as separate cooperatives.

In 1986, the agribusiness department of the Entrepreneurial Division took a further step by forming a cooperative group, EREIN, for agriculture and agribusiness. EREIN differs from the other cooperative groups in two important respects. At least for the initial period of its creation and development, EREIN's director general, Mario Zubía, continues to serve as director of the agribusiness department of the Entrepreneurial Division. This arrangement reflects one major difference between the cooperatives of EREIN and the industrial cooperatives: The latter are all in a small geographical area, permitting easy communication among them, whereas the seven cooperatives forming the EREIN group are spread across the Basque provinces. There is also a difference in organizational structure. Whereas the chairmen of the governing councils of constituent cooperatives form the governing council of the industrial cooperative group, in the case of EREIN, the group governing council is made up of the managers (chief executives) of the constituent cooperatives.

By 1985, the EREIN group consisted of two strong and well-established cooperatives and five small units still in the early stages of development. Well over half the worker-members of the seven units were employed by Lana, and well over 90 percent of the farmer-members were associated with either Miba or Lana. With the greatly increased support of agribusiness development within the Mondragón complex and the strong support of the Basque government, this situation should change over the next decade as new cooperatives are created and those established earlier gain economic strength and increase the numbers of worker-members and associated farmers.

The director general of EREIN, Mario Zubía, stresses the potential for growth in the following areas: EREIN now is committed to the development and application of the most advanced technologies of agricultural production. Zubía expects that before 1990 cooperatives will be started specializing in floriculture and in sheep raising and that new projects will be developed in fish products and cereal grains. He especially emphasizes the importance of Eroski in this projected surge of development, noting that relations between EREIN and Eroski go far beyond those of buyer and seller in that Eroski actively supports both the development of the raw materials and the processing of the products it will market.

In the development of new agribusiness cooperatives, the Entrepreneurial and Financial divisions work closely with Eroski and existing agricultural cooperatives and farmers' associations. In describing the process of creating Artxa, for example, Otamendi spoke of monthly meetings and frequent informal communications among representatives of the cooperating organizations.

The growth of the agribusiness sector proves the value of building a cooperative complex in which the member cooperatives help one another. We have described the early years of Lana, as it grew and spun off new cooperatives, with the assistance of the Caja. A broader network of mutually supporting organizations also developed as a result of the creation of the new agribusiness cooperatives in the 1980s. Miba's sales of fodder greatly expanded with the creation of Artxa and the increased scale of operations of the swine farmers of Anoga. The direct involvement of Eroski has greatly simplified the problems of feasibility studies, and its willingness to purchase the total output of Artxa eliminates the need for people in the middle.

The agribusiness sector still faces serious handicaps, beginning with the decline over the years of Basque agriculture and reinforced by the lack of advanced agricultural education in the Basque provinces. The increasing support of the Basque government and recent changes in its support policies should strengthen Mondragón's efforts in this area. Mario Zubía told us in 1986 that at first the government had allocated its agricultural funds so as to maximize the number of farmers receiving assistance. Although this policy had obvious political advantages, it was difficult to provide enough capital to mount efficient and modern agribusiness enterprises. The government has modified this policy, opening the way to the approval of larger loans and subsidies. Furthermore, the policies prevailing in 1986 provide more support for a cooperative enterprise than for an individual farm family. This shift in policy may have been influenced to some extent by concerns expressed by Mondragón people, but it also had a general political and economic justification. If an individual farmer is given a loan or subsidy, only one family benefits, whereas the same loan or subsidy to a cooperative can support many individual workers and associated farmers and their families.

The rise of Eroski and the agribusiness cooperatives testifies to the resourcefulness and flexibility of the leaders of the Mondragón movement. It also illustrates their responsiveness to community needs. Initially, they had no interest in, or special knowledge of, retail marketing or agribusiness. Eroski was created in response to calls for help from failing consumer cooperatives. Lana arose in response to a plea for guidance from farmers. Because the conventional structure of a farmers' cooperative enables the farmers to dominate the workers, the organizers of Lana devised a structure that ensured equal rights for both classes of members and a formula for distribution of income that prevented farmers from exploiting workers—or vice versa. Pay standards established with the Caja Laboral Popular provided further ensurance that the workers would not exploit the farmers or be exploited by them.

Since the mid-1980s, Eroski and the Caja have been the most consistently profitable and expanding cooperatives. As they work ever more closely together, they will undoubtedly provide powerful support and guidance for the acceleration of agribusiness development.

17 Mondragón in the 1980s

In the evolution of the cooperatives, the 1980s have been a crucial period marked by substantial sacrifices and structural readjustments. The 1980s have also called for increasing investments in human and material capital and the resumption of organizational growth, even though expansion has not been nearly as rapid as in earlier decades.

Readers are reminded that our research was concentrated in and around the city of Mondragón, and particularly within the FAGOR group. The extent to which our interpretations apply to other parts of the complex must be weighed with caution.

More than half of those gainfully employed in the Mondragón area work in the cooperatives. The ways the cooperatives are organized, operate, and develop socially and economically have a pervasive influence on the entire community. Naturally, relations between the community and the cooperatives are not nearly as frequent and powerful outside Mondragón and especially not in areas where few cooperatives are linked together. We are also told that the members of FAGOR are much more tightly knit than those of other cooperative groups. This does not simply reflect the natural pride of the people of FAGOR. It is also evidenced by FAGOR's being the only group that pools 100 percent of the profits and losses of each cooperative. In the other cooperative groups, there is considerable variation in this policy, so that some pool varying percentages of profits and losses and others none at all, although they cooperate in other respects.

INVOLVEMENT IN THE REGIONAL AND NATIONAL POLITICAL ECONOMY

In the early years, the Mondragón cooperatives were a miniscule element in the regional and national scene. They were hardly noticed by anyone outside the Basque country. Now the complex is a major element in industrial and job development for the region and is receiving increased attention and interest from the national government.

Members and former members of the cooperative complex have played important roles in the development of policies and programs of the Basque government. Some have moved back and forth between the Mondragón cooperatives and the autonomous government, and some have remained with the government. The annual publication of the Caja on the state of the Basque economy has become a basic economic planning document for the Basque government. And the community clinic, established with the support of the cooperatives in Mondragón and earlier operated by Lagun-Aro, was recently taken over by the regional government. Furthermore, the clinic has been adopted by the government as a model for the development of clinics in small cities throughout the region.

As the Mondragón complex has become important regionally and nationally, its leaders have become increasingly involved in consultation and negotiations with government officials on issues of development policy, as well as on particular measures of interest to Mondragón. In recent years, the leaders of the Caja, FAGOR, Lagun-Aro, Ikerlan, and Eroski have become prominently involved in public policy discussions with government officials. As the Congress of Cooperatives and the Council of Cooperative Groups begin to function and gain public and government recognition, we can expect leaders of those organizations to play even more important public roles. At the same time, this success and prominence pose delicate political problems for the complex and for the regional government. Both parties must seek to avoid the impression that government policies are especially designed to favor the complex.

CHANGING REQUIREMENTS FOR
THE CREATION AND MAINTENANCE
OF EMPLOYMENT

The nature of industrial development within the Mondragón complex that made possible its early growth now poses severe problems of readjustment and revitalization. The cooperative complex began with a strong base in mature mass-production industries, those very sectors of the world economy that have been the hardest hit by recession and intensified competition. Mondragón is struggling with some of the same problems that have affected mature industries in the United States. To survive, industrial companies and cooperatives have had to shift from mass production toward flexible manufacturing, from producing large volumes of standardized items to meeting the needs of customers who require high quality and variety. As competition has become based more on quality, customers have been more demanding in the standards of performance they accept.

In the early years of Mondragón, those in charge of production held the dominant positions. As competition increased and customer requirements became more varied and exacting, those in marketing became more influential. In interviews carried out in Ulgor and Copreci by a small group from Cornell University in November 1985, we saw the impact of this shift in power on the first-line production supervisors. Their schedules were frequently disrupted by demands from marketing for quick changes in products or models to meet the needs of important customers. Their working lives were greatly complicated by the imposition of the "just-in-time" policy of production and inventory control. In some departments, the implementation of this Japanese manufacturing strategy had resulted in a 50 percent reduction in the materials available at work stations in the plant. Previously, supervisors had a bank of components at their work stations, ready for use on any new order. Now, with the drastic reduction in this materials bank, some supervisors told us that they were constantly worrying about whether components would be ready for the next operation. Of course, a skillfully operated just-in-time system can result in substantial reductions in the money tied up in inventory, but the policy also places additional pressures on first-line supervisors, who are now required to fine-tune operations that previously required only loose coordination.

Modernization of technology for worldwide competition now requires massive investments. With the resources of the Caja, and at times the support of the national government, the Mondragón cooperatives are in a stronger position than most private companies in Spain. Advances in automation and robotization, however, mean fewer jobs. Executives in Spanish private companies facing such changes have the problem of how to discharge surplus workers given the restrictions imposed by government, but when that problem is solved, they do not have to worry about the fate of the workers who have been laid off. The leaders of Mondragón may have more options than private employers in reducing the work force, but they are obligated to provide alternative employment or to make very substantial support payments to unemployed members. This places Mondragón under heavy pressure to accelerate the creation of new enterprises.

Leaders of private firms base decisions primarily on estimates of the potential profits and consider only secondarily how many people must be employed to generate the output and income required. *In Mondragón, the generation of profits or surplus is a limiting condition but not the primary driving force.* The distinction is between *means* and *ends.* Leaders of Mondragón recognize profits as *the essential means* for achieving their *ends* of social and economic development.

Professionals in the promotion department of the Entrepreneurial Division are constantly searching for opportunities to create new enterprises and new jobs. The limiting condition is that the new enterprise cannot be financed until the banking officials are persuaded by a feasibility study that there is a reasonable chance that the firm will survive and grow. We have seen this process lead to the creation of jobs in URKIDE. The drastic reduction of the work force of Zubiola, for example, led the group's management to push research and development to create a new firm that would employ some of Zubiola's surplus workers.

As the director general of the Caja, José María Ormaechea, wrote in reflecting on the ten years since the death of Don José María, lack of capital has not been the problem in creating jobs. "The total resources of CLP will have reached about 220 billion pesetas [by the end of 1986]. But, of these funds, only 45 billion pesetas are dedicated to financing the cooperatives" (Ormaechea 1986, 10).

In the early years, the Caja could expect newly created cooperatives to be profitable within two years. Ormaechea noted that "firms now become profitable only in the fourth or fifth year and every job one wishes to create constitutes a risk and an important cost" (page 10). He stated that only a small percentage of the Caja's funds were devoted to the creation of new enterprises because only a few viable projects could be supported given the limits of capital the Caja could allocate to the creation of each job.

He noted also that during the decade before the death of Arizmendi, employment was growing at the rate of about 15 percent annually, in a national market that was growing at the rate of 6 to 7 percent of gross national product. In the decade 1977–86, new jobs were created at a rate of only 3.3 percent annually, and most of the gain was in the first five years of the decade. Still, compared to the general conditions in the Basque country, the performance of the cooperatives must be considered extraordinary.

From 1976 to 1986 we have been able to create 4,200 jobs, when in Euskadi [the Basque country] more than 150,000 jobs were lost in the same period.

As you see, that is not a brilliant result, but only a process of adjustment carefully calculated, reflecting the spirit of solidarity, and audacity has made it possible to avoid having any cooperative member unemployed. (page 5)

Ormaechea recognized that maintaining employment also put a financial burden on all the members. He pointed out that members had 2.35 percent of their pay withheld for unemployment support in 1986 (compared to 0.5 percent in 1980, when the payroll tax was created).

Ormaechea's evaluation of the economic health of the cooperatives was entirely compatible with the independent analysis done by economists Keith Bradley and Alan Gelb (1987), who had been following the evolution of the Mondragón complex closely in the preceding years. They noted (page 84) that Spain's industrial output grew at the annual rate of 1.5 percent in the period 1976–83, while Mondragón averaged 6 percent during those years. The contrast is shown in figure 17.1.

As Bradley and Gelb pointed out (1987, 88–89), in 1978 and 1979 the average pay in the complex was higher than in Spanish industry but dropped somewhat below the national average in 1980 because of the financial sacrifices made by the members of FAGOR. The gap was narrowed in the following years. They noted, however, that Mondragón members have substantially better social security support than workers in private industry because Lagun-Aro "provides far better value; to obtain a comparable level of benefits from the national system is calculated to be 1.75 times as costly" (page 92). Their analysis indicated that, to support continued growth in output and jobs, Mondragón members have made sacrifices in their short-run rewards but have maintained an exceptionally strong social security sytem.

STRENGTHENING EDUCATION

Between 1962 and 1964, the Caja joined with cooperatives and individual members to invest 74 million pesetas to build the Escuela Politécnica and the student residence. In recent years, Mondragón has placed great emphasis on strengthening its educational institutions. New construction and remodeling of the Escuela in the 1980s has cost the Caja 200 million pesetas (Ormaechea 1986).

Enrollment in the Escuela Politécnica, which offers an education com-

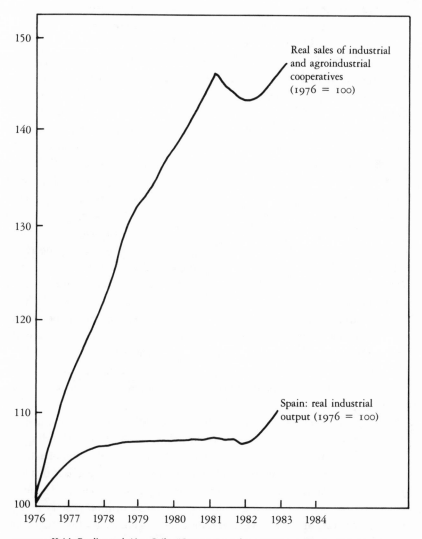

Real sales of industrial
and agroindustrial
cooperatives
(1976 = 100)

Spain: real industrial
output (1976 = 100)

150

140

130

120

110

100

1976 1977 1978 1979 1980 1981 1982 1983 1984

SOURCE: Keith Bradley and Alan Gelb, "Cooperative Labour Relations: Mondragón's Response to Recession," *British Journal of Industrial Relations* 25 (1987): 85.

Figure 17.1.   Industrial Output and Sales (1976–83): Mondragón and Spain

parable to three years of a four-year undergraduate program in the United States, continues to expand. Its engineering program has grown from 365 students in the academic years 1983–84 to 720 for 1986–87, and the five lower grades had almost identical numbers for the two years (773 and 772). In the neighboring town of Oñate, the Escuela Técnica Empresarial de Oñate (ETEO), a school of business administration founded in 1961, enrolled 868 students in 1985–86.

In addition to investing in physical structures, the Caja and the cooperatives have joined to support the creation of other educational institutions closely linked with the Escuela Politécnica and Ikerlan. Saiolan was created for students who have completed their university education beyond the level of the Escuela. It offers a two-year program in which students alternate between formal instruction and working with personnel from the Escuela, Ikerlan, and the cooperatives. This collaboration is designed to create and develop new products or processes, thus helping the participants link their theoretical education with the practical concerns of the cooperatives. Another school, Iraunkor, was formed to provide leaders and members of Mondragón cooperatives with specialized and intensive instruction in new developments in engineering and manufacturing. In addition, Mondragón has been sending people to Milan to study in the European Center for Industrial Design. Some of the graduates of this program established the Instituto de Diseño Industrial at Mondragón, where students and members of the cooperatives can do advanced work in industrial design. In 1973, the cooperatives created Ahizke-CIM, which provides intensive instruction in English, French, German, and Euskera, the Basque language. In 1982–83, enrollment in Ahizke-CIM was 1,289, including 210 members of cooperatives.

Recognizing the need to send students to other parts of Spain and abroad for an upper-university-level education, the leaders of Mondragón organized a foundation, Gizabidea, whose income supports scholarships and fellowships for advanced study. This foundation was the last of Don José María's ideas to come to fruition. According to its director, Gizabidea borrowed the initial financing from the Caja: 100 million pesetas at 13 percent interest, at a time when the foundation could loan the money at a market rate of 18.24 percent, thus creating a continuing flow of funds. By 1985, Gizabidea had received gifts of 7 million pesetas from FAGOR, a total of 5 million pesetas from other cooperatives, and 19 million pesetas from individuals.

In 1984, the Caja converted an antique manor house into Ikasbide, a modern educational center complete with offices, seminar rooms, equipment for simultaneous translation, and living quarters for up to thirty-five people. The center was designed and executed entirely by the Caja. Because other cooperatives were not involved in planning Ikasbide, they are still in the process of discovering how they can use its facilities and services.

In spite of the great emphasis Mondragón places on educational development, the changing economic conditions are demanding a level of education that the complex cannot meet alone. The five Ulgor pioneers began work in factory jobs while they were getting their degrees in engineering. When they started Ulgor, they remained close to Don José María and his circle of young people by discussing new ways of organizing firms and society. That they had more education than their fellow members presented no barrier to mutual understanding. Now that the more technologically advanced cooperatives are recruiting graduates of university engineering programs, the leaders of Mondragón are becoming concerned with balancing the need for people with high-level technical and scientific knowledge with the desire for people who understand the values and operating methods of the cooperatives. The cooperatives are competing for executives with private firms that pay much higher salaries than the cooperatives can offer. Even with the expansion of the salary range to 4.5 to 1, a few of the cooperatives have been forced to hire nonmembers as executives. Because no cooperative is permitted to have more than 10 percent nonmembers, and those hired on contract are limited to four-year terms, cooperatives that have contracted for their top leadership face problems at the end of that period.

The pay scale for Mondragón has been comparable to that in private industry at the unskilled and semiskilled level, but, because of the policies limiting the differential between the bottom and the top, the salaries of executives in Mondragón are substantially lower than those of executives in private industry. A study by the Entrepreneurial Division (*Trabajo y Unión*, January 1986) indicated that the salary scale for executives in the cooperatives, depending on their position, was 18 to 43 percent lower than that of comparable personnel in Spain; the differential for the Basque country ranged from 3 to 42 percent.

In 1975 we were told that executive turnover had not become a serious problem. We also learned that most of the executives who had left the cooperatives for jobs in private industry had *not* been educated in the Escuela Politécnica. Those who had been educated and trained in the cooperative movement seemed much less attracted by the prospect of receiving higher salaries elsewhere. During the period of rapid expansion, every graduate of the Escuela Politécnica was likely to find a job in the cooperatives. Membership was officially open to all comers, but graduates of the school had the advantage of having experience in the cooperative governance of the school. For those who financed their education by working half time in Alecop, the experience was even more closely comparable to that of a regular member of a worker cooperative. A student with a good record in Alecop would come to the attention of management. In the 1980s, as industrial employment within the complex has declined, fewer graduates of the Escuela have been able to move directly into one of the worker cooperatives. Except for those graduates of the Escuela who go on to universities, the graduates of universities who come to Mondragón do not have experience with the cooperatives.

Before 1980, recruitment for higher-level positions in the cooperatives was primarily from within. People advanced because of their job performance and by studying new technologies and methods part time. Now the leaders of the cooperatives face two problems: how to socialize the highly educated newcomers into the ways of working and thinking in a cooperative and the frustration of workers who have been moving up in the organization and now find their careers blocked because they do not have advanced degrees.

In response to growing concern over the ability of Mondragón to attract and retain executive talent, the Entrepreneurial Division surveyed 94 percent of the cooperatives on turnover in the top four executive positions for the period 1980–85 (*Trabajo y Unión*, February 1986). During this period, the turnover ranged from 80 percent for administrative directors to 112 to 115 percent for the other three executive positions. The study pointed out, however, that much of this turnover involved movement from one cooperative to another within the Mondragón complex. Marketing directors, who have the highest frequency of contact outside the cooperatives, were the most likely to leave the complex; only about 39 percent of their movement was from one cooperative to another. Intercooperative shifting of positions accounted for 50.5 percent of the turnover among directors of production, 57 percent among administrative directors, and 60.2 percent among managers (the chief executives).

The study also showed considerable variation among the cooperative groups in their capacity to retain executives. For example, 69 percent of those leaving INDARKO took jobs outside the cooperatives, whereas only 11 percent of those leaving FAGOR took such jobs. These results are not surprising considering how much stronger the culture is in the cooperatives that are in or near the city of Mondragón, such as FAGOR, compared to those that are loosely linked in a group and some distance from Mondragón, such as INDARKO in Guernica, some thirty miles away.

The situation in FAGOR is of special interest because it is a training ground for a large number of workers who move on to executive positions in cooperatives outside the FAGOR group. Working within the largest cooperative group, which contains some of the most technologically advanced firms, provides supervisors and middle-management people with rich learning opportunities, which make them especially attractive to other Mondragón cooperatives and enable them to advance into positions not currently open in FAGOR. Leaders of FAGOR take pride in employing almost no nonmembers, yet the pay range is extraordinarily narrow. Leaving out 1 percent of the members who are at the lowest pay levels and 1 percent who are at the highest levels, the differential for the remaining 98 percent is no more than two to one. Thus members who have demonstrated ability within FAGOR but are not in the top fifty-eight to sixty positions have greater financial opportunities when they move into top positions in other cooperatives.

COMMUNICATIONS PROBLEMS

The communications problems Mondragón faces are quite different from those in private industry in the United States. In U.S. private industry, union leaders often demand the right to detailed financial and operating information. This right has been vigorously resisted in most companies as an invasion of managerial prerogatives. Executives consider such information proprietary and therefore to be withheld from workers as well as competitors. If management resists union pay demands on the grounds that the company cannot afford them, the National Labor Relations Board has ruled that the company must then open its books to the union leaders. In the United States, it has taken a long struggle to gain access to such information, and freedom of access is available only to the 20 percent of workers who are represented by unions and then only when management claims inability to pay.

In Mondragón, the problem for worker-members is not in gaining access but in coping with the abundance of technical and financial information that is available. The severity of the problem depends in part on the size of the organization. In a small cooperative, members can readily grasp the relation between their labor and skill and the overall performance of the cooperative. In a large cooperative, and in a cooperative group, the information must necessarily be communicated in a more abstract and general form, which makes it more difficult for members to understand the relation between their labor and the overall figures. The size and complexity of Ulgor and FAGOR greatly complicate communications problems. Because all the members have a right to vote on the business plan of the cooperative and also on whether they approve or disapprove of the performance of management, the leaders are concerned about finding ways to simplify the process of providing and discussing the information while still presenting economic and technological realities.

The communication of figures and plans is not a simple step from the preparation of materials by management to the presentation of the facts and figures to the membership at the annual meeting of the cooperative group. In the FAGOR cooperatives, for example, groups of members are taken off their jobs on company time for the presentation and discussion of issues that will be voted on in the annual meeting. The General Assembly of FAGOR, made up of elected representatives of the member cooperatives, then discusses these issues with the members before they are voted on. The Central Social Council also has one or more sessions each year at which business plans and annual reports are presented and discussed. Furthermore, when major structural changes are proposed for the cooperative group, as in the recent reorganization of FAGOR, an enormous amount of time is invested by management in preparing informational materials and in training those who are to present and interpret them to the rest of the cooperative group. The costs of this process, including materials preparation time, training time, and time for which workers are paid but away from their jobs, are very substantial. For example, planning and discussion meetings before the general assembly meeting in Ulgor to vote on the business plan for 1985–86 cost management an estimated 14 million pesetas, which is 7,000 pesetas, or more than $50, for each of the approximately 2,000 members of Ulgor. Meetings to plan the 1986 reorganization of FAGOR cost 172 million pesetas, well over $1 million.

We have not studied the communications process, but we wonder whether the members of FAGOR are suffering from information overload: being inundated by a larger and more complex volume of information than most are able to absorb in the limited time available. We were impressed by the dedication of management and personnel people to providing as complete information as possible and by the emphasis they gave to the communications process, as indicated by the training of presenters and the financial cost of the process. As of this writing, however, FAGOR has not conducted systematic interviews with members to determine what they understood from the informational meetings and how they evaluated the communications process. If Mondragón devoted as much attention to research on communications as to technological and economic research, substantial gains in efficiency might be achieved.

DOES COORDINATION MEAN CENTRALIZATION?

Leaders of the cooperative complex have seen that to deal effectively with the increasingly competitive economic environment there must be more internal coordination among the member units. One way this is being achieved is by imposing within the complex the economic discipline that would be imposed by the market if each unit were operating independently. In other words, the Caja and its Entrepreneurial Division and the management of the cooperative groups have taken over some of the responsibilities of the individual cooperatives. Whatever the rationale, the result has been a trend toward increased centralization of decision making, especially in the most highly developed cooperative group, FAGOR.

The reorganization of FAGOR has established an intermediate or divisional level of management between the individual cooperatives and general management. For the individual cooperative, the advantages of belonging to FAGOR are clear. The group management is able to concentrate on strategic planning, since it is in a position to take a broad view and to seize opportunities that might not be grasped by the managements of the individual cooperatives. The capacity of the group to shift personnel instead of laying off members is also extremely important. Ulgor, for example, had approximately 3,500 members at the time of the 1974 strike; by 1985, it had fewer than 2,000. Those Ulgor workers who became surplus in this twelve-year period were absorbed in other cooperatives, particularly in newly created or expanding firms in the FAGOR group.

In our interviews, we found no management people who believed that their cooperative would be better off as an independent unit, but we did hear concern expressed about what some people in management saw as an increasing tendency toward centralization. This trend is evident particularly in the policy of pooling the profits and losses of the cooperatives in the FAGOR group.

Depending on the financial performance of the cooperative, this policy can have welcome or unwelcome consequences. A cooperative experiencing serious financial losses gets help essential for its survival. To be sure, such help does not come without cost; the management of FAGOR is intimately involved in working out structural and personnel changes and in negotiating program and policy changes with the affected cooperative. (The Caja may provide necessary refinancing but has not been involved in the reorganization of FAGOR.)

In interviews conducted in November 1985, researchers from Cornell University found that the management of Arrasate, a cooperative that had experienced several years of substantial losses, recognized the great importance of the support it was receiving from FAGOR. The pooling policy had quite different implications for the leaders of Copreci. More than a decade earlier, Copreci had experienced a financial emergency. Since then, it had been the most consistently profitable FAGOR cooperative. Although it did not basically question the economic and social rationale of pooling profits and losses, the management of Copreci was restive under this policy. Because Copreci did not retain its own profits, those proposing a new project had to persuade not only the management of Copreci of its value but also the management of FAGOR and probably the management of the Financial Division of the Caja. (With the establishment of the divisional structure in 1986, such a project would also have to be submitted to the management of the division before being considered by FAGOR's top management.)

The management people in Copreci who discussed this problem with us were concerned both about the number of bureaucratic levels their proposals had to pass through and the work required to make the case at each level. Even after all this work, the proposal could still be blocked by someone assigned to review it in FAGOR's Central Services.

As we discussed this issue with a group that included people from FAGOR's Central Services and from the individual cooperatives, an official of FAGOR argued vigorously that the concerns were based on a misunderstanding. He pointed out that decisions on proposals were made not by staff people but by the Governing Council of FAGOR, where each cooperative had a representative. A Copreci official replied that what the man from FAGOR said was technically correct. She pointed out, however, that the members of the Governing Council of FAGOR were very busy, combining work for their individual cooperatives with their responsibilities for the governance of FAGOR. No one except the Copreci representative would have adequate time to devote to a detailed study of a proposal. Inevitably, they would be considerably influenced by the conclusions of the FAGOR staff person who was responsible for the study and evaluation of the proposal. A FAGOR official replied that he knew of no case in which the Governing Council of FAGOR had rejected a proposal made by Copreci.

We should not exaggerate the importance of this problem in retarding growth and creativity. It is reasonable to assume that, in the Mondragón cooperatives as elsewhere, not only the facts and figures in a proposal are evaluated but the reputation of the individuals making the proposal and the organization supporting it. Thus executives of highly successful organizations are more likely to get approval for proposals than executives whose organizational records are not as strong. The success of Copreci over the years must therefore favor approval of its proposals.

PARTICIPATION IN GOVERNANCE AND IN THE MANAGEMENT OF WORK

How does the quality and extent of worker participation in the Mondragón cooperatives compare with the prevailing situation in private industry in Spain? We know of no broadly based national surveys, but in studies conducted by Keith Bradley and Alan Gelb (1981, 221–22) the responses of members of Mondragón and workers in two large private firms, Unión Cerrajera in Mondragón and Mayc in Vitoria, were strikingly different. On a question about whether workers were inhibited from expressing their opinions, 59 percent of 1,004 Mondragón respondents replied that they were not inhibited, compared to 45 percent of 212 respondents in the private firms (a difference statistically significant at the 0.005 level). To a question on the perceived division between management and workers, 21 percent of 994 Mondragón respondents reported a "large division," compared to 62 percent of 265 workers in the private firms (a difference significant at the 0.005 level). To a question on the "perceived degree of participation in important decisions" offering four alternatives—direct participation, indirect participation (through representatives), not very extensive participation, and none at all—the contrast was again striking. Of 993 members of cooperatives, 37 percent reported either direct or indirect participation, compared to 7 percent of 269 workers in the private firms. At the other extreme, 30 percent of the Mondragón respondents reported that they did not participate at all, compared with 80 percent of the workers in the private firms (a difference significant at the 0.005 level).

To go beyond *perceptions of participation*, it is important to examine actual behavior and to distinguish between *participation in governance* and *participation in the organization and management of work*. For this further step, we cannot report comprehensive quantitative data, but we have learned enough from interviews, group discussions, and documentary records to warrant an interpretive analysis.

By governance, we mean the establishment of strategies and policies designed to guide and control the operations of people in management and workers throughout the organization. By the management and organization of work, we refer to the planning and implementing of the particular arrangements through which work gets done and information is communicated through established channels. This process is guided only roughly by the policy makers controlling the governance of the organization. To be sure, the distinction between governance and management is more sharply made in the structure of the Mondragón complex than in private industry in the United States, where the chief executive officer is nearly always a member of the board of directors and often holds the position of chairman of the board. It seems conceptually useful, however, to distinguish between the governance and the management of work because the possibilities and limitations of participation are different in these two areas.

There is a marked contrast between the Mondragón cooperatives and U.S. private companies regarding participation in governance. In most U.S. firms, employees have no representation on the board of directors. In recent years, with the growth of employee ownership in various forms, particularly where unions have negotiated with management over pay sacrifices, worker representatives have gained positions on boards. In nearly all cases, however, they constitute a small minority and have little influence. In Mondragón, all major policy changes are subject to final decision by a majority vote of the members. Our studies of FAGOR's painful readjustments in the 1980s make it clear that the worker-members do not simply rubber-stamp the proposals of management and the governing council.

The leaders of Mondragón cooperatives are very much aware of the difficulty of maintaining democratic control in increasingly complex organizations where the issues to be decided are highly technical. Javier Mongelos, general manager of FAGOR, had this concern in mind when he pointed out that some leaders in the social councils were pressing to have more power over the complicated issues of governance, although they had taken no initiative in the organization and management of work, an area in which they and their fellow worker-members had great experience-based competence. He particularly noted the reluctance of the social councils to become involved in the redesign of work.

As we have seen, work redesign in FAGOR has been planned and con-trolled by management. In the redesign of the refrigerator department of Ulgor, there was an advisory committee that included two members of the social councils of Ulgor, but the basic redesign was carried out by engineers in Ulgor and in the Central Services of FAGOR. When the initial plans for the new refrigerator line were presented to the social councils of Ulgor, some members vigorously objected that the engineers had simply devised a plan to install better machines without changing the dehu-manizing characteristics of the conveyor belt assembly line. These objec-tions resulted in the design team going back to their drawing boards to work out a design that would be more acceptable to the social councils.

It is important to distinguish between *reactive* and *proactive* participation. In reactive participation, workers or their representatives have opportu-nities to make criticisms and suggestions on management plans, with some prospects of changing the plans. In proactive participation, workers or their representatives are involved in all stages of working out the plans for the reorganization of work or other issues. Workers in Mondragón seem to have far more opportunities for reactive participation than workers or their representatives in most U.S. private firms. We have found, however, that in a few firms in the United States workers or their rep-resentatives have gone beyond Mondragón in the extent to which they are involved in proactive participation.

The Xerox Corporation, which has one of the most advanced systems of participation developed in the United States (Lazes and Costanza 1984), is one such company. Based on a strongly supported collaboration between top union leaders and top management, the program began with the establishment of "study action teams" in departments where management had found that the company could save millions of dollars if components or products made by Xerox were instead bought from outside vendors. The program began in the wire harness department. The challenge for the first study action team was to discover how the department could cut its costs by $3.2 million and thereby save jobs.

The first study action team was selected jointly by union leaders and management. It consisted of six volunteer blue-collar workers representing the various jobs in the wire harness department and two members of management, one from the line operation and one staff engineer. The team was allotted six months of full-time work, paid by the company, to devote to the project and was granted access to all technical and financial information it might require, including the right to consult any individual within the organization or outside it.

At the end of the six-month period, the team brought in a report describing in systematic detail changes that could save $3.7 million a year—well beyond the target figure. Impressed by this unexpected result, management, working with the union, established study action teams in other departments that were threatened with closing because their operations were noncompetitive. Furthermore, management and the union institutionalized this process by negotiating a clause in the union contract that when a department was found to be seriously noncompetitive, management and the union would establish a study action team, with the same time and support arrangements as the initial team, before laying off workers. After some months of further collaboration, in the 1986 three-year contract with the union, management included a guarantee that no worker who had been with Xerox since 1983 would be laid off for reasons of outside competition. Management reserved the right to shift employees to other jobs, but in making this exceptional guarantee clearly expressed significant confidence in the participative program.

In the following months, Xerox and the union expanded the study action team program considerably by involving workers and technicians in the planning and implementation of research and development projects and in the design of new plants. Typically, workers become involved in a research and development project only when it moves into production, at which time the problems workers are sure to recognize are very difficult to correct. The management of Xerox now states that involving workers and technicians in the early and middle stages of research and development projects has enabled them to move plans for a new product from the drawing board to full-scale production in half the time it took under the conventional arrangements (Dominick R. Argona, personal communication). Similarly, involving workers and technicians in both the design and construction of a new plant allows them not only to bring to bear their experience and voice their opinions regarding future working conditions but to have a major voice in the selection of machines and in the design of work flow in ways that will make production work easier and more efficient.

To be sure, these examples are the exceptions. Nevertheless, just as the Mondragón complex is an exceptional set of organizations from which outsiders can learn a great deal, so too the people of Mondragón could learn much about proactive participation in the management and organization of work from organizations elsewhere.

THE ROLE OF THE SOCIAL COUNCILS

The social councils are a Mondragón invention of considerable importance. This is widely recognized in Mondragón, and yet there is considerable ambiguity and ambivalence regarding their nature and functions. On the one hand, some members of the complex criticize them for having no power and simply rubber-stamping decisions of management. On the other hand, some members of the social councils are reluctant to challenge management because they feel that this is not in accord with their established role in the cooperatives. Management naturally would not welcome such challenges.

Our interpretation of the role and nature of the social councils is generally rejected by the leading figures in the Mondragón complex, yet we can find no other acceptable rationale. As we see it, the governing councils are primarily concerned with the interests of members as co-owners, whereas the social councils are primarily concerned with representing the members as workers. This dual structure gives the Mondragón cooperatives strength in decision making not available in large worker cooperatives elsewhere. When worker-members have to make decisions about the future of their organization, they are naturally ambivalent. On the one hand, they want to strengthen their organization to ensure long-run profitability and survival; on the other hand, they want to increase their income and to make working conditions more humane and attractive. Ambivalence is not a good position from which to make decisions. We therefore believe that organizations as large and complex as some of the Mondragón cooperatives and cooperative groups have a distinct advantage in having two official bodies: It enables them to achieve balance (*equilibrio*) in representing the interests of members as workers and their interests as owners.

The basic argument against this interpretation is that, because the members of the governing councils are popularly elected, they represent the interests of members as workers as well as their interests as owners. Furthermore, the members of the social councils have a right to, and are expected to, consider the business needs of their organizations. This is undoubtedly true in ideology and to some extent in practice. Our impression is that the members of the governing councils do consider the interests of members as workers to a much greater extent than managers do in private companies, and we have noted an increasing tendency for members of social councils to become involved in evaluating and criticizing the business performance of management.

In practice, we see this duality of interests being acted out in the two bodies. It is also reflected in the job status of their members. The members of the governing council are elected at large, and workers in higher-level positions who have greater visibility to the rank and file are more likely to be elected. Because membership in the social councils is based on representation from departments or work groups, the average job index of the members of social councils is below that of the members of governing councils. This difference was anticipated from the very beginning, since the original constitution of Ulgor (1959) specified that anyone elected to its governing council who had a job index of 1.6 or below would automatically become a member of the social council. Clearly, the original rationale was to favor representation of rank-and-file workers on the social councils.

Useful here is a comparison of the relationship of management and the governing councils to the social councils and the situation in those U.S. firms where union and management work closely together to improve productivity and the quality of working life. In the United States, the union continues to process members' grievances and to argue with management on pay and policy questions but at the same time is actively engaged with management in improving the organization and planning of work.

Leaders of Mondragón generally reject any perceived similarity between their social councils and American unions, but this may be based more on the history of labor relations and current experience in Spain and the Basque country than on social theory, which might indicate how a union could play a role quite different from the conventional one of confrontation and adversarial bargaining. Some union leaders in the United States, for example, feel that they have established their good faith with workers over the years by hard bargaining and continue, when the economic environment drastically changes, to represent workers' interests by co-operating with management to increase the competitive strength of the company and therefore the workers' job security—provided management is willing to open up channels of participation and truly share power with workers.

In our review of the history of the social councils, we find cases in which members were divided over how far they should challenge management. This issue raises the question of whether the social councils should act like unions. When the issue is defined in this form, the members of the social councils tend to back off—but not necessarily by surrendering to management, since the final decision is made by a vote of the members. We also note that this tension regarding the appropriate role for social councils has recently been resolved in the reorganization of FAGOR in a way that strengthens the analogy between the social councils and unions. For the first time, the chairperson of the FAGOR Central Social Council is elected by the members of that body, whereas previously that person was chosen by management. The new statutes also explicitly recognize the right of the social councils to negotiate with management and with the governing councils on a broad range of issues. Negotiation had been taking place in practice, but it is nevertheless important that the right is now formalized. Does this resolve the ambiguity or only compound it? Can an organization have an advisory body that does not simply advise but that actually negotiates with management?

One of the questions on Bradley and Gelb's survey (1981, 221) casts light, albeit indirectly, on whether the social councils adequately represent the interests of the members of the cooperatives. When asked whether they would favor a "large trade union role" in their firms, only 25 percent of 971 Mondragón respondents responded yes, compared with 86 percent of 261 workers in the private firms (a significance level of 0.005). This result confirms our impression that the desire for unionization is not strong among the members, yet, in that one out of four members favored such a role, it suggests that many members may not have been satisfied with the representation they had through the social councils—or through other structures of participation. (We should add a word of caution in interpreting any single survey item: Much depends on the conditions respondents were experiencing at the time of the survey. Bradley and Gelb's survey was administered when the Mondragón cooperatives were entering a period of painful financial sacrifices.)

We have been surprised by how little the social councils have been involved in the redesign of work, considering that some leaders and members of local unions have been actively involved in this area in the United States. Perhaps the organization of work has been conventionally defined in the Basque country as a responsibility of management, which would suggest that it is not the business of social councils to help management carry out this responsibility. Some of the more active members of social councils may be concerned lest they seem to be coopted by management and thus unable to represent the workers. Workers and union leaders in the United States, however, are finding it much easier to participate effectively in the reorganization of work than in the governance of the plant or company.

One of the problems of the social councils is how difficult it is to interpret the facts and figures on which management decisions are made. Mondragón people point out that the same facts and figures management uses are freely available to the social councils. The facts and figures are so complex and technical, however, that staff must spend considerable time to understand and interpret them. This weakness has long been recognized, and some remedial steps have been taken, such as allocating more staff time and making the personnel departments responsible for working with the social councils. The members of the social councils are expected to advise management on social and organizational questions, on which they can speak from experience, without the support of formal study. One wonders whether the development of social research within FAGOR might become a special field of interest and involvement of the social councils.

SOCIAL EDUCATION AND RESEARCH

For purposes of economic development, the Caja probably has the strongest research capacity of any organization in the Basque country. Various observers have reported that Ikerlan has become a world-class applied industrial research institute. Between them, the Escuela Politécnica and ETEO have developed engineering instruction and economics courses, but although Mondragón's founder was a serious student of sociology and an extraordinary applied sociologist, Mondragón's educational system has lagged in instruction in the social sciences, except for economics. As of this writing, little instruction is being offered in organizational behavior, except for what is needed in practice in business administration. Furthermore, courses in business administration primarily present ideas and information derived from foreign studies in private industry. We do not assume that the literature on business administration in private industry is irrelevant to the Mondragón cooperatives. In fact, leaders of Mondragón are familiar with the literature on participative management. Nevertheless, the absence in both the Escuela Politécnica and ETEO of courses specifically focused on the organization and administration of worker cooperatives seems to be a serious handicap.

Foreign visitors to Mondragón often comment on this gap in the educational system. A common explanation is that the leaders want to avoid giving students the impression that the educational system is brainwashing them. Because most of the existing literature on cooperatives has been written by true believers, motivated more by a missionary spirit than by scientific interests, this explanation has some merit. Most of this literature is normative in character rather than an examination of the actual problems of organization and development. To be sure, Ikasbide and other organizations provide seminars and short courses on cooperative management to members of the cooperatives, and particularly to their leaders, but most of this material also is normative in character, orienting the participants to the way their cooperative should operate to meet legal, economic, and social requirements.

Because no other cooperative organizations anywhere in the world resemble the Mondragón complex even remotely, it would be difficult for Mondragón's leaders to learn from social research on cooperatives elsewhere, even if the literature were much more scientific. Mondragón therefore needs to develop its capacity to do such research, which could produce reports of practical value to the cooperatives and publications of great interest to a growing outside public fascinated with Mondragón. The research could contribute to the development of teaching materials, so that those in leadership positions in the cooperatives could learn from the study of Mondragón rather than only from material published by outsiders and focused on private industry.

Active participation in the Mondragón cooperatives provides large numbers of members with opportunities to learn from experience about their organization, its problems, and its management. FAGOR's personnel department is seeking to determine whether this experiential learning can be strengthened by combining it with social research designed to fit the characteristics and requirements of FAGOR. From 1984 to 1986, members of personnel departments of FAGOR, working with a group from Cornell University, took the first steps toward what may become FAGOR's social research program and a primary source for the development of teaching materials—provided these efforts prove to be as fruitful as we all hope. People in personnel might thus improve their capacity to inform and advise management and the social councils about the social and organizational problems of their cooperatives and their cooperative group. Playing a role in the research process and in the interpretation of its results might strengthen the social councils, whose responsibilities and capacities have been so unclear. People from Cornell University have helped to begin this process, but its future will depend on how social research can be developed by Mondragón people themselves.

MONDRAGÓN'S STRENGTHS

In this chapter we have discussed some of the problems facing the cooperative complex. It is also important to recognize the strengths that have enabled it to deal with these problems.

We have been impressed by the dedication to cooperative ideals manifested by Mondragón's leaders, both in operations and in personnel departments. They are not simply technocrats. To fulfill their responsibilities, they must have a high degree of technical competence, combined with a social vision. Following the vision of the founder and adapting that vision to changing conditions—as the founder himself emphasized—they have built a distinctive organizational culture, which we will analyze in chapter 19. This does not mean that all, or even a majority, of the members of the organization are strongly committed to the core values of this culture. Comparing the values of the leaders with those in the rank and file would require research far beyond this study. For a cooperative organization to survive and grow, however, it is not necessary for all its members to share the key values of the leaders, as long as the organization provides its members with social rewards arising directly out of their experience in the cooperative.

Another of Mondragón's great strengths is the high value it places on continuous critical examination of its own experience. Here Mondragón departs markedly from what we have come to expect in organizations that have been designed and developed out of a social vision. As these organizations grow and face changing conditions, in many cases the leaders are so strongly committed to their initial principles and beliefs that they are unable to make the changes necessary for survival and growth. In Mondragón we see a hero worship that is similar to what we find in innovative organizations founded by a charismatic leader, but there are two crucial differences: The founder himself constantly emphasized the need for self-criticism and to adapt to changing conditions, and he never held an executive position that would have enabled him to impose his views on others.

The employment security provided by Mondragón is another extraordinary strength. As noted in chapter 13, according to definitions customarily used in the United States, only 0.6 percent of the members of cooperatives were unemployed in 1985, when unemployment in the Basque country was 27 percent.

Employment security should not be seen simply as providing benefits to individual members. Because workers do not feel threatened, we would expect much less resistance to change from workers and managers in the Mondragón complex than from workers and managers in private firms, where employees are much more likely to feel their employment security is threatened.

Another strength of the Mondragón cooperatives is their capacity to invest for future growth and modernization. In this regard, they have far surpassed private industry in their region.

Even though cooperative employment in manufacturing makes up only about 3% of the Basque population employed in manufacturing, a measure of the dynamism of the group is that cooperative investment was about 77% of all Basque industrial investment in 1981. (Milbrath 1983, 11)

The key structures on which the cooperatives are based, and those linking the cooperatives, are also important sources of strength. In many cooperatives elsewhere, the chief executive is elected directly by the membership. This arrangement may be considered more democratic than the indirect selection of chief executives by the governing councils. In Mondragón, however, chief executives have a degree of job security that may be essential to concentrating on problems of administration and development without having to be constantly concerned with the possibility of being voted out by the membership. To be sure, chief executives are accountable through the governing council, which is elected by the members, and, in any case, are appointed for only four-year terms. Furthermore, should the members of a cooperative and its governing council become seriously dissatisfied, an executive can be relieved of his or her duties before the end of a term. In other cases executives have asked to be relieved of their positions when they felt they could no longer meet their responsibilities. Thus the Mondragón system cannot be considered simply an arrangement for management entrenchment, although it may provide a degree of stability essential for efficient performance.

In spite of the criticisms directed against it from time to time by the members, it seems to us that the social council is an important social invention. This position seems to be supported by the contribution of the social councils during the period of economic readjustments and sacrifices beginning in 1979. We doubt the necessary changes could have been worked out with as little conflict and difficulty had there been no social councils. They were important in improving the quality of communication from management to the workers and from the workers to management and also in negotiating and mediating between the workers and management.

Many managers (chief executives) have had experience as representatives on governing councils. This background in analyzing and determining policy serves them well in their executive positions and makes them effective in dealing with the governing councils. Some managers also have served on social councils. In fact, although the governing councils have more prestige, some members aspiring to top management positions make a point of seeking election to a social council to gain experience in dealing with the social concerns of the members. Movement through these bodies, plus experience on various committees, constitute an extraordinarily effective management-development program.

The leaders of Mondragón have been highly successful in building an integrated mini-economy. They have built strong base organizations and strong support organizations that link all the units so that each depends on some of the others and each contributes to the total complex.

The most impressive evidence of the importance of grouping cooperatives under a joint management is provided by FAGOR, which links some of the oldest and largest cooperatives and includes a number of the cooperatives with the most advanced technologies. In other cooperative groups, especially the most recently formed, which are linked much more loosely, the strengths of group management are less apparent. Nonetheless, we have seen evidence of the importance of group management in the way the URKIDE group worked through the very difficult problems of economic readjustment in the 1980s.

The advantages of group management are illustrated particularly well in the area of personnel, where the maintenance of employment security has been possible only because the group, assisted by Lagun-Aro and the Caja in cases of extreme economic difficulties, could shift members from one cooperative to another within the same group. Thus Ulgor could reduce its total membership from approximately 3,500 in 1974 to just under 2,000 in 1985, while contributing to the creation and expansion of other cooperatives within FAGOR.

Joint management makes it possible to centralize and build the capacity for strategic planning that enables member firms to be expanded and contracted and for new firms to be created within the same group. By itself, a small cooperative lacks the staff to engage in such planning. Some of Ulgor's most important strategic initiatives originated in the management of FAGOR rather than in the management of Ulgor itself. Of course, it is desirable for each cooperative to develop some capacity for strategic planning, and there is always the danger of allowing the group management to play too dominant a role in shaping the development of individual cooperatives. Nonetheless, the problems of how to balance the capacities of individual cooperatives with the capacity of the management of the group should not obscure the advantage of group management.

The program to introduce and develop work redesign among the FAGOR firms might have lost momentum had it been left entirely to the management of the individual cooperatives. Because of the initiative of FAGOR's management, the program moved ahead.

In both FAGOR and URKIDE, we have seen impressive demonstrations of the importance of the group's management in intervening to rescue and revitalize cooperatives on the brink of closing. In such cases, of course, the group's management did not act alone. It linked up the failing cooperative with the Caja for technical assistance and financial support and worked with Lagun-Aro to help relocate surplus members.

Finally, group management provides another source of strength that is less readily apparent: the capacity to facilitate key changes in leadership positions within a given cooperative when such changes are vital to a cooperative's survival. Suppose an isolated cooperative encountered a crisis in which its survival depended on its ability to replace its top executive. In a cooperative that stood alone, and especially one whose success in its early period of growth had depended on one individual remaining in the top position, it would be exceedingly difficult to remove this key person and bring in someone better able to manage current problems and conditions. Under the threat of losing his job and with no employment opportunities within the cooperative, the executive would probably struggle to hold on, even if he himself doubted his ability to handle the problems. At the same time, members who wanted to get rid of him would be worried about finding and attracting someone who could do better.

In contrast, executives in FAGOR firms who have lost confidence in their abilities have occasionally volunteered to leave their positions, knowing that the group management would make every effort to place them where they could be expected to perform adequately. These executives still suffer the psychological pain of being eased out, but the change is more acceptable to all those concerned. For example, one man who had been the manager of a cooperative for many years described quite dispassionately the change he experienced. In describing a performance review, he said that the general manager went over his strengths and weaknesses in a considerate and gentlemanly manner. The manager did not entirely agree with the assessment of his weaknesses, but he emphasized that the process was carried out correctly and that the general manager had the power and responsibility to act in response to evaluations of his performance by the governing councils of his cooperative and of the cooperative group. As the review session closed, the general manager said that he was authorized to let the manager choose one of three important positions, all within his cooperative group. After some reflection, he chose a newly established position that gave him important responsibilities for the future development of the group. He emphasized that the man who replaced him was an excellent choice and was doing an outstanding job. We might add that the former manager's performance in his new position is generally regarded as outstanding. Replacing the chief executive of an organization is never easy, but the existence of the cooperative group provides a way to make strategic replacements in a manner that is both more humane and more economically efficient than is possible in an organization that stands alone.

PART FIVE

Lessons from Mondragón

18 Understanding Mondragón's Founder

Don José María Arizmendiarrieta resisted any attempts to honor him and thus personalize the movement he and his associates founded. Now that he is gone, symbols and images of Arizmendi pervade the cooperatives in Mondragón. The technical school has been named after him. The street linking the school, Lagun-Aro, Ikerlan, and the Caja Laboral Popular now bears his name. Portraits and busts of Arizmendi, made after his death, are in the lobbies of major organizations that support the cooperatives. Quotations from his writings are liberally used in reports for publication and internal circulation and are displayed, along with his portrait, in branch offices of the Caja.

The description that follows is based on our all-too-brief acquaintance with Mondragón's founder and on interviews with his disciples, especially three of the five Ulgor pioneers still active in leadership positions during the period of our visits. Additional information was provided by Ana Gutiérrez-Johnson, who participated in all of our interviews with Don José María in 1975 and interviewed him again after we left Mondragón.

OUR INTRODUCTION TO THE FOUNDER

The man we met in 1975 was of medium height and appeared slim and frail. He had sparse, receding gray hair, sunken cheeks, and a sallow complexion. He was approaching the last year of his life and depended on a pacemaker, but those who had known him in the early days of Mondragón had always found it difficult to reconcile his inexhaustible energy with his body, which had not seemed built to support it. He talked with us on the day of our arrival, in the living room of the Hostal Txerrita, where we were staying. Settling into an upholstered easy chair,

Don José María seemed to recede into the furniture. His dark glasses, which he had worn since he lost an eye in a childhood accident, made him seem even more retiring.

Don José María was a man of simple tastes who never sought any material comforts for himself. In spite of the urging of his followers, he never drew on Church funds to buy himself an automobile or allowed others to raise money for one. He was still getting around on a bicycle.

He spoke to us in a soft voice, hesitating from time to time as if searching for the right words to describe what he and his associates had created. Our most vivid impression of our first meeting was of his hands— the long, thin El Greco-like fingers—constantly moving as if to help shape his thoughts. By now, the ideas he was expressing must have been familiar to him, but he still seemed to be struggling to express his thoughts in exactly the right way.

During our second interview, which took place in the school he had founded, Don José María permitted us to use a tape recorder, but, after that, he barred the machine, claiming that we were attaching too much importance to him and his words. He always minimized his personal role and spoke of collective achievements. In fact, in speaking about past events, he rarely used the first-person singular, saying instead, "Se pidió," which, literally translated, means, "It was asked." Because such a phrase is awkward and misleading in English, we have written "I asked" whenever it was clear from the immediate context or from other information that Don José María did the asking.

Don José María gave us a depressing picture of the city of Mondragón as he found it in 1941. By this time political opposition and labor union leaders had gone underground, and the city had become a dangerous place for activists. As he told us:

> We lost the Civil War, and we became an occupied region. In the postwar period, the people of Mondragón suffered severely in the repression. I had known some people of Mondragón, but when I came after the war they all had either died, or were in jail, or in exile.

During our interviews, he interpreted the beginnings of the movement:

> One of the main goals commonly shared . . . was to promote opportunities for practical education without discrimination. That naturally implied sensitizing people to the concept that it is necessary to socialize knowledge in order to democratize power because in fact knowledge is power. . . .

It was a process of mobilization, consciousness raising, and training, of theory and practice, of self-government and self-management, in which young people, in order to face the serious problems of financing, organized raffles, festivals, and other public events. This not only facilitated the financing but also gave the youth—especially the most dynamic young people—the opportunity to learn practical lessons from experience. Simultaneously, in this process of interaction, they had the chance to build up credit with the community in a broader sense. It was this youth that later on would become the protagonists of the cooperative experience. Practically, it was they who did everything, because I was the one who reserved for myself the easiest task—to think aloud. All that I did was to raise ideas and provoke the young people, and nothing more.

We might add: and nothing less!

It was not his purpose to guide his associates in the building of better small groups or small firms, or even larger firms, but rather to change the whole society. As he said to us:

> It was not our custom to distribute all the profits, because we were not trying to build a cooperative-*cofradía* [layman's religious brotherhood] but rather a cooperative firm. . . .
>
> The protagonists of the cooperative enterprise were conscious of their role. They were trying to be protagonists of an expansive process, with a realistic sense of direction. The origins of the enterprise they founded lay in the solidarity and mutual support of a contingent of people developing a program. That is, solidarity is not good as we usually understand it— simply as mutual help—but when it is transformed into a reciprocity that extends beyond the limits of the individual enterprise, on a broader scale. In a *cofradía* people participate only for themselves and for their fellow members.

AS SEEN BY HIS FOLLOWERS

In 1975, Don José María's friend and biographer, Jesús Larrañaga, described his and his associates' early experience with the founder to us:

> In our first contacts with Don José María, really he put us to sleep talking about his ideas, we had no understanding of the implications of these ideas. What we did, following the leads he opened up for us, we did simply because we were men who felt the desire to do things, and also because of the confidence in himself he built in us through his tenacity and stubborn-

ness, which motivated us and made us think. . . . At this time, frankly, his speaking ability in Spanish was poor—although he wrote very well, he lacked oral facility, and it was hard work for him to communicate with us. But he was tenacious. Once he confessed to me that this difficulty was a form of penance that God had imposed on him because what he wanted to do most was transmit ideas, and yet he had the least talent for that. This led him to force himself to transmit the essence of his ideas, and the lack of fluency made him think more deeply. He has been a man of enormous drive who always went for the essential and not for the superficial. He was always pointing us in different directions, with a practical sense. His theory of education was that young people—even when very young—had to accustom themselves to taking practical actions, they had to participate in initiatives of any kind, from making things for Christmas to taking steps in any other activity. The important thing was that there be continual practice, so that initiative, responsibility, and commitment can be developed and demonstrated. In this way, he led us to develop channels that were then open to us. Because it was an era of political hibernation, in the sense that there was no opening for political action, the only institution that had certain options open was the Church.

José María Ormaechea, one of the founders of Ulgor and chief executive of the Caja Laboral Popular for many years, also recalled his early years with the founder.

Don José María never distinguished himself as an orator. Fundamentally, his gift was a capacity for personal dialogue . . . besides, contrary to what was customary, instead of flattering us when we went to consult him, he treated us with affection but urged us every day to make a greater commitment to the labor movement and to the future economic and social transformation of society. Misled somewhat by capitalistic thinking in our first phase, we thought the solutions could be found in social reforms of a paternalistic type within capitalist society. But Don José María always insisted that the solution was not to be found in casual reforms but rather in structural reforms; that is to say it was necessary to change the sovereignty of capital to the sovereignty of labor.

In speaking to Ana Gutiérrez-Johnson in 1975, Alfonso Gorroñogoitia, one of Ulgor's founders and at this writing chairman of the governing councils of the Caja Labor Popular and of FAGOR, reflected on Don José María's philosophy.

Don José María is a typical man of the countryside, very pragmatic, with practical judgment, and inclined to orient his ideas toward realities. Beginning with the conception that the idea that can't be expressed in words is not a good idea, and the word that can't be translated into action is not a good word, he guided Acción Católica along original and unorthodox lines. In that era Acción Católica was busying itself with things of minor importance—whether or not dancing should be permitted. We were disciples who year after year educated ourselves, thanks to the teachings of Don José María, along lines of social concerns and toward a translation of religious ideas into something that would link up with our real world. Don José María imbued us with the idea that being a man meant to occupy one's self and do something. That is taken for granted now, but in those days there was a spiritual, scholastic, and puristic atmosphere in the Church. In other places, Acción Católica taught different ideas, people dedicated themselves to Castilian mysticism. Don José María was different in that he was telling us that men have problems and must work in the building of their world. From Don José María I learned that work was not a punishment—which I had been taught earlier—but rather the realization of the Creation and collaboration with the plan of God. . . .

Thanks to the establishment of the Escuela Profesional, we developed the idea that in order to do things we needed technical competence as well as spiritual witness and personal effort.

As Gorroñogoitia noted, the drive toward personal competence and mastery did not submerge social and religious values.

What surprises other entrepreneurs is the poetic-philosophic vein that we have as entrepreneurs. This humanistic inclination that surprises them we owe to Don José María, because we could never dissociate our entrepreneurial attitudes from a philosophy, a concept, an ideology, after the contact we had had with him. We could not be pure technocrats, who know perfectly the processes of chemistry or physics or semi-conductors but nothing more. We have never been pure technocrats. We see the development of these firms as a social struggle, a duty.

EVOLUTION OF HIS IDEAS

Don José María never developed his ideas systematically in a book, but he spoke and wrote constantly. Copies of his writings for *Trabajo y Unión*, the monthly publication of the Mondragón movement, and sermons and other essays have been collected in fifteen volumes. Although we have not undertaken to read those volumes, we have taken advantage of a book published in 1984 by the Caja Laboral Popular, *El Hombre Cooperativo: Pensamiento de José María Arizmendiarrieta* by Joxe Azurmendi. Azurmendi made an exhaustive analysis of Don José María's writings and placed them in the context of the political and economic development of his times, supported by interviews with people who knew him best. Quotations to support our analysis of the founder's thoughts are drawn from that volume, and, unless otherwise indicated, the page numbers following each quotation refer to Azurmendi's book. To place the thoughts of the founder in context, some comments regarding his writing style and the evolution of his ideas are in order.

His style presents a peculiar paradox. On the one hand, the writing is full of complex, multiclause sentences that are difficult to follow and would have been even more so when spoken. On the other hand, when he did get around to making his point, Don José María had a gift for explaining an idea in brief and potent sentences. The maxims and slogans he created lived after him and are constantly quoted in print and in discussions.

It is important to place the thoughts of the founder in the context of his times, his personal development, and the changing political scene. In his early years, Don José María endorsed traditional Catholic doctrine on such matters as contraception and abortion, but as time went on, he gave little attention to such matters of personal morality. Similarly, in his early years, he was a close student of orthodox Catholic theology but later paid less and less attention to such sources. Azurmendi describes the evolution of his thinking:

(A) In his first writings [sermons, conferences with parents, conferences with youth of Acción Católica] the crisis [of the times] is seen fundamentally as one of faith, although faith itself is understood in a broad sense as a general system of Christian-humanist values.

(B) By about 1945–1950 Arizmendiarrieta was centering his attention on the so-called social question. The idea of universal crisis (of authority, of faith, and of reason itself) continued in evidence. But the nucleus of this crisis was not a problem of faith any longer, but rather the question of property. After this epoch distinctly religious themes tend to disappear almost entirely from the writings of Arizmendiarrieta. The quotations from traditional Christian authors, especially from the papal encyclicals, markedly diminish, while at the same time there are increasing numbers of citations from people outside the Church, above all from labor politicians, as he arrived at his own conception of the cooperative, in the 1950s. (page 36)

As Azurmendi pointed out (page 85), the founder's library contained hardly any theological books published after he had completed his studies for the priesthood. The most notable exception was a volume by Hans Kung, a Catholic theologian noted for his outspoken opposition to traditional Catholic theology.

Although years later many progressive Catholic speakers and writers would be citing the new policies of Vatican II and the encyclicals of Pope John XXIII, "in the writings of Arizmendiarrieta the wide use of pontifical texts almost disappeared by the late 1940s" (page 89).

Along with this evolution in his ideas, Don José María shifted his primary interest from the family to the factory. This shift in emphasis accompanied the change in the focus of his activities. In his first years in Mondragón he was busy coping with the pressing problems of housing and health. As time went on, he focused ever more strongly on the workplace. In fact, one woman in Mondragón who regularly went to Don José María for confession told us that he sometimes became so interested in questioning her about workplace conditions and problems that she had to remind him that she was there to confess her sins.

Among secular authors, the founder was a close student of the writings of the French leftist social philosophers Jacques Maritain and Emmanuel Mounier. Azurmendi found Paulo Freire's book *The Pedagogy of the Oppressed* in Arizmendi's library. He had underlined many passages. The founder's copy of the sayings of Chairman Mao also had a number of underlined passages.

Don José María was generally sympathetic to the Marxist critique of capitalism but rejected important aspects of Marxist doctrine. He knew the Marxist literature much better than many ideologically committed Marxists, and he frequently used quotations from leading Marxist writers. As early as 1965, before he and the Mondragón cooperatives came under attack from leftist extremists, he was using quotations from leading Marxist writers to support his views. For example, he cited a statement by Lenin written in 1918 to the effect that cooperatives should be preserved and another written in 1923 that, when the proletariat had triumphed, cooperatives would be valid elements of a socialist society (page 767).

FACING CULTURAL AND POLITICAL
REPRESSION

The early years after the end of the Spanish Civil War were marked by
intense repression in the Basque country, particularly of priests and other
intellectuals, and by a strong campaign against Basque culture. According
to Azurmendi:

> Creating this cultural desert applied even more to Euskadi [the Basque
> country], where the Basque language was proscribed, and those speaking
> it were persecuted. Many years passed before Arizmendiarrieta again wrote
> anything in Euskera, even private notes. Euskadi remained culturally and
> politically decapitated. More concretely, the Basque Church saw its arch-
> bishop, Mateo Múgica, exiled and its clergy submitted to blind persecution.
> (page 38)

Azurmendi reports that sixteen Basque priests were shot (including
Don José María's immediate predecessor in Mondragón), and hundreds
were sent to concentration camps, were deported, or escaped into exile.
Francisco Javier Lauzurica y Torralba, archbishop of the Diocese of Vitoria,
was a dedicated follower of Franco. Azurmendi quotes him as stating that
"I am one more General under orders from the Generalissimo to smash
nationalism"—by which he meant Basque nationalism (page 39).

Although most Basques were opposed to the Franco government, the
active underground movements were divided over the value of Basque
language and culture and even of Basque nationalism. Many socialists
considered Basque nationalism a romantic concept and had no use for the
Basque language. Don José María's stance on these issues changed over
time. In his student days, he was known to his fellows for his great
attachment to the Basque language and his intimate knowledge of Basque
culture and history. Between 1940 and 1950, the founder's writings
deemphasized the importance of minority languages and cultures, in favor
of social class issues (page 653).

In June 1966, *Trabajo y Unión* published an angry letter from a reader
who did not want the publication any more because it failed to give
attention to "the Basque man." He wrote that he had had enough of the
paper's Marxism. Don José María replied that Mondragón had gone further
than other cities in producing active people who defended local and
regional interests.

After 1968, when it became possible to publish openly in the Basque language, *Trabajo y Unión* printed increasing numbers of essays by Don José María in Euskera. From the 1960s on, he was more inclined to emphasize the characteristics of the Basque culture as fundamental to the cooperative movement.

Under the Franco regime, Arizmendi sought to avoid outright confrontations with government, while at the same time stimulating and guiding organizational activities of working people. Because the line between social and educational organization and labor militancy was not clear, he was playing a delicate and risky role. Government authorities did not draw this line uniformly, however, so that, although some regarded him as a dangerous radical, others saw him as a constructive social influence.

At times, the founder also clashed with local authorities. In March 1952, he addressed a long letter to the civil governor of Guipúzcoa complaining that officers of the Guardia Civil (national police) had entered the facilities of Acción Católica and torn notices off the bulletin board and required officials of the organization to come to the government office to defend themselves.

At the time of widespread strikes in Mondragón, in 1956, Don José María was threatened with exile, according to Azurmendi (page 648), "because he was considered 'unanimously', according to the civil governor, as the principal person responsible for these [strikes] in Mondragón." The author adds that the archives of the founder contained many papers evidencing his involvement with labor problems, contract issues, campaigns for reform of private companies, and so on even after the first cooperatives had been well established. *Trabajo y Unión* periodically had problems with the Spanish censors. One issue was seized, and two serious warnings were issued, one in writing and the other by telephone, threatening punishment and suppression of the magazine. These problems arose in response to articles on political prisoners, violence—the failure to condemn it unequivocally—and, before 1968, the use of terms referring to the Basque country and the Basque language.

In the same period, important government officials in Madrid knew and respected the founder. As we have noted, José Luis del Arco, head of the government agency for cooperatives, played a key role in helping Arizmendi fit the constitution and bylaws of the cooperatives into the framework of national legislation and regulation, without violating any of the basic principles pursued by the Mondragón movement. In the early years of Ulgor, Don José María played the key role in securing a major loan from the national industrial bank. The man who was head of the bank at the time noted later that Don José María had all of the important facts and figures at his fingertips and was able to make a very convincing case. "I just thought it was a good loan. I found him a very impressive individual" (from a personal interview conducted by Davydd Greenwood).

Arizmendi's reputation in some quarters of Madrid was confirmed in a highly public way in 1965 when he was awarded the Medalla del Trabajo, a national medal of honor, for his work with the Mondragón movement. This honor conveyed a mixed message. To some of the most radical opponents of the Franco government, anyone receiving a medal from the government had to be an enemy of the Basque people and of the working class. (Perhaps it is because Arizmendi received this honor that some socialists in the government even today associate the Mondragón movement with Franco's fascism.) Arizmendi never defended himself directly for accepting it. Rather, he took the position that the Church should be criticized for its relations with the national government only if those relations had resulted in the Church's estrangement from the people it served. "To find a motive for criticism," Arizmendi said, "one should seek it in that the Church becomes detached from the people, not that it deals with the authorities" (page 53).

From time to time, and particularly in critical moments of labor disturbances within the cooperatives, the founder and the leaders came under fire from the left. These attacks, however, were neither continuous nor represented unanimity among Basque radicals.

The Basque political opposition to the Franco government was divided by differences of beliefs and values regarding the use of peaceful pressure versus violence and Marxism versus Basque nationalism. The most militant tended to support ETA, the organization that has become internationally known for political assassinations. Although the most vocal people in ETA considered themselves Marxists and in the 1970s were attracted to the communism of Chairman Mao, ETA itself could not maintain a united front against the government. Over the years it split up into competing and mutually antagonistic factions. Thus we cannot say that there was any unified opposition on the radical left to the founder of the Mondragón movement. Nevertheless, he and his followers suffered sharp attacks from those quarters. For example, the awarding in 1965 of the medal of honor to Arizmendi moved one anonymous critic to charge the cooperative movement with double treason—to the Basque country and to the working class. This charge was publicly rejected, however, by the leaders of ETA (page 615).

In 1973, the founder was again attacked, this time for refusing to justify ETA's most spectacular act of political violence: the assassination of Franco's prime minister, Carrero Blanco. In *Trabajo y Unión*, Don José María expressed his sorrow about the incident and repudiated violence, but at the same time stressed the importance of building a new society based on "solidarity and cooperation." A statement distributed by the Leninist faction of ETA attacked Arizmendi, charging that *Trabajo y Unión* "is impeding the *real solidarity* of the working class, which is the only guarantee of real struggle against capitalism and the regime" (page 721).

The attack went on to say that Arizmendi's expression of grief over the death of the prime minister was traitorous to the working class: "Only the violence of the exploiter is to be condemned by the working class in the class struggle. . . . In the struggle an assassination is for the workers only an assassination by one of the oppressed" (page 722).

As noted in chapter 9, the 1974 strike at Ulgor and Fagor Electrotécnica provoked especially bitter attacks by ETA on the leaders of the Mondragón movement. It is worth noting that the founder refrained from taking sides in this argument; instead he wrote of the dangers of organizational growth leading to bureaucratization.

RELATIONS WITH THE CHURCH

Don José María had several close friends and admirers among the clergy, but the Catholic Church did not provide institutional support for his work or for the Mondragón cooperative movement. One of his closest friends, Miguel Altuna, a classmate in the seminary who was active for many years in neighboring Vergara, told us that Don José María was an able student in the seminary and was highly respected by his fellows. Later, within the diocese, he had few friends and active supporters among the clergy. He seldom participated in diocesian meetings, where he found little response to his ideas. On one occasion he gave a talk that outraged some of his more conservative fellow priests. One of them left the meeting, shaking his head, saying, "That fellow thinks only of economics" (Larrañaga 1981, 77). In some conservative circles in and around Mondragón, the founder was known as "the Red Priest."

He was highly critical of religion in general and of his church. From personal conversations, Jesús Larrañaga quotes Arizmendi as saying:

In the name of religion, what barbarities have been committed. We must be on guard against any type of dogmatism, regardless of what type it is. . . . Religion has been well marketed, but what good has that done? It has led us to feel the attraction of the universal and the abstract. Theologians, sociologists, and philosophers have operated from the top down when the correct way to think is in the opposite direction. (Larrañaga 1981, 84–85)

Arizmendi criticized the Church in these words:

The Church, and above all the Catholic Church, is an organization that is completely authoritarian. But today we note within it movements of local communities and others that demand that they be responsible for themselves and name their own representatives. (page 809)

He noted the alienation of working people:

All or almost all workers, even those who externally continue to practice the religion and to go to church, are also inwardly cut off from the Church because they have lost confidence in it. (page 71)

He claimed that

we have the singular case today that we encounter much more Christian doctrine in those parties and those groups which have been rejected [by the Church] as enemies of Christ and of Christianity than in many programs of parties and groups that call themselves Catholics. (page 153)

As early as 1945, he had stated that workers saw the Church as allied with the dominant military and political forces. "The armed forces, the clergy and the Falange are the three basic claws of the capitalist" (page 75).

Although Don José María was highly critical of his church and had few friends among the priesthood in his diocese, he recognized that the Church provided an indispensable shelter from government attacks, and he did not find the Church a barrier to achieving his socioeconomic objectives. We learned from José Luis Olasolo that Norwegian social psychologist Einar Thorsrud asked how a priest at the bottom of an authoritarian organization had been able to create such a democratic social movement: "How can it be that you have achieved such remarkable results when you serve under the archbishop of your diocese, the Catholic authorities in Madrid, and the Pope in Rome?"

Don José María answered in four words: "Rome is far away."

POLITICAL IDEOLOGIES

Arizmendi presents an impossible problem for anyone who insists on placing an influential person in the context of traditional political ideologies. As his biographer said: "He was allergic to all isms . . . including cooperativism. 'Isms imprison and oppress us, without providing any final answers' " (Larrañaga 1981, 83). On occasion, he spoke of himself as a socialist, but he had his own definition of socialism, arguing that cooperativism was true socialism not just one way to achieve it. Azurmendi (pages 776–77) comments, however, that he wrote few statements on socialism and that they were very limited in content.

The founder wrote of cooperativism as

> the third way of development equidistant from individualistic capitalism and soulless collectivism. Its center and axis is the human person in his social context. (page 777)

> It is the third way distinct from egoist capitalism and from the mastodon of depersonalizing socialism. We want cooperatives which constitute a new social potential and, thus, are built by those who are not impelled by a myopic and limited egotism or by a simple gregarious instinct. (page 779)

Arizmendi was in favor of the nationalization of private companies under particular circumstances but against nationalization as an overall policy:

> Nationalization should not only be applied where private initiative does not operate, but also when private initiative is operating imperfectly or when we must combat monopolies. (page 768)

> Cooperativism seeks to create a new state of conscience, of culture in a word, through the humanization of power through democracy in economic affairs, and through solidarity, which impedes the formation of privileged classes. Here and now it assigns a functional value to property. That is, property is valued in so far as it serves as an efficient resource for building responsibility and efficiency in any vision of community life in a decentralized form. (page 608)

On a number of occasions he expressed negative views of capitalism. He spoke of the capitalist system as having been developed "with hardly any positive influence of any ideal or moral principle, fueled only by egotistical and material desires" (page 751).

On another occasion, he wrote:

> It is a social monstrosity that a system of social organization is tolerated in which some can take advantage of the work of others for their exclusive personal profit. . . . The cooperativist distinguishes himself from the capitalist, simply in that the latter utilizes capital in order to make people serve him, while the former uses it to make more gratifying and uplifting the working life of the people. (page 757)

He was somewhat acquainted with the literature of scientific management and commented, "Taylorism has failed as a philosophy because it has considered man as an instrument to such an extent that it makes him a mere complement to the machine" (page 410).

Although hostile to capitalism as an overall economic system, Arizmendi believed that there was much the workers in cooperatives could learn from capitalism:

> To build cooperativism is not to do the opposite of capitalism, as if this system did not have any useful features, when in reality it has been a very interesting experience in organization and economic activity, and its efficiency cannot be doubted. Cooperativism must surpass it, and for this purpose must assimilate its methods and dynamism within the limitations and with the improvements necessary to support supreme human and personal values. (pages 759–60)

In private conversations, the founder spoke of the Soviet Union as having a highly repressive and brutal government, but he never attacked the Soviet Union in any of his criticisms of the all-absorbing socialist state. Why not? No one who knew him intimately has undertaken to answer this question, but we might venture a speculative answer. Condemnations of Communism and of the Soviet Union were common currency in the discussions and pronouncements of spokespersons for the Franco government, so adding his voice to theirs would only have served to identify him more closely with the government. Also, he was trying to build bridges with radical Marxists, to persuade them of the value of cooperatives, and perhaps he saw no need to antagonize them by attacking the Soviet Union.

He described his political philosophy as pluralist:

> In the minds of the cooperators is the idea that future society probably must be pluralist in all of its organizations including the economic. There will be action and interaction of publicly owned firms and private firms, the market and planning, entities of paternalistic style, capitalistic or social. Every juncture, the nature of every activity, the level of evolution and development of every community, will require a special treatment, but not limited to one form of organization if we believe in and love man, his liberty, and justice, and democracy. (page 787)

He added:

> Cooperation is one organizational option among others, that for effectiveness and spontaneous acceptance should be achieved with its own characteristics, but without challenges and tensions with other entities present in the same economic field. (page 788)

He believed in democracy in both political and economic affairs. In the 1970s, while Spain was still under the dictatorship, he wrote:

> From our point of view we believe that the failure of charismatic men and their successors is inevitable, because of the illness of the system in which they are sheltered. For this reason, we prefer to elect our leaders periodically, leaving open those roads that will permit men who bring with them new charisma to flourish. We the workers have clear ideas. We do not like men who define themselves as undisputed leaders or who are declared such by interested groups. (page 677)

> Democracy loyally and honestly felt and practiced cannot limit itself to the formalities and administrative expedients of the elective process, but rather must have its impact and be reflected as much in the educational and social fields as in the economic and financial fields through building it into the institutionalization process. (page 679)

Don José María refused to imprison his mind in any conventional political ideology. He was not apolitical, but he was unorthodox. It may be that this lack of a political orthodoxy made it difficult for conservative or radical ideologues to mount a successful political attack against him.

FUNDAMENTAL GUIDING IDEAS

There is no question that education was central in the thinking of the founder. Above all, he was a student and teacher. "In the Escuela Politécnica," a former student told us, "he taught classes in religion and sociology—and really his religion class was mainly sociology." While teaching, Don José María continued his own education at the Escuela Social of the seminary of Vitoria, where "his interest extended from economics and sociology to philosophy and pedagogy" (page 173).

He saw the cooperatives as being built on a foundation of education, and in turn providing education for economic progress toward a new social order. He defined the cooperative experience as

> an economic effort that translates itself into an educational action or . . . an educational effort that employs economic action as a vehicle for transformation. (page 729)

> Cooperatives are schools and centers of training and maturation of those many men that the new order demands. (page 811)

In *Pedagogy of the Oppressed*, he underlined Freire's statement that education "must be developed *with* and not *for* him [the student]" (page 190).

Don José María saw education being acquired both through formal study and through the experience of working in a cooperative.

> One is born male or female, but not lathe operator or pattern maker, and much less doctor or engineer. To become a good official or technician one must have many hours of apprenticeship or study and normally one needed teachers. . . .
>
> One is not born a cooperator, because to be a cooperator requires a social maturity, a training in social living. For one to be an authentic cooperator, capable of cooperating, it is necessary to have learned to tame one's individualistic or egoistic instincts and to adapt to the laws of cooperation. . . .
>
> One becomes a cooperator through education and the practice of virtue. (page 231)

His conception of education was not limited to the classroom and the library; he believed in learning from experience.

Life is a fabric of relations between the past and the present, and the future is not built in a vacuum: experience, that of others as well as our own, is enriching, a positive resource. (page 741)

It is better to make mistakes than to do nothing. Besides, by making mistakes we end up learning how to act correctly. (page 482)

We have recognized that theory is necessary, yes, but it is not sufficient: we build the road as we travel. (page 481)

The last phrase, "*se hace camino al andar*" (quoted from the Spanish poet Antonio Machado), recurs again and again in his writings, and it has been quoted many times in the literature of the Mondragón cooperative movement. In that many of the problems Mondragón has faced have had no precedent in cooperative movements elsewhere, it has been important for the people of Mondragón to recognize that they themselves are building the road to their future by reflecting on their past.

The most appropriate philosophical label for Arizmendi is pragmatist. He was always urging his followers to channel their actions within the range of possibilities, without losing sight of their ideals.

We must confront realities rather than hypotheses, and reflect upon data and concrete facts more than pure ideological formulations. (page 673)

We are not working for chimerical ideals. We are realists. Conscious of what we can and cannot do . . . we concentrate on those things that we have hopes of changing among ourselves more than on those things that we cannot change in others. . . . Dedicated to changing those things we can and that we are in fact changing, we are conscious of the force that this movement produces. (page 719)

Problems concerning ideals appear to be minimal, but it is not so regarding the methods to bring them about. Here there are incompatibilities between the so-called maximalists and pragmatists or realists. (page 727)

The ideal is to do the good that we can and not that of which we dream. (page 728)

To be realists and pragmatists does not mean giving up our ideals, which must not be confused with chimeras and beautiful dreams, but rather accepted as objectives to accomplish. (page 728)

Don José María believed in revolution, but the revolution he sought would come gradually and peacefully. He spoke of Jesus Christ as the greatest revolutionary in history (page 746).

> Daily revolution consists of effective transformations built upon new structures. . . . It is like a growing chain that can reach beyond what we can imagine. (page 742)

On achieving revolution through violence, he wrote:

> Violence will prevail and power will pass from one party to another, but when the smoke has cleared and the bodies of the dead are buried, the situation will be the same as before; there will be a minority of the strong in power, exploiting the others for their own benefit. The same greed, the same cruelty, the same lust, the same ambition, and same hypocrisy and avarice will rule as before. (page 746)

In 1966 he wrote:

> We are totally in agreement with the revolutionary formulation of the clear sighted Christian thinker, Mounier. The economic renewal will be moral or it will not exist. The moral revolution will be economic or it will not take place. (page 748)

He inveighed against those who focused attention solely on the political sphere. One of his close friends, Simon de Arroiabe, described the founder's conception of the revolution:

> For him the revolution should not be centered as much in the political sphere as in the infrastructure of society from the most primary and elemental cells up to the most global [the nation]. Many times I have heard him attack the obsession with the political, for polarizing the revolution in terms of political power. Basically he saw the danger in converting the political into an absolute, from which one would accomplish the revolution. Any group, he would say to me, that considers itself revolutionary must overcome this mentality, or its revolution will be simply a taking of power to install another tyranny of different coloration, but basically a tyranny and a dictatorship. For him the revolution had to be based on other perspectives, taking more into account the "cultural" infrastructure. . . . The revolution that the cooperators must bring about is primarily a cultural revolution. (page 772)

He believed in *solidarity* and—within limits—*egalitarianism*. On the one hand, he looked on egotistical individualism, which he found even in Basque society, as the enemy of the social solidarity necessary to build the cooperative movement. On the other, he noted the dangers of coercive suppression of individualism. In reflecting on the changes in Europe through the last century, he wrote, "From dissolving individualism we have passed on to degrading collectivism" (page 149).

> To teach only how men should behave with each other, without attacking their egotism, is like plowing in the sea. . . . Before teaching them public relations and courtesy, we have to get them accustomed to forgetting about themselves. (page 245)

He favored solidarity especially within the working class and spoke of the cooperatives as "an element in the vanguard of the labor movement" (page 791). Yet he was constantly striving for interclass solidarity.

On the rights of organized labor, he wrote:

> Like other social and economic organisms, the union has a right to independent existence. That is, it has a right to existence and self-government independent of the will of the state, to determine its own programs of action and administer its resources. The autonomy of the union in relation to the state is at least as important as the autonomy of the companies. (page 122)

> Catholic doctrine, which defends inequality among classes, condemns the class struggle. However, it argues for equality of opportunities for all men and for a just distribution of wealth. (page 695)

> We need each other; we are called upon to complement each other. The man who can stand solitude is either a god or a beast, as a celebrated philosopher has stated. And this means that social classes need each other and should collaborate; this means that the people and the authorities must not live divorced from each other. This means that the institutions must offer mutual aid, that when we sincerely pursue what we claim, that is, the common good, the good of all, there is no reason for exclusivity, for particular personal interests, even when they claim to cover themselves with formalities, and the most specious reasons do not hide anything more than vanity, pride, or the urge to dominate. For this purpose it is not enough that the bosses undertake and do good things. It is necessary that the workers participate in those things, so that a real communion among them exists. It is not enough that the workers dream of great reforms, if the bosses or

entrepreneurs do not contribute to their realization, providing their zeal, their technical knowledge and skills, their experience. It is not enough that the authorities propose great objectives, because to reach them something more will always be missing than what they have in their grasp, that is the enthusiasm, the zeal of the subordinates. Where this fusion and spontaneous and generous collaboration has not been achieved, there is no real social life, and it will be difficult in such an environment to have fruitful coexistence. The existing peaceable relations will be superficial or fictitious. (page 700)

Without ever denying his commitment to the working class, Don José María never gave up hope of securing collaboration from private business and government. He always refrained from attacking those who failed to support the cooperative movement. This policy bore important fruit, for even the major private enterprise in Mondragón, the Unión Cerrajera, eventually closed its school for apprentices and began contributing to Mondragón's educational program. As we have noted, the Mondragón cooperators received important support from the central government in Madrid, even during the Franco regime, and later from the autonomous Basque regional government.

The founder began his pastoral service with fairly traditional views regarding the place of women, but his views changed with time and experience. By 1964, he was openly criticizing the assumed superiority of males. By 1968, when he had become involved with the establishment of Auzo-Lagun, he wrote, "Let women decide their fate for themselves. . . . half of adult people do not have any right to rule the destinies of the other half" (page 309).

On equal rights on the job, he noted that

based on the recognition of the equality of man and woman, all jobs, except those specifically prescribed for medical reasons . . . will be distributed without any discrimination. We repeat, the only valid arguments are of a physiological character, whose definition depends upon the medical service. (page 708)

He believed that the major social changes he desired could only be brought about gradually.

Advance a little each time, but without ceasing. . . . Step by step and without pausing. (page 730)

The new social order that we cooperators contemplate is not attainable except little by little. The community that pleases us at any moment is displeasing to others. . . . we must accept present reality, even as with all our forces, we continue to be dedicated to modifying it, and for this we reserve and direct all our forces and resources. . . .

The good ideas are those which we know how to translate into realities and the good words are those which everyone knows how to support with deeds. (page 732)

He recognized the relations among beliefs, actions, experience, and the structures that shape them.

Insofar as one is capable of living according to the ideas he professes, it is also certain that he who does not live as he thinks ends up thinking as he lives. (page 726)

Good men with poor instruments rarely accomplish anything good, and the most lamentable and prejudicial for the community is not that bad people with good instruments do harm, but rather that good people with poor instruments must be condemned to poor results. These instruments are nothing more than the institutions and the structures that make up these institutions. (page 332)

Don José María warned against the complacency that often comes with success and stressed the need for *constant reevaluation* of the cooperative experience.

My friends, we must take the steps to stimulate greater self-criticism and criticism among ourselves, in our dialogues and meetings. The procedure most appropriate to safeguard the health of our institutions is the use of criticism and self-criticism, opportunely and with foresight. This is appropriate in any case and in not a few cases it is necessary. . . . Let us move ahead with criticisms and self-criticisms, more than with criticisms of others. (page 574)

This spirit of self-criticism has been institutionalized, especially in the form of the social council.

In many of his writings and speeches, Don José María stressed the need for people with open and flexible minds, capable of adapting to constantly changing conditions.

Our problem is men with closed minds. (page 241)

Water which does not flow becomes stagnant. (page 242)

To live is to renew one's self. (page 280)

We must emphasize the fact that the firm is a peculiar entity in permanent process of evolutionary change, and therefore needing the constant attention of its leaders: it must renew and revitalize itself at all times due to the inevitable consequences of the changing technology and economy of our world. (page 405)

The Mondragón cooperative experience is not a completed file, it is an open process, it is a comparison of methods with results, with several contingents of workers thinking aloud, submitting for examination the results of all types of experience, interpreted fundamentally in terms of the human conscience. (page 561)

He constantly urged his fellows toward new achievements to meet changing conditions, often expressing his views in quotable maxims.

There is no respite. . . . There is always one more step to take. . . . We must keep moving, continue advancing. . . . There is still much to be done. . . . Every day we must go forward to new conquests. . . . The cooperative firm is a daily task. . . . The cooperative must be reconstituted and renewed constantly. (page 561)

The greatest risk that a man can run today is to feel satisfied with what he has accumulated so that he can live on the fruits of past accomplishments. . . . to be satisfied is an intolerable luxury. . . . to live is to renew one's self . . . renew one's self or die. (page 562)

Don José María made frequent use of the concept of *equilibrium*, speaking of a "society in dynamic equilibrium" and writing also about "economic equilibrium" (page 551). He also spoke of "an equilibrium in movement" and of a tendency toward "an order that is permanently in evolution" (page 561).
Equilibrium was a key concept in his conception of democracy.

Men spend themselves and become exhausted: democracy is a resource for renovation. A community acts because every one of its components feels a stimulus to action, but in the final analysis it must harmonize its interests with those of others, because it is then when, with a common effort, all end up gaining. Democracy must serve to find the point of equilibrium. (pages 577–78)

ON THE COOPERATIVE MOVEMENT

Arizmendi's views regarding the potentialities and limitations of the cooperative movement changed with time and experience. In 1962, he wrote:

We are not among those who believe that cooperativism is an exclusive formula that can be applied equally to all types of economic activities. Activities in which the labor content in all of its forms is high fit better into the cooperative formula than those others in which capital plays a preponderant part. There the systems of capitalism or socialism are more appropriate. (page 484)

As early as 1964, he was opening his mind to broader possibilities:

We admit that there are fields of economic activity in which the cooperative formula may not be the most appropriate for rapid development. However, it does not seem to us that in this respect the experience of the past throws sufficient light to discern the possibilities of application of the cooperative formula. Man and circumstances today are different from yesterday and thus we see institutions, vigorous in the past, surviving today providing they have been able to profoundly modify their structures. It is not difficult to observe that once powerful institutions have decayed, while others once considered utopian are gaining strength. Explanations based on the past are not valid for the present when we deal with cooperativism, whose principal support is the level of education and living together, which is precisely what is subject to the most rapid acceleration. (page 484)

At the time the leaders of the cooperative movement were grappling with the problems of organizational growth he wrote:

One question that arises repeatedly on the lips of those who observed the growth of the cooperative is whether the massification of large scale, imposed by economic reality, is compatible with the experience of the cooperatives, which have always been thought viable only in small organizations. It has been accepted as a generalization that the garden in which the cooperative can germinate and develop permanently comes up against the barrier of numbers. . . .

Undoubtedly affection and other moral values have their most logical development within small circles and consequently (with growth) we quickly lose the optimum point for man that is in harmony with the laws of production for a variety of activities. . . .

Any attempt to organize on a competitive level must necessarily deal with technical exigencies, which condition economic development. Consequently it would be suicidal to avoid the establishment of larger human concentrations demanded for an economically viable entity, in order to satisfy some supposed or real exigencies of living together cooperatively. (pages 485–86)

The founder considered growth inevitable and believed that its disadvantages must be faced.

It would not be acceptable to blame the cooperative solution for inability to deal with human masses when no other type of organization has done so. (page 486)

Don José María was very much involved in designing structural arrangements to try to harmonize the cooperative system with economic and technological realities.

In 1963, two years before the formation of the first cooperative group, he recognized the importance of linking the cooperatives.

We must think in terms of intercooperative solidarity as a unique resource through which we can advance toward other problems of growth and maturity: we must think of providing living space adequate to the circumstances. (page 558)

We will not interpret the linking together of firms necessarily as absorption, which gives rise to a new uniformity, monolithic and even monstrous. Rather we must design a type of concentration that links together centers and functions that are multipliers of the totality, while keeping decentralized those aspects that in their nature constitute substantive elements with a separate unity that, being linked and associated with superstructures, engage in exchange relations which mutually enrich them. (page 559)

Don José María recognized that organizational growth required that the leaders give more attention to business administration.

Our region has never been strong in this discipline, considering the cost of administration a waste of money or at least a luxury that only large firms could permit themselves. In the opinion of many, the people who really were working were those in the shop, and the rest were considered a heavy burden, which in consequence must be reduced to the minimum. Many cooperatives have been formed with these criteria, and it is costly to adjust to the requirements demanded by a sound policy for administration. (page 515)

He often stressed the importance of credit and investment.

We must resolve to be something more than more or less fortunate consumers: we must also become investors, because as simple consumers what we will definitely be doing is giving to our exploiters with one hand what we try to take from them with the other. We have two hands and we must accept the responsibility for two functions that must accompany each other, that of necessary consumption to replenish our strength and to compensate our efforts, and that of investment, indispensable for looking after our future and exercising solidarity across generations. (page 702)

One cannot think of a vigorous and expanding cooperative movement without its involvement in the field of credit. . . . cooperativism lacking this resource is weak, necessarily fragile, being confined to fields of artisanship, and must live in a small world, in a domestic and modest circle. . . . credit is something like blood, the sap that must invigorate all members of the community. (page 537)

Our cooperativism must develop itself so that, in relation to availability of capital, technology, and organizational flexibility it does not find itself in an inferior condition. . . . A cooperative must not condemn itself to the sole alternative of self-financing. (page 763)

As he was working to pave the way for Ikerlan, he wrote:

Our people require of our men the development of the means to scale the heights of scientific knowledge, which are the bases of progress. (page 553)

Later he wrote:

Today the great industrial and economic battles are decided in the field of research and scientific discovery, and the various states turn to this field to support their dominant position. (page 765)

While emphasizing what must be done to build the cooperative movement, he never lost sight of the goal of laying the foundations for *a new and more humane social order*. As his disciples have testified, he constantly urged them to think beyond the limits of their particular enterprise, to encompass the broader community and the challenge of building new social and economic structures.

As early as February 28, 1941, shortly after he had arrived in the city, he wrote that "the ideal of the youth of Mondragón is to make of this community a model among the industrial towns of Guipúzcoa" (page 816). This ideal probably was not widely shared at the beginning of his tenure in Mondragón, but his work with the young people led them toward it, and thirty years later he could say, "Mondragón is today a new city" (page 816).

On the Ulgor pioneers, he wrote:

They have not studied for individual advancement, but rather to work; and they work not only to gain their daily bread but also to pursue new forms of society. (page 818)

Our cooperative commitment cannot lose sight of the goal of a new social order. (page 815)

We do not hide from ourselves that the simple functioning of cooperative firms cannot be the goal of those who have mature consciousness of the problems of the world of work. For this purpose, quite apart from the more or less satisfactory results of our respective firms, cooperators must continue to be nonconformists to the extent that the whole vast economic-social world is not organized according to the postulates of the dignity of the worker and the requirements of his work or we will fall into an insularity and myopia that is inexcusable. Those who are satisfied will not build a new world, a new social order that is humane and just, nor will it be given us without risk and common effort. (page 816)

Don José María as a Leader

Was Don José María a charismatic leader? He is so described today by those who knew him and by many others, but that characterization explains nothing and is misleading. We are accustomed to thinking of a charismatic leader as one whose eloquence moves people to follow him. In a profession that required him to preach, his performance in the pulpit, as even his most devoted followers have told us, never rose above mediocrity. Outside the pulpit, he lacked the gifts of the orator.

First, last, and always, Don José María was a teacher—but a very unusual teacher for his times and place and indeed for any time and any place. He was most effective in group discussions and in conversations with individuals. If he sometimes had difficulty putting his thoughts and feelings into words, there were no deficiencies in his ability to listen so that others knew he was interested in them, valued them, and above all wanted to understand them.

Over the years, we have tried to think of the words that would most parsimoniously explain the effects this extraordinary man had on his followers and the institutions they built. We arrived at two words: *challenge* and *support*. He challenged those learning with him to undertake tasks that they had thought were beyond their abilities. And he supported their efforts by helping them succeed and thus build the strength of mind and will to go on to meet ever-greater challenges—which he repeatedly placed before them.

The remarks quoted from the interview with José María Ormaechea are worth repeating, for they capture well the founder's combination of *challenge* and *support*.

> Contrary to what was customary, instead of flattering us when we went to consult him, he treated us with affection but urged us every day to make a greater commitment to the labor movement and to the future economic and social transformation of society.

The Mondragón Arizmendi encountered in 1941 was a city depressed in spirit as well as in material resources and opportunities. Don José María provided the spirit that opened up access to resources and opportunities.

One of his first challenges was to organize a sports club. The first task was to get public attention and support to acquire a field for practice and soccer matches. To promote this campaign, Don José María provided the slogans the young men painted on posters. In the meeting marking the tenth anniversary of his death, the general manager of the Caja remembered one slogan in particular: "Sports unite us. Give us a field, and we will become champions" (Ormaechea 1986, 12). In 1944, just three years after Don José María settled in Mondragón, his Juventud Deportiva defeated by five to one a team from a much larger city (Tolusa) to win the soccer championship of Guipúzcoa.

The founder's vision of the future constantly pressed his followers to move beyond any immediate success and confront new challenges. When he could not convince the Ulgor pioneers that they had to create a bank, he managed to present them with a fait accompli and then led them to achieve what they had thought was beyond their abilities. He saw the need for a research organization, encouraged the young teachers in the Escuela to pursue the dream, and then pushed for the major investment in building and facilities when others believed the project involved too great a financial risk.

In our first visit in 1975, Javier Retegui, then director of the Escuela Politécnica Profesional, interpreted the founder in this way: "He sees the future and makes us face it."

Don José María provided both affective and intellectual support. He had a warm, affectionate relationship with those who worked with him. He let them know that he believed in them—in fact, particularly in the early stages, he believed in them more than they did in themselves. Then, when they had risen to new challenges, they came to share his confidence.

His belief in people was not indiscriminate, but he was a shrewd observer of behavior and judged abilities to master future tasks by how people had performed in meeting earlier objectives. For example, Manuel Quevedo lacked the educational background and academic credentials one would normally have expected of someone who was to lead in the development of a first-class industrial research institution, but his performance in the early stages of building the research program led Don José María and a growing number of others to believe that Quevedo and his team would be equal to the challenge.

In 1983, a member of the intervention department in the Entrepreneurial Division described how he managed the conversion of a bankrupt private firm into a successful cooperative. He explained that the principal owner had been making all the decisions for his department heads and supervisors, but because none of them had had any real management experience, it was very difficult to judge how they would perform without the autocratic boss. Would he have to bring in a new management team? In dealing with the workers and supervisors, he became convinced that many of them had the training and talent to build an effective management, so he decided against bringing in outsiders. In explaining his decision, he told us that he too had been a student of Don José María, and the founder had led him to believe that such people, if given the chance, could measure up to the challenge.

Don José María was not a social philosopher in that he did not have a fully worked-out systematic philosophy. He was interested in philosophy and social theory only to the extent that they helped him link words to actions and beliefs to practice. Combining his reflections on philosophy and social theory with what he was learning from experience, his guidance provided his associates with the *intellectual support* needed to think through the elements for building the cooperative culture of his vision and theirs.

19 Ethnic and Organizational Cultures

Were the Basque culture the primary basis for the creation and development of the Mondragón cooperative complex, then the practical implications to be drawn from Mondragón for other societies would be extremely limited. We do not deny that Basque culture has influenced the shaping of Mondragón, but we reject claims that it was culturally determined. At the same time, we recognize that the leaders of Mondragón have built a distinctive organizational culture and that we can better advance our understanding of Mondragón by analyzing this culture than by concentrating on the ethnic culture of the Basque people.

As applied to societies or communities, culture is a widely used concept in the social sciences and particularly in anthropology. Recently the concept has become popular in U.S. management circles, and the demand has increased for consultants to tell executives how to build a company culture that will foster improved organizational performance. In both academic and business circles, there is a growing recognition of the importance of culture, and yet there is no agreement on the meaning of the term.

For our purposes, the culture of a people is a system of widely shared beliefs and values and a set of characteristic behaviors used in organizing social processes. The culture includes an ideology, a cognitive map or framework within which people explain their own characteristics and their relations to others of different cultures.

The concept can be applied at the organizational level, and that is the level at which we will concentrate in this chapter. Although we recognize the importance of culture, we do not assume that it is a self-perpetuating entity that continues to shape behavior and values in the same way however environmental conditions change. A culture arises out of the efforts of a people to solve social, economic, and political problems. The existing culture depends for its maintenance on certain institutional and structural supports—some of which we will examine in our study of the culture of the Mondragón cooperatives. When those supports are altered, we expect changes in culture to follow.

The statement that a culture arises out of the efforts of its people to solve their problems does not mean that the existing culture offers optimal solutions to those problems. Whether the culture facilitates or impedes the search for such solutions is an empirical problem. We are simply pointing out that generally people do not make decisions on an ad hoc basis, responding only to the immediate incentives or deterrents readily apparent in the situation. Out of their experience of living in a family, a community, and an organization, they develop ideas that are both descriptive and normative. That is, they develop ideas about how the world operates and also about how they and others *ought* to behave. This social learning provides a context within which people evaluate options and make choices. This framework is what we call culture.

BASQUE CULTURE

In reviewing the history of the Basque people, we have noted certain features of their culture. They themselves speak of "our associative tendencies." They manifest strong ethnic pride and commitment to egalitarian values and democratic governance. And they believe in the dignity of labor—of any kind, although, of course, they recognize differences in prestige among jobs and occupations. These features are certainly compatible with the main features of the Mondragón movement, but they occur elsewhere where no such movement has arisen. Furthermore, it is not clear to what extent the general ethnic culture has influenced the evolution of the Mondragón cooperatives.

In the course of the history of the Basques, their associative tendencies have manifested themselves in the formation of tightly knit groups or organizations, closed to outsiders. From its inception, the Mondragón complex has been an open system. Membership is open to anyone with the educational and technical background required for the available job, and in fact about 25 percent of the members are not Basques. Ethnic pride may have been an influence supporting social solidarity, especially in the early years when most Basques regarded themselves as an oppressed people, suffering under the dictatorship. But if ethnic pride can support the development of cooperatives, apparently it can also foster the terrorism of ETA in pursuit of its dream of an independent Basque country. Like other characteristics of the Basques, ethnic pride can manifest itself in a wide variety of organizational forms.

It does appear that the Basque culture provides fertile soil for the development of worker cooperatives. In fact, the Basque country is home to far more worker cooperatives outside the Mondragón complex than within it. That interpretation breaks down, however, when one notes that worker cooperatives are also fairly common in other parts of Spain, where the ethnic cultures are quite different. Furthermore, the Mondragón complex is unique in the Basque country and the world.

If we look beyond the incidence of cooperatives toward the structural features of the Mondragón complex, we find explanations based on ethnic culture of minimal value. Unlike cooperatives in other parts of the Basque region, those in Mondragón have an organizational culture—and the support system to maintain it—that has the flexibility to adapt to changing environmental conditions.

THE CULTURE OF THE COOPERATIVES

To understand Mondragón, we need to understand its organizational culture, including the support system that maintains that culture and influences its ability to change in adaptive ways.

We think of the culture of the Mondragón cooperatives in terms of two categories of concepts: the cognitive framework and the shaping systems.

The cognitive framework is the set of ideas and beliefs about basic values, organizational objectives, and guiding principles that form the foundation of any organization. Basic values refer to people's deeply held beliefs about themselves and their co-workers. Objectives refer to the goals or targets leaders set for their organization—which can be supported, rejected, or modified by the members. Guiding principles refer to the ideas (explicitly articulated or implicit) that shape the general direction people take in trying to move from their basic values toward their objectives.

Shaping systems enable an organizational culture to be maintained or to change. A culture does not maintain itself but is shaped by forces such as major policies, structures, and instruments of governance and management.

Our interpretation of the nature of the cognitive framework is based not on surveys of the attitudes, perceptions, and beliefs of a sample of the members of the Mondragón cooperatives but from studying the processes of decision making. These processes can be studied by observing individual and group actions and interactions, by interviewing members of decision-making and advisory bodies, and by examining the documentary record of meetings leading to decisions or recommendations. We have never had the opportunity to observe group meetings, but we and others have had substantial opportunities to interview members of Mondragón, and we have found the documentary record extraordinarily valuable for our purposes. For example, the reports of social council meetings in Ulgor and in FAGOR describe not only the proposals presented and the decisions made but the arguments for and against all major proposals.

Focusing attention especially on decision-making bodies may appear to bias our interpretations by giving much less attention to the thoughts and feelings of the rank-and-file members. At the same time, however responsive to the rank and file the leaders wish to be, it is they who make the major proposals and the decisions. It is the workers who react to these decisions and proposals, and, by studying especially controversial issues (the 1974 strike and the change in policies regarding pay and capital contributions in the 1980s), we get some sense of the reactions of rank-and-file workers to their leaders. In any case, neither we nor our Mondragón associates assume that there is or should be any uniformity of views between leaders and other workers or even among the leaders themselves. We have found many conflicting opinions on particular issues. Yet it is a strength of Mondragón that the leaders and rank-and-file members have created an organizational culture that enables them to resolve conflicts and pursue vigorous social, economic, and technological development.

Following our description of the cognitive framework and the support systems, we will examine how they fit together in shaping social processes and behavior.

THE COGNITIVE FRAMEWORK

Basic Values

Equality. All human beings should be considered as having been created equal, with equal rights and obligations. This does not mean that Mondragón people are oblivious to differences in social class and in organizational position, but it does mean that the impact of these distinctions should be minimized in interpersonal and organizational relations.

Solidarity. Members of a given cooperative should rise and fall together; individuals should not gain while others lose. The concept of solidarity also applies to relations among the cooperatives and between a given cooperative and a support organization. To some extent this concept can apply to relations between the members and their cooperative and between the cooperatives and the Basque community, working people in general, and so on.

Dignity of labor. Clearly, this value relates closely to the two values described above. The idea is that there is or should be dignity to any human labor, blue-collar as well as white-collar or managerial work.

Participation. Members have a right to participate as much as possible in shaping the decisions affecting them. They also have an obligation to participate.

Objectives

The principal objectives were determined by the leaders of the complex in the early years. To what extent they are shared by the membership is an open question. We should keep in mind, however, that the objectives set at a given time tend to create a shaping system that leads toward these objectives, even when many members are indifferent to them.

We see the following objectives as being of primary importance.

Job creation. The creation of jobs was a primary objective from the very beginning, and the cooperatives retain a strong commitment to it.

Employment security. Every member in good standing should be able to expect continuous employment up to the age of retirement. Note that we have not said "job security," which implies that the member retains an indefinite right to a given job. It would be unrealistic, given the dynamic nature of economic forces, to expect that any given job could be maintained indefinitely. Because economic progress necessarily involves eliminating certain jobs and leads to unemployment unless an adequate number of jobs are created at the same time, the commitment to employment security also implies a commitment to job creation.

Human and social development. We find many references in discussions of work to the importance of making the work itself humane and to the need to foster the social development of the members.

Autonomy and self-governance. The leaders have been committed to developing autonomous and self-governing organizations that are linked together to help in coping with national and international economic conditions.

Economic progress. The leaders of the complex have not looked on making profits as the fundamental purpose of their organizations, but they have, by necessity, recognized the need to generate profits or surplus as a limiting condition. Without the strength that comes from financial success, they cannot expect to attain the other objectives.

Guiding Principles

We see Mondragón as having nine guiding principles.

Balance. In discussions of important decisions, the word *equilibrio* appears again and again as a justification for any action proposed. The basic idea is that life in a cooperative should not be carried on as if it were a zero-sum game in which some win and some lose. There must be a balancing of interests and needs; we hear it said that technological imperatives must be balanced with social objectives and that the financial needs of the firm must be balanced with the economic needs of the members.

The word *equilibrio* appears prominently in discussions of relations within groups—between one cooperative and another and between member cooperatives and the management of the cooperative group. It also appears in discussions of relations between a cooperative or cooperative group and a support organization. We find it further in discussions of relations between the cooperative and the community in which it is located.

Future orientation. From the beginning, the leaders of Mondragón have emphasized that planning must be oriented toward a future well beyond the time when the immediate problem has been solved.

Organizational self-evaluation. What now exists must never be considered perfect and immutable. It is important to carry out frequent self-critical evaluations, to examine the functioning of the organization, and to figure out ways to make improvements. This process provides an important means of implementing the principle of future orientation.

Openness. Nondiscriminatory in nature, the cooperatives are open to anyone with the requisite skills and training.

Pluralistic political orientation. From the beginning, the leaders of the cooperatives avoided identification with any established political party or political ideology. Individual members may freely express their own political views and belong to any political party, but the organization itself avoids such commitments. This is in marked contrast to the situation in other countries, particularly Italy, where cooperatives are affiliated with unions or political parties. Of course, such political identification would not have been possible under the Franco regime, but the orientation necessary in the beginning has become a guiding principle even now when such political commitments are possible.

Freedom of information. If the members are to make intelligent decisions, they must, as much as is practical, have access to all information relevant to those decision-making rights and responsibilities.

Intercooperative complementarity. Individual cooperatives should buy from and sell to one another, except when it is clearly disadvantageous to one of the parties to the transaction. Mondragón applied this principle when it used the rapid growth of Ulgor as a basis for creating firms to produce components for Ulgor—and then for developing a market beyond Ulgor and other cooperatives. In the agribusiness sector, we saw the same process when Lana's growth facilitated the development of related cooperatives. The collaboration of the Financial and Entrepreneurial divisions of the Caja with Eroski is another example of complementarity.

General Secretary Iñaki Imasa of Eroski explained the implementation of the principle of complementarity. Eroski is not required to buy any product offered it by a Mondragón cooperative, and no cooperative is required to sell its total output to Eroski. For example, Eroski buys a major part of Lana's total milk production and would be willing to buy the total output, but Lana prefers to maintain other marketing outlets. Suppose a cooperative offers its product to Eroski but Eroski prefers to buy that product from a private firm? In this case, an official of the producing cooperative may ask purchasing officials for an explanation. The Eroski officials will then explain the considerations (price, quality, efficient delivery, and so on) that led to the decision to buy from the private firm. They will also offer advice and information on the conditions that need to be met before they will buy from the cooperative in the future. In other words, both parties recognize the value of being of help to one another—but not when providing such help would impose a serious sacrifice on one of the parties.

Formation of cooperative groups. To achieve economies of scale and broaden and strengthen solidarity within the movement, it is important for individual cooperatives to join together. This leads to the grouping of cooperatives in the same local area under a general management and to collaborative efforts in marketing and other services by cooperatives in the same industrial sector but different geographical areas.

Size limitation. This principle is based on the assumption that it is difficult for an organization to remain flexible, democratic, and efficient when it grows beyond a certain size. Whenever feasible, a new line of products initiated in one cooperative should lead to the line being spun off to create a new cooperative. The basic values and other guiding principles of the complex provide a general framework for this process: Employment must be maintained, and the equal rights and economic opportunities of the members involved must be upheld. Retaining the new cooperative within the cooperative group ensures the efficiencies of larger scale but also that each cooperative has considerable autonomy.

SHAPING SYSTEMS TO MAINTAIN OR CHANGE THE ORGANIZATIONAL CULTURE

We visualize the forces shaping organizational culture as falling into three categories: *major policies, structures,* and *instruments of governance and management.* Some of these shaping systems attest to the extraordinary creativity of Mondragón in producing social inventions: new ideas put into practice to meet important needs of the cooperatives. We should not assume, however, that Mondragón's success has depended entirely on such social inventions. Whenever an idea, policy, or practice developed elsewhere serves Mondragón's purposes, it makes sense to adopt or adapt it, and clearly Mondragón has been resourceful in bringing in a wide range of technical and social information from other parts of Spain and abroad. We place particular emphasis on social inventions because they embody those unique contributions of Mondragón that merit study by those seeking to draw their own lessons from the cooperative complex.

Major policies. Policies regarding the rights and obligations of members are of great importance. Membership is based on labor rather than capital. This is the case for worker cooperatives generally, but the implementation of this policy is of special interest. No stock is issued. The members' initial financial contributions are treated as money loaned to the cooperative.

Members' capital accounts and the policies on distribution of profits to members are key features of the complex. Since 1965 all the surplus allocated to members has gone into their capital accounts rather than being distributed in cash. This policy has contributed enormously to the strength and stability of the cooperatives.

The 10 percent limit on the number of nonmembers in each cooperative is not unique to Mondragón but deserves special emphasis. This limit is imposed not only in the constitutions of the cooperatives but in Spanish legislation. But just because the law imposes this limit does not mean that Mondragón's internal control is superfluous. The Spanish government cannot always be counted on to enforce its laws in the labor field.

The policies for job creation and for employment security are mutually reinforcing. In the face of rapidly changing technologies and market conditions, no cooperative can guarantee that it will maintain all of its jobs indefinitely. To remain competitive, the firm must be able to increase output while reducing the number of workers producing any product. Because the cooperatives are not free simply to lay off surplus workers, they are driven to create new cooperatives and expand employment.

Structures for governance and management. Mondragón has created both significant internal structures and a crucially important network of collaborating and supporting organizations. For all the criticisms leveled at it by many members, the social council seems to be an important social invention. In addition to their functions in representing members as *workers*, the social councils are the particular organs involved in applying the principle of *organizational self-evaluation*.

The grouping of cooperatives under a common general management provides an important means of balancing economic imperatives against social values. The group management has the primary responsibility for maintenance of employment by shifting members among the constituent cooperatives and by creating new cooperatives and new jobs.

Solidarity is further strengthened by the network of organizations that support the cooperatives and that are supported by them. The Caja Laboral Popular is not only a key supporting organization; it also plays a leading role in holding member cooperatives to the basic values and principles developed in the early years by Don José María and the Ulgor pioneers. The right of the Caja to cancel the contract of association with any cooperative that violates these values and principles is an essential element in making Mondragón a cooperative complex rather than a loose federation of cooperatives.

As well as providing for social security and unemployment compensation, Lagun-Aro plays an important role in placing members in other cooperatives when any cooperative group is unable to provide jobs for all members within its own group. Similarly, Ikerlan has become essential in the process whereby the cooperatives become equipped with new technologies and manufacturing methods necessary for their continued economic viability.

The educational system, beginning with the Escuela Politécnica and strengthened by the development of Alecop, ETEO, Saiolan, Leunkor, Ahizke, and Ikasbide, continues to provide the members with knowledge and skills essential to Mondragón's future. Although these institutions do not provide formal courses in the management of cooperatives (as distinguished from general management courses), their educational programs in the context of the cooperatives and the Mondragón community help to socialize members and potential members to the ways of working in a cooperative.

Some of these organizations seem to embody important social inventions. Mondragón invented a financial institution specifically designed to support the development of cooperatives. This is indeed an innovation. The Caja's Entrepreneurial Division can be seen as a set of inventions designed to guide and support collective entrepreneurship. Similarly, although Mondragón did not invent the applied industrial research institute, Ikerlan's network of linking and mutually supporting relations constitutes a set of distinctive social inventions.

Mondragón also has several *instruments of management*: systems and practices for shaping the work process. Some of these have been borrowed from abroad. For example, Mondragón modeled its initial management program on the principles of scientific management as promulgated by Frederick W. Taylor and his followers. As they became increasingly aware of the limitations of these principles, Mondragón's leaders reached out to Norway and elsewhere for ideas and information on the redesign of work. In its training programs, FAGOR has used literature from abroad on worker participation and management by objectives—but has adapted the ideas significantly. In the United States, worker participation and management by objectives are treated as two separate concepts; FAGOR's leaders speak of "participatory management by objectives" and are trying to find ways to promote "working by objectives" at the level of the rank and file. In 1983, management people in the FAGOR cooperatives were undergoing intensive training (with a U.S. consulting firm) on zero-based budgeting. In our own fieldwork in 1984 and 1985, we saw the changes (and some of the resulting problems) caused by the implementation of the "just-in-time" manufacturing system developed in Japan.

Our studies with the personnel people of FAGOR suggest that some of the Mondragón cooperatives have gone beyond most U.S. private firms in developing a leadership role for personnel people in working with top executives on organizational design, work redesign, and management development. In the past, most U.S. personnel departments have been confined to recordkeeping and trying to "put out fires" in labor relations and have had little opportunity to engage in the strategic planning that might prevent the fires from breaking out. From the outset, the social orientation built into the process of development at Mondragón has enhanced the influence of personnel people and has enabled them to play proactive roles in shaping the growth of their organizations. Furthermore, though they see themselves as primarily accountable to the governing council and to the management of their cooperatives and groups, they also recognize that they are accountable to their social councils.

Mondragón does not simply adopt a technology or methodology invented elsewhere. In some cases, the import is adapted or linked with distinctive Mondragón social inventions. We illustrate with the following example.

Javier Retegui, the manager of the Entrepreneurial Division, told us that by the fifteenth of every month his division had in its data bank the financial and operating records for the preceding month from the more than one hundred associated cooperatives. To demonstrate, he pressed several buttons on his desk-top computer to display the operating figures of a given cooperative for the preceding month. He then pressed other keys to bring forth, automatically computed, what he called the "level of alarm." According to the program worked out by the division, the scale goes from zero to ten. Zero means the cooperative is in excellent condition. Ten means that the cooperative is in desperate condition, at the edge of bankruptcy. In this case the number flashed was five. Then, pressing several more keys, he brought forth the level of alarm for this cooperative for the preceding month: 7.5. By comparing the monthly figures, it became clear that, although this cooperative had serious problems, it was making progress.

Some of the instruments of management involved in this case were simply adaptations of standard hardware or software. That is, the division did not invent the computer, and no doubt many, if not all, of the categories of data used are standard in the accounting field. The level-of-alarm operation, however, depends on a computer program devised within the division that can integrate a large number of figures so as to produce a single figure reflecting the condition of the firm.

The culture of the Mondragón cooperatives is not unrelated to the underlying ethnic culture of the Basque people. Any attempt, however, to explain Mondragón as simply a product of this ethnic culture is bound to produce serious distortions and oversimplifications. The leaders of Mondragón have selected from among the elements of the Basque culture, while devising a support system to reinforce those aspects they value and to create other elements that are not present (or at least not prominent). In this way, they have created a *distinctive organizational culture*.

Mondragón's cognitive framework—its basic values, organizational objectives, and guiding principles—provides the leaders of the complex with a sense of where they want to go. The shaping systems—major policies, structures, and instruments of governance and management—tell them, in general, how to get there. The cognitive framework and the shaping systems should be viewed as mutually dependent rather than as controlling one another. If the shaping systems are not helping them achieve their desired goal, responding to the guiding principle of organizational self-criticism, they will often reexamine and change some elements of the shaping systems or rethink and decide to modify their objectives.

Mondragón's organizational culture shapes the decision-making process. The leaders and members are not free to decide issues based on the interests of the moment. The cooperative culture guides actions within preexisting channels. Changes, however, are not simply ad hoc responses to particular problems. Indeed, we have been impressed with the flexibility of Mondragón in adapting to changing conditions and meeting new imperatives.

20 Implications of the Mondragón Experience

Evaluation of the implications of the Mondragón experience naturally falls into two topics: (1) the influence of Mondragón on worker cooperatives elsewhere and (2) a theoretical analysis of the practical lessons to be drawn from the complex.

The striking economic success of Mondragón has conveyed worldwide the message that a worker cooperative need no longer be considered simply a utopian ideal of a few visionaries on the fringes of an industrial economy. The complex is attracting increasing attention and interest from both practitioners and scholars searching for better ways of organizing production and distribution and the relations between labor and management.

The attempts to derive practical lessons from Mondragón are already so numerous in so many countries that it is impossible to provide a comprehensive overview. Here we will limit ourselves primarily to the influence of Mondragón in the United States.

MONDRAGÓN'S IMPACT IN AMERICA

Mondragón has already had a substantial influence on American legislation on worker cooperatives and employee ownership. Until 1982, organizers in this field were handicapped by the absence of state legislation. They had to fit their designs for worker cooperatives into laws pertaining to private corporations or consumer or farmer cooperatives. The Employee Cooperative Corporations Act (chapter 104, Massachusetts General Laws, 1982) fills this gap in the legislative framework. Maine, New Hampshire, New York, and Vermont followed Massachusetts in enacting identical legislation (National Center for Employee Ownership 1988). Staff members of the Industrial Cooperative Association worked closely with legislative staff in drafting the Massachusetts act and ensured that it provided a supporting framework for those seeking to apply elements of the Mondragón model to their own worker cooperatives.

Mondragón's influence on national legislation has been less direct but nevertheless is important. Mondragón has helped to bring worker cooperatives to the attention of some members of Congress and White House staff. In consulting with Congress on legislation on employee ownership (Whyte and Blasi 1980), Joseph Blasi and William Foote Whyte used the Mondragón example in arguing that worker cooperatives (as well as employee-owned firms) were worthy of attention in designing public policy. Through John McLaughry, then senior policy adviser to President Ronald Reagan, Blasi arranged to have the British Broadcasting Company's documentary on Mondragón projected on videotape to all the offices in the White House. Blasi also invited Senator Russell Long to lecture on ESOPs at Harvard University and used the dinner before the lecture as a chance to ask the senator whether he favored only the one form of employee ownership. The senator replied that he believed in employee ownership in general and recognized that it could take a variety of forms. In that case, Blasi asked, "Why not extend to worker cooperatives the same tax advantages you have provided for ESOPs?" Senator Long agreed to consider that possibility.

In his speech that evening, Senator Long did in fact insert a broad endorsement of other forms of employee ownership, including worker cooperatives. Blasi followed up in discussions with Jeffrey Gates, then staff aide to Long and to the Senate Finance Committee. This information flow and lobbying may account for why the Deficit Reduction Act of 1984 extended to "eligible worker owned cooperatives" (EWOCs) some— but not all—the tax advantages authorized for ESOPs. (The principal exclusion at that time concerned interest payments on loans to finance ESOPs. The 1984 act allowed financial institutions to exclude for tax purposes 50 percent of the interest income received from loans to ESOPs but not from EWOC loans. This provision has persuaded some banks to reduce their interest charges on ESOP loans.)

Mondragón has also aroused interest among European national federations of worker cooperatives and leaders of support organizations. At the 1984 international conference on worker cooperatives, held in Montreal, representatives from these national organizations were eager to learn from Mondragón how they could build more integrated support structures. In London, Robert Oakeshott has established Job Ownership Ltd., which promotes the development of worker cooperatives along the lines of Mondragón.

In the United States two national organizations have emerged out of the movement toward employee ownership. Supported by ESOP companies, the ESOP Association publishes a monthly bulletin, engages in lobbying, and sponsors informational conferences. The National Center for Employee Ownership (NCEO) has a wider scope of interest, including worker cooperatives but particularly ESOPs, the area in which major changes have occurred in recent years. NCEO publishes a semi-monthly bulletin, engages in research, and organizes national and regional conferences for the general public, including special meetings for union leaders and union supporters.

This surge in interest in worker ownership has given rise to a growing number of support organizations, some of which are explicitly committed to trying to apply some of the lessons of Mondragón in the United States. So far the most active of these organizations are the Industrial Cooperative Association (ICA) located in Somerville, Massachusetts, and the Philadelphia Area Cooperative Enterprises (PACE). In addition to providing information and organizational and technical assistance to groups working in, or hoping to create, worker cooperatives or ESOPs, both organizations manage revolving loan funds. By 1986, building on an initial grant from the Ford Foundation, ICA built up a fund of more than $1 million. PACE, which also had a support grant, was building a fund approaching that level. These funds are minuscule compared to those of the Caja Laboral Popular, but in its early years the Caja was also a frail organization with limited funds. It took two or three decades to build the material and human resources that the Caja offers its member organizations today. Neither ICA nor PACE depends entirely on its own loan fund for financing worker-owned firms. In both cases, the leaders use the revolving fund as seed money to bring in more substantial funds from private sources.

By 1985, North Carolina had become a fertile field for the development of cooperatives; there were sixteen worker-owned firms and six supporting organizations (*Workplace Democracy* 1985). The Center for Community Self-Help in Durham and the Twin Streams Educational Center in Chapel Hill provide technical assistance and educational services. With more than $1.5 million in assets, the Self-Help Credit Union has provided loans to twelve worker-owned or democratically managed firms. Guilford College has an undergraduate program in democratic management and holds an annual conference on the subject, and faculty members have consulted with worker-owned firms. As its name suggests, the Center for Women's Economic Alternatives was organized to help women form worker-owned businesses. The Legal Services Corporation has helped people set up such businesses.

During the 1980s, we have witnessed a marked shift in the attitudes of union leaders toward worker ownership. In the early 1970s, they tended to dismiss the idea. Recently a number of unions have recognized that, whether they like it or not, employee ownership is becoming more common in the United States. Leading officials of the United Steelworkers of America have openly stated that the survival of the steel industry will depend in large measure on the transformation of a growing number of steel companies into wholly or partially worker-owned firms. Local 1357 of the United Food and Commercial Workers (UFCW), in the Philadelphia area, very skillfully countered a threatened shutdown of A&P Supermarkets by bargaining with management for profit sharing and participation in decision making in exchange for financial sacrifices. The contract made possible the purchase from A&P of two abandoned supermarkets, which were reopened as worker cooperatives. UFCW continues to work with PACE toward the development of more worker cooperatives and employee-owned firms (Whyte 1986). (The BBC documentary on Mondragón figured prominently in the training organized by PACE and UFCW for prospective members of the worker cooperative supermarkets.)

Unions in the building trades are becoming interested in worker cooperatives as a means of providing employment for their members. In many parts of the country, these unions have a strong position only with contractors engaged in large commercial projects. Some of their leaders see the possibility of serving and extending their membership by forming cooperatives that would bid against nonunion contractors for residential building and renovation and small commercial projects.

Jack Joyce, president of the Bricklayers Union, visited Mondragón to learn about cooperatives in the construction field. His union has already organized a worker cooperative in Birmingham, Alabama, and has been planning other initiatives in this field. Furthermore, Joyce has been so impressed with Mondragón that he has been exploring the possibility of arranging for translation of Azurmendi's book *El Hombre Cooperativo*, so that the thoughts of Don José María can be available to a broader American public (Chris Mackin, personal communication).

Local 675 of the International Union of Operating Engineers (IUOE) in Pompano Beach, Florida, has become strongly committed to the development of worker cooperatives and democratically controlled ESOPs. The leading figures in the IUOE program have been the union's business manager, Dennis J. Walton, and attorney Jayne Zanglein. Early in her career as a labor attorney in Buffalo, New York, Zanglein joined the informal academic-activist network for promoting the development of worker cooperatives. Walton has been innovative in leading his union into new fields. With technical assistance from the local's full-time economist and consulting relations with marketing research firms,

> Walton has pioneered in the use of union pension funds in real-estate investments. Since winning a decisive victory in Federal Court in 1985 he has guided his own local's Fund into several multi-million dollar real-estate deals, all of which have generated high returns and 300 million dollars worth of work . . . from union building sites in Broward County, Florida. (Shostak)

Walton and Zanglein introduced the union membership to worker cooperatives through the BBC documentary on Mondragón. The first IUOE worker cooperative, United Crane, emerged out of an agreement between the union and a contractor who was facing bankruptcy and had major unpaid fringe benefit obligations to his workers. The local worked out a deal whereby five of its unemployed members contributed $2,000 each, supported by a $40,000 line of credit, to establish the IUOE's first union-sponsored cooperative firm.

> The other major venture to date, Park Central Services, Inc., a wholly owned subsidiary of the local's $45 million joint labor-management Pension Fund, has been a black-ink, steadily growing success since its initiation. Its landscaping unit was created to service a 95-acre office park funded by the Pension Fund (at a very handsome profit to it). So popular was the unit that outside clients clamored to sign contracts, one of which grew out of the union's apprenticeship program, was opened only to service customers at the emerging office park complex, but, in short order, was drawing area-wide customers as well. (Shostak)

In the fall of 1987, leaders of the local were studying plans to acquire a nearby bank and an insurance company. Thus the union was on its way to building its own cooperative complex.

Some union leaders have recognized that in this hectic era of corporate takeovers and threats of takeovers, the reshuffling of ownership creates enormous debts for the victorious raiding company or for the company that successfully withstands the raid. This growth of debt then drives managements to shut down or sell off plants and lay off thousands of workers. Until now, workers and unions have been pawns in the takeover game, but now some union leaders and their allies are seeking to raise funds so that they can operate on their own. A new investment banking firm, American Capital Strategies, has been formed for this purpose. With help from this firm, workers and union leaders threatened by a takeover or potential plant shutdown could raise the money to buy the plant or company, thereby setting up a worker-owned company.

One union, the Amalgamated Clothing and Textile Workers, has its own bank, but so far it has operated very much along conventional lines. It could, however, be a source of support, providing union members with personal loans to establish worker-owned firms. Many unions have their own credit unions, and personal loans from the UFCW credit union were the main source of equity financing for the members of the O&O Super-market cooperatives in Philadelphia.

The National Cooperative Bank, established during the Carter admin-istration, has concentrated primarily on loans for consumer and housing cooperatives, but it is empowered by its constitution to loan to worker cooperatives. So far the bank has done little in this area, and probably financial institutions at the state level would be more useful in developing worker-owned firms.

Labor and government officials in New York State and Pennsylvania have been exploring the possibility of tapping the pension funds of union-ized workers and of state and municipal employees to support employ-ment. Current legislation, which requires pension funds to be invested in very conventional and conservative ways so as to protect the interests of the individual employees, presents a legal barrier, but not an insur-mountable one. It appears possible to use these pension funds for employee ownership in an indirect way through what are known as "countervailing funds." For this purpose, the agency controlling the pension funds works out a cooperative arrangement with a bank. For example, the agency purchases a million dollars in certificates of deposit in that bank, on the understanding that the bank will use a million dollars of its own funds as loan capital in a designated employee ownership project. Because the bank is now lending its own funds, no banker would comply simply on the request of the agency. The bankers would need to satisfy themselves that the loan is financially sound. The elimination of the legal barrier, however, could make possible a large-scale shift to financing employee ownership in the interests of labor.

Cornell and several other universities have become involved in conducting applied research in worker cooperatives and employee-owned firms and in providing them with technical assistance. It seems likely that state universities providing extension education in industrial relations will give increasing attention to the needs of and opportunities for developing such organizations.

Churches may become a major force in expanding worker ownership in the United States. Because the Mondragón movement was founded and led by a priest, Catholics can justifiably take pride in its achievements. A growing number of priests and nuns have become interested in Mondragón, and some have visited the cooperatives.

The most prominent member of the Catholic hierarchy to take an interest in Mondragón was the late archbishop of Boston, Cardinal Humberto Madeiros. The cardinal invoked the vision of Mondragón during the Church's effort to help lobstermen fend off real estate developers and retain a pier in Boston harbor. As *Newsweek* (July 9, 1984) reported:

> The Boston archdiocese is now sponsoring an economic experiment along the lines of a coop (*sic*) in Mondragón, Spain, which a Basque priest helped workers to organize. In 25 years the Mondragón coop has expanded to include 80 commercial and industrial manufacturers and nearly 20,000 workers. "We can't transplant Mondragón, but we can use it as our model," says the Rev. Michael Groden, head of the Boston archdiocese planning office.

Cardinal Madeiros's successor, Archbishop Bernard Law, has continued to involve the archdiocese in the development of worker cooperatives and employee-owned firms.

Clearly the message of Mondragón is getting through to an expanding public around the world. We now turn to an analysis of the meaning of that message.

MAINTAINING WORKER OWNERSHIP AND CONTROL

The record shows that a worker cooperative is likely to find itself in a catch-22 situation: It disappears if it goes bankrupt or if it is highly successful. When stock provides the basis of ownership, a successful firm must deal with the problem we call collective selfishness. As new workers are needed so that the firm can expand or replace those who leave, the original worker-owners recognize that they can increase the value of their investment if they resort to hiring labor. Thus, in some plywood cooperatives in the United States between 30 and 40 percent of the personnel are now hired labor. The 1984 Montreal conference on worker cooperatives reported that, on average, French cooperatives had 40 percent nonmembers and those in Quebec 20 percent. As one of the leading students of the U.S. plywood cooperatives has reported:

> The shares of the successful firms have attained values that make sale by a retiring owner to a potential worker-owner almost impossible. As this condition increases, the successful cooperative can either "go public" or sell out to a major producer. The relatively uncomplicated nature of the latter seems more likely. (Bellas 1975, 212)

Unless the problem of collective selfishness is prevented in the way the firm is initially structured, we can expect this scenario to occur in financially successful cooperatives: The worker-owners will be reluctant to include new workers as owners; when they retire, they will be glad to sell to co-workers, but the value of their stock will make this impractical. The structure and financial policies of Mondragón prevent this problem from occurring. No stock is issued, and the constitution and bylaws of the individual cooperatives impose a 10 percent hiring limit on nonmembers. Because their capital accounts are nontransferable and no stock is issued, members cannot profit from selling shares to outsiders. There remains just one theoretical possibility for collective selfishness. The original members of a growing cooperative could vote to change their constitution and bylaws to allow more than 10 percent of their employees to be hired labor. In that case, the value of the individual member's share in profits would increase. This has never happened in Mondragón. The culture of Mondragón blocks the tendency to collective selfishness, but, more important, such a decision by an individual cooperative would place it in violation of its contract of association with the Caja. The penalty for such violation would be cancelation of the cooperative's contract with the Caja, thus cutting the cooperative off from very great financial and technical resources. Going beyond the 10 percent limit would also place the cooperative in violation of Spanish law, but this barrier is not likely to be as powerful as that imposed by the contract of association.

Legislation on employee stock ownership may provide a way out of the catch-22 bind, as the employee-owners of a San Francisco garbage-collecting cooperative, Golden Gate Disposal Company, recently discovered. The cooperative had become highly profitable. As could be expected, the initial owners decided to limit the profit sharing to themselves, so that over the years the labor force came to be predominantly hired labor. Because the value of an individual share of stock had risen to $100,000, it was out of the question for the hired workers to buy the shares of the retiring owners. Rather than sell their shares to outside investors, the retiring worker-owners arranged to transform the cooperative into an ESOP. This was accomplished in the now-familiar manner: With the aid of attorneys and financial advisers, the retiring worker-owners established an employee stock ownership trust, which then borrowed the money necessary to buy them out. Thus the hired workers were immediately made co-owners, even though the stock held in trust for them was to be paid for out of company earnings over a priod of years (*San Francisco Chronicle*, January 20, 1987).

This maneuver, which is likely to be practiced increasingly in the future, illustrates the broad range of possibilities involved in ESOP legislation. Louis Kelso, the inventor of the idea, and Senator Russell Long, the chief exponent of ESOPs in Congress, had no initial interest in employee involvement in management. Nonetheless, ESOPs can be an important instrument for ensuring that workers retain ownership over the long run and for giving them the possibility of participating in decision making. ESOPs do not guarantee that the workers will participate in decision making, or even gain control of management, but it does keep such possibilities open.

According to ESOP legislation, management can establish an employee stock ownership plan that is limited to managers and white-collar workers, but if blue-collar workers are included in the plan, by law any newly hired worker must share in ownership.

According to usual practice, voting rights for the control of an employee stock ownership trust are allocated based on the number of shares a shareholder has, and stock is allocated based on one's level of pay. This of course provides managers and more highly paid employees with substantially more voting power than the rank and file. ESOP legislation, however, provides for an extraordinary range of possibilities in the design of the plan. In 1981, attorney Jack Curtis designed an employee stock ownership plan for the employees of Rath Packing Company that separated the power to vote for the trustees who would control the stock from the power of individual stock owners (Whyte et al. 1983). Under the Rath plan, when the employees gained 60 percent of the company's stock in a buyout, the trustees who voted that stock and thereby controlled the board of directors were elected on the basis of one vote for every employee–share owner, regardless of the number of shares held. Futhermore, stock was originally allocated equally to each employee-owner. Rath went out of business in 1985. If Rath had survived, however, the plan would have made it impossible for higher paid workers and salaried people to gain a disproportionate influence—unless the stock in trust was distributed later to the individual employee-owners.

BALANCING OWNERS' AND WORKERS' INTERESTS

The Mondragón experience demonstrates the need in a worker cooperative to balance the interests of members as owners and as workers. When a worker cooperative operates fully democratically and all or nearly all the workers are co-owners and have equal voting power, the need for this dual form of representation is not immediately apparent. As we have pointed out, the dual role of owners and workers necessarily involves some ambivalence. As workers, they would like to increase their immediate financial benefits and improve the quality of working life, but as owners, they also must be concerned about the long-run financial and organizational strength of their cooperative. Ambivalence is not a good position from which to make decisions. Rather than expecting each leader and each worker to make these choices individually, it is advisable to have separate structures and processes to ensure that the balancing problem becomes a focus of open discussion and debate.

In worker buyout cases in which workers are members of a union, there is a tendency for the workers to retain their union affiliation, although members of management and even some rank-and-file people may question the need for it. Our conclusion on the basis of research in the United States is that a union can be important in an employee-owned company. If the ESOP provides the workers with very little influence on management, the union's role in providing the balance and representing workers' interests is obvious. But even if the structure of the ESOP permits worker participation in the management process, the union can still play a constructive role in representing workers' interests and balancing them against ownership interests. This requires a substantial reorientation of the role of the union. The union needs to move from the conventional adversarial role toward cooperation with management—without becoming simply the tool of management. This means that the union must bargain with management to arrive at mutually agreed upon bases of cooperation.

This analysis offers an answer to the question most frequently raised by union skeptics in the early stages of the employee ownership movement: "How can you bargain with yourself?" The answer is that the union leaders are not really bargaining with themselves. They continue to bargain with management but the negotiations are focused primarily on the terms and conditions for cooperation, including how to share the costs and benefits of that cooperation. Whatever the form of ownership, there will always be the possibility that individual workers, or groups of workers, will feel that they have been unfairly treated and will demand that their grievances be considered. The union should continue to receive and process such grievances.

If a group of workers that has never had a union forms a worker cooperative or employee-owned firm, one can hardly expect management or the workers to see at once the need for more representation than they have gained through ownership, so it would be unrealistic to urge them to unionize. Judging from the Mondragón experience, however, the leaders of such organizations should consider the possibility of establishing something like a social council to ensure that workers' interests are represented in dealing with mangement, which necessarily must give primary consideration to the business needs of the firm. In a small, newly formed worker cooperative where relations are on a very informal basis, the members are not likely to see the need for dual forms of representation. As the cooperative expands, there will be an increasing need for a structure and a process to ensure that workers' interests are balanced with those of management.

In some cases, such as the supermarket cooperatives in Philadelphia organized under the leadership of the United Food and Commercial Workers Union (Whyte 1986) and the cooperatives created by the International Union of Operating Engineers, the initial members of the organization may be union members and maintain that affiliation. As leaders in various unions see a growing need to maintain employment for their members through employee buyouts, or through startups of worker cooperatives or employee-owned firms, we are likely to see increasing union involvement in worker ownership.

COMPLEMENTARITY AND SUPPORTING ORGANIZATIONS

There is one proposition on which all students of worker cooperatives agree: The long-run prospects for a cooperative trying to survive in a sea of private enterprises are very poor. One aid to survival is to group cooperatives so that they can exchange services and share expenses. We also see from Mondragón that a financially successful cooperative can stimulate the creation of cooperatives in fields that support the interests of both the parent cooperative and one another. For example, as worker cooperative supermarkets continue to expand in the Philadelphia area, we can expect their leaders to develop plans for the creation of food-processing and food-packaging cooperatives. A similar development strategy is illustrated in the Pompano Beach program of the IUOE.

In addition to exchanging and sharing among individual units, worker cooperatives need supporting organizations. We are unlikely to see the development of such a tightly integrated network of complementary and supporting organizations as in Mondragón. Nevertheless, various countries have national or regional organizations that offer expanding services to worker cooperatives, and here and there technical assistance organizations, such as Job Ownership Ltd., in London, have been created. Similar organizations in the United States were described earlier.

LEADERSHIP

It is impossible to reproduce Don José María, but we can learn from his example. A review of the history of worker cooperatives indicates that they often arise because a single individual has inspired, organized, and built the organization—and then continued to dominate it. His followers become dependent on him. When he leaves the organization or dies, the cooperative tends to deteriorate and eventually disappear.

Don José María differed sharply from this pattern. He provided an unusual combination of challenge and support. Furthermore, except in the case of the creation of the Caja, he did not make decisions for the members. Rather, he provided a framework for growth, change, and development. He never held an executive position, which would have given him the power to dictate decisions. He introduced ideas for new directions of development, but he never attended regular business meetings of the governing councils of the cooperatives. He was the primary strategic thinker and planner, but he left it to others to make the necessary decisions in following the course that he had helped them chart.

Don José María was a man of strong convictions, and he did not hesitate to argue with his co-cooperators. His strong commitment to anticipating future trends guided his followers in their openness to change and their organizational creativity.

In most cases, the founder of a worker cooperative is also its primary leader at the outset and probably for a considerable time. Most leaders will therefore not be able to stand aside as Don José María did, exercising influence without directly making decisions. The leader, who will probably occupy an executive position, is likely to find it difficult to restrain himself and guide the members so that they will be able to make independent and intelligent decisions when he can no longer exert guidance and authority. He must guard against the natural tendency to let his original ideas dominate members' thinking.

Organizational Culture

As one learns about the distinctive social inventions in Mondragón, one might conclude that some of the structures, policies, and social processes could be lifted out of the complex and fruitfully applied, with little modification, in quite different organizational settings. That would be misleading, for Mondragón is not simply the sum of these structures, policies, and processes. Members of the personnel group in FAGOR with whom we have been working have realized that Mondragón is a set of organizations that has its own distinctive culture. It is because of that culture that the various elements are linked together into an integrated whole.

In any organization that has persisted for as long as FAGOR has, members do not act and react to one another simply in anticipation of the potential rewards or penalties inherent in the situation. Rather, the way they interpret events and problems occurs within the context of the organizational culture they have created. In private companies, executives tend to assume they understand this culture simply because they are generally familiar with private enterprise from their own experience, what they hear from friends and relatives, and what they read. To forge new relations between labor and management, however, leaders of private companies will need to reflect on and discuss the culture they want to build for their organization.

In designing and shaping a worker cooperative or an employee-owned firm, organizations for which there is little popular knowledge or experience, leaders need to think, from the very beginning, of building an organizational culture and to reexamine and rethink this culture as conditions change. This does not mean that an organizational culture can be created by fiat, simply by identifying the cultural elements that are supposed to guide the organization. As we have seen in Mondragón, the elements of culture need to be compatible with one another and mutually reinforcing. They cannot be simply expressions of desirable conditions, laid out at random. Futhermore, one cannot assume that the culture consists of what is written down and disseminated in company policy statements: the "espoused theory." One infers the nature of a culture from the study of behavior, which leads to the "theory in use." At the same time, it is important for a company to write down and disseminate the basic elements of its culture so as to provide behavioral guidance for members and reference points for further study and debate. It may be important to move back and forth between the written statements of the company's culture and the study and discussion of current behavior. Such a process can help members recognize points at which actual behavior has departed from the espoused theories of behavior and thus promote fruitful discussion of the need to change elements of either the culture or the behavior. (For discussion of espoused theory and theory in use, see Argyris et al. 1986 and Schön 1983.)

While recognizing that the people who will work within an organizational culture need to be the ones to develop it, we nevertheless believe that certain elements of the culture of Mondragón may have applications elsewhere. One particularly important element is its future orientation. The leaders of an organization must guide present actions in relation to some conception of the future. Combined with this future orientation, organizational self-criticism is also important. For participation in decision making to be effective, members and leaders of the organization must be able to step back from issues needing immediate decisions and reflect critically on the way their organization has been functioning.

Especially in the case of worker cooperatives, it is important to avoid the dead weight of dogma. We have found, in reflecting on the American experience since the surge in the growth of small worker cooperatives and informally organized work collectives, that such organizations tend to attract "true believers" who embrace cooperative values with religious zeal. In some cooperatives, for example, the leaders and members have believed so strongly in participation and direct democracy that they have insisted that virtually all decisions be made by group consensus or near consensus. Even in a small organization, this policy tends to produce long, frustrating discussions that exact a high psychological toll from members and constitute a significant drag on organizational efficiency. Of course, if the cooperative gets larger, this policy becomes completely unworkable. In other instances, founding members may believe that all worker-members should receive the same pay and rotate their jobs. Because the technical requirements of various positions may be quite different, these companies may have difficulty attracting or retaining highly skilled people.

To guard against the problem of dogmatism, it is important to adopt the *equilibrio* or balancing principle used so effectively in Mondragón. If an organization is to survive and grow, there must be systematic means for balancing economic and technological imperatives with social values and objectives (Whyte and Blasi 1982; Rothschild-Whitt 1979).

Although we do not recommend simply imitating the culture of Mondragón, it is important for leaders of any organization, and particularly leaders of cooperatives or employee-owned firms, to try to build a coherent organizational culture. The culture of Mondragón may provide an approach and a set of categories useful for studying and interpreting other organizational cultures.

REGIONAL ECONOMIC DEVELOPMENT

Finally, the lessons drawn from the Mondragón experience have more general implications for regional economic development in America and abroad. The Mondragón experience suggests the increasing importance of growth through horizontal exchange and service relations, rather than through vertical hierarchies in which leaders of the organization try to bring under their control as much as possible of the human and material resources needed to produce their goods and services. In the early decades of industrial growth in the United States, leaders of expanding companies assumed that the only way to control resources and operations was to build predominantly in the vertical dimension. In recent years, the rigidities and inefficiencies of organizations designed on this model have become increasingly apparent. Even large companies have begun to recognize that it is frequently more advantageous to buy goods and services from another organization than to finance, manage, and control the provision of those goods and services.

Mondragón is a prime example of a set of organizations that has grown in large measure by following the principle of complementarity in sharing goods and services among autonomous organizations. Mondragón thus represents a shift from vertical to horizontal thinking and also from domination to cooperation.

For similar reasons, the dynamic and expanding small-business sector in northern Italy has been exciting the interest of students and practitioners of regional economic development (Piore and Sabel 1983). Giorgio Alberti (personal communication) has found that the entrepreneurs are increasingly developing relations with other small firms in the area with which they share expenses and exchange services and create supporting organizations. Thus they appear to be developing among themselves a mini-economy in which the relations among legally independent firms somewhat resemble relations developed among the Mondragón cooperatives, cooperative groups, and their supporting organizations. This trend has stimulated managerial economist Alan McAdams (personal communication) to visualize the proliferation of "virtual factories." In contrast to the factory of an earlier era, whose leaders aimed as much as possible to concentrate production and service operations within the same physical structure and within the same company, we may be seeing the spread of the virtual factory, in which a number of relatively small independent organizations work together to develop, produce, and market goods and services that were provided much less efficiently by large organizations.

Mondragón's ability to maintain employment *in part* by adjusting labor rates to market conditions suggests that the cooperatives are providing a practical example of the principles stated in *The Share Economy* (Weitzman 1984). We should not assume, however, that the results achieved by Mondragón can be duplicated elsewhere simply by using a formula linking pay to the economic performance of the firm. In adjusting to weak markets, the Mondragón cooperatives have worked out an integrated set of procedures and policies, among which pay sacrifices are only one element. Furthermore, in Mondragón the pay sacrifices are not simply imposed on rank-and-file workers but are accepted by all members throughout the ranks and are accompanied by thorough reorganization of firms in financial difficulties.

In the United States, managers tend to think there are two separate and unrelated labor markets: one for labor and another for managers and professionals. In the recession of the 1980s, leaders of private companies, claiming that their financial problems were caused by the high cost of labor, persuaded union leaders to accept worker pay concessions as a price for saving jobs—even though in many cases direct labor costs amounted to only 15 percent of total costs. Contrary to common practice in Japan, American managers seldom accept comparable pay sacrifices for themselves. Nor is it yet common for American managers, when seeking pay concessions, to invite union leaders and workers to join with them in analyzing all costs so as to guide in a reorganization of firms in financial difficulties. American workers would more readily accept the idea of linking their pay to the performance of their firm if they expected necessary pay sacrifices to be equitably shared among all company personnel and if they or their representatives were invited to participate in plans to reorganize and revitalize the company.

Americans pride themselves on their entrepreneurial spirit and rugged individualism, which leads people to take risks to create new businesses and industrial firms with a greater frequency than in many other cultures. It is now well recognized that growth in employment in the United States does not stem from an increase in the number of jobs in large corporations. In fact, the record in the 1980s suggests that, although large companies do create new jobs, at least as many jobs are eliminated. Because employment growth depends largely on the creation and expansion of new firms, it is a vital matter of social policy to understand the conditions fostering growth and survival so that both the potential entrepreneurs and government agencies or other supporting organizations can strengthen and support entrepreneurship.

So far neither business schools nor governments have done much through research or public policy to support entrepreneurship, thus leaving entrepreneurs to succeed or fail in response to the dynamics of social Darwinism: the survival of the fittest. Consider the costs involved in this model. In their exploration of the entrepreneurial career, Orvis Collins and other researchers gathered intensive life histories from 110 Michigan industrial entrepreneurs of firms founded in the period from 1945 to 1958 (Collins et al. 1964). All of these firms were at least marginally profitable, and most of them employed twenty or more people, yet the researchers found that many of the entrepreneurs had gone bankrupt at least once and some more than once. Collins and his colleagues interpreted the experience of going bankrupt as an important stage in the learning process that enabled these men eventually to succeed. No doubt it was, but one wonders about an economic system that imposes such frustrations and punishments on the very individuals it is counting on to create new enterprises, provide new goods and services, and expand employment.

This is not to suggest that the risks can or should be removed from entrepreneurship. In the Mondragón system, a newly created cooperative has no guarantee that it will be successful, and all parties involved recognize the difficult struggle before them and the heavy risks they are assuming. Nevertheless, the Entrepreneurial Division and management of the cooperative groups provide a body of research on the market available and the technology required as well as training and guidance for the leader of the new firm. These services protect the individual and the group founding the firm from embarking on an enterprise that is bound to be a lost cause. The entrepreneurial group faces a challenge, but it also receives support, not only in the form of encouragement but in technical, economic, and social guidance.

Mondragón is also important for its capacity to recognize the interdependence of financing and technical assistance. In the United States the pattern has been one of separation and specialization. For example, in its early years the National Cooperative Bank provided grants to agencies offering technical assistance to worker cooperatives but stipulated that such grants could not be used for technical assistance until *after* the bank had approved its loan to the cooperative. This meant that the organizers received no technical assistance from the bank during the period of organizing and planning the cooperative and making the many decisions that would shape its development for the months and years to come. The policy has since been changed, but the fact that such a policy could have been imposed suggests a failure to recognize the necessary interdependence of financing and technical assistance.

One of the major problems for entrepreneurs in the United States who need technical assistance is the specialization and competition among consultants. The small-business entrepreneur is likely to need the assistance of a lawyer and an accountant and may also need technical assistance in manufacturing, marketing, and organizational development. The problem here is not simply that different people need to be called upon— assuming their services can be afforded—but that specialists do not generally limit their recommendations to the field covered by their specialization. Thus the lawyer, the accountant, the marketing specialist, and the technological consultant are all likely to give general advice on how to establish and manage an organization, and more often than not present conflicting and mutually incompatible views. In Mondragón, consultants work within a system in which information and ideas are worked out and presented in an integrated fashion.

The United States may never develop as integrated a socioeconomic system as in Mondragón, but leaders of business organizations and of the agencies seeking to help them should be concerned about the problem of specialization and conflicting recommendations. This suggests the need to distinguish between the organizational consultant/facilitator, who works with the organization on a more or less continuing basis and gains an intimate knowledge of that organization, and experts who are called in for specific technical information and ideas. The consultant/facilitator needs to be an intermediary between the organization and the technical specialists, someone who helps the organization secure the technical information and ideas when needed and then integrates these ideas with the organizational and business development strategy.

Whatever the future holds, we are clearly in an era of rapid social, technological, and economic changes. In such an era, conventional strategies for organizing and producing goods and services are no longer adequate. For those who hope to find ways of following a humanistic vision while confronting hard economic and technological realities, Mondragón can serve as an inspiration. Mondragón demonstrates that it is not easy to meet this challenge but that it can be done.

Appendix
Evolution of Our Research
on Mondragón

What began in 1975 as our individual research has evolved since 1983 into a collaborative research program implemented jointly by Cornell University and FAGOR (formerly ULARCO). Tracing the course of this evolution should be useful in providing a context for this book and future publications developing out of this collaborative relationship.

We cannot claim credit for the discovery of Mondragón. In the English-speaking world, that contribution was made by Robert Oakeshott (1973). At the time, during the Franco era, leaders of the cooperatives were deliberately maintaining a low profile, and even few Spaniards outside the Basque country had any idea of what was going on in Mondragón. Oakeshott's discovery occurred in a library in Paris as he was leafing through the pages of an obscure series of publications by the Centre de Recherches Cooperatives and happened upon the first research report on Mondragón, published in 1967 (Aldabaldetrecu and Gray). The cooperative complex had already grown to formidable size: 4,800 worker-owners in forty-two cooperatives linked together through the Caja Laboral Popular. The discovery excited Oakeshott, and he thereupon decided he had to see Mondragón for himself.

I reacted as Oakeshott had when in 1974 I noticed an article he had written about Mondragón (1973) on a bulletin board at Cornell University. Like Oakeshott, I was determined to study Mondragón.

Our field study began in April 1975 when Kathleen King Whyte and I spent two weeks in Mondragón. As far as we know, we were the first native speakers of English to interview people in the complex in Spanish. A Peruvian graduate student in Cornell's New York State School of Industrial and Labor Relations, Ana Gutiérrez-Johnson, joined us a day after we arrived and remained for seven weeks after we left. During our two-week visit, Ana, Kathleen, and I carried out all of our interviews together. After we left, Ana conducted additional interviews and gathered basic documentary material. As part of the research for her master's thesis (1976), she also conducted a survey of Basque students in the Escuela Politécnica Profesional in which she measured their reactions to questions on equity—a research area for which she had comparative material in the United States and Holland. The field work resulted in an article (Gutiérrez-Johnson and Whyte 1977) that we believe was the first research report on Mondragón published in English.

Ana made two more visits to Mondragón up to 1979. By then she had spent a total of nine months in the field, far longer than any other foreign scholar had up to that point. She completed her doctoral thesis on Mondragón in 1982.

Our contacts with Mondragón from 1975 to 1983 were limited to visits to Cornell by Tomasa Zabaleta, administrative secretary to the central social councils of Ulgor and FAGOR; Maria Angeles Amenabar, administrative secretary of the Governing Council of Zubiola; and later Manuel Quevedo, manager of Ikerlan. They stayed at our home during their several days in Ithaca, providing us with an opportunity to renew acquaintance and talk extensively about developments since our visit in 1975.

By the early 1980s, I had put my other research commitments behind me and begun to shift my attention to Mondragón. I drew heavily on the research of Ana Gutiérrez-Johnson for the period up to 1979, but her field work had ended before the complex had felt the impact of the worldwide recession, which affected Spain and the Basque country much more severely than most other industrialized nations. Previous research explained the creation and development of the complex, but clearly our understanding of Mondragón could be greatly enhanced if we could now focus on how it was coping with serious economic difficulties. We knew that because of the recession the once-dynamic cooperative complex was now struggling to hold its own in the marketplace. But we had also heard that, as difficult as the struggle was, Mondragón was achieving extraordinary success in ensuring the survival of its enterprises. The problem was to explain how Mondragón was able to cope with the recession so much better than private firms in Spain.

Kathleen and I returned to Mondragón for three weeks in October 1983. We devoted this period to interviewing key informants in various parts of the complex and to gathering basic documents. Toward the end of this visit, I suggested to Tomasa Zabaleta that we meet with some of the people we had interviewed to discuss our impressions of the complex. After I had talked informally with the group, José Luis Gonzalez, director of personnel for FAGOR, suggested that I present the group with a proposal and budget for the next stage of our research. His enthusiastic reaction took me completely by surprise. I had not thought of our meeting as anything more than an opportunity to express our thanks to the Mondragón people for what we had learned and to give them a little something back.

Gonzalez's response posed a dilemma for me. I was fascinated by Mondragón, but at the age of sixty-nine I was not prepared to organize and promote as ambitious a program in organizational behavior research as was needed. I was also skeptical about how much a foreigner could contribute to such a highly developed democratic and participative system as Mondragón. I thought first of trying to attract Spanish social researchers to work with the Mondragón people, but the social sciences had been crippled by the Franco dictatorship and were just beginning to recover. I knew of no Spanish social scientists who had a track record in research in organizational behavior. I was attracted by the idea of getting members of the Mondragón cooperatives involved in doing their own research. I recognized that they had many bright and dedicated people who would be interested in such an undertaking, but they lacked an educational background in social research or organizational theory. At the time, this seemed a serious handicap.

On returning to Cornell, I presented my dilemma to Davydd J. Greenwood, director of Cornell's Center for International Studies. I knew Greenwood only casually at the time but had read his impressive study of a Basque community (1976) and recognized that he knew the Basques and Spain far better than I.

Greenwood suggested that we seek support from the Spain–United States Committee on Educational and Cultural Exchange to explore the possibility of establishing an interinstitutional relationship for research and educational collaboration between Mondragón and Cornell. Together we drafted a proposal, which resulted in our receiving a grant for one year to support a series of visits between Mondragón and Cornell for the purpose of exploring to what extent we had mutual interests. (The committee later awarded a second grant to support the program that evolved out of the exploratory visit.)

Because the Mondragón complex has no central administration, it was not clear to what organization or to what individual we should address our idea regarding the exchange. As a first step, I sent a preliminary paper to Tomasa Zabaleta. She was a good friend and a respected person in an important advisory position in FAGOR, although not in the position to make decisions for FAGOR or any other unit. I simply asked her to share the preliminary paper with key people in FAGOR, the Caja Laboral Popular, and Ikerlan. At this stage, José Luis Gonzalez was the only person in the complex who expressed a strong interest in collaborating with Cornell, but he secured the support of Javier Mongelos, general manager of FAGOR, and that was sufficient to provide the basis for the joint program.

In February 1985, José Luis Gonzalez came to Cornell to get acquainted with people in the School of Industrial and Labor Relations, the Center for International Studies, the Johnson Graduate School of Management, and the College of Engineering.

In April 1985, a group of Cornellians made a two-week visit to Mondragón. Kathleen and I were joined by Davydd Greenwood and Virginia and Richard Lance (professor of theoretical and applied mechanics in the College of Engineering). Kathleen and I stayed on for a third week to conduct additional field work.

Greenwood returned to Mondragón for the month of July for an intensive seminar in FAGOR to launch participatory action research. The seminar was devoted to a study of Ulgor, the largest and oldest cooperative in the complex. The development of that program will be reported on in a future volume written and edited by Greenwood and José Luis Gonzalez, in collaboration with other members of our joint program.

In September, Alex Goiricelaya visited Cornell for two purposes. He was accompanied by professors from what is now the Escuela Politécnica José María Arizmendiarrieta and ETEO, the school of business administration. While they explored teaching and research in Cornell's colleges of engineering and management, Goiricelaya consulted with Greenwood and me to plan a second stage of the participatory action research program. He told us that the people who had participated in the July seminar with Greenwood were enthusiastic about the experience and that Mongelos had encouraged them to undertake an even more ambitious project the following year focusing on FAGOR, the oldest and largest group of cooperatives. Goiricelaya also met with Donald Kane, director of management programs and co-director of Programs for Employment and Workplace Systems in the extension division of Cornell's New York State School of

Industrial and Labor Relations, to explore the possibility of having Kane work with Mondragón to strengthen FAGOR's management-development program.

In November 1985, Kane led a four-person Cornell team (that included me and graduate students Sally Klingel and Fred Freundlich) to Mondragón to do a needs analysis for FAGOR. We spent two weeks interviewing Mondragón people from first-line foremen to top management in three of the largest cooperatives (Ulgor, Copreci, and Arrasate). Although the analysis was not specifically focused on research, it provided useful information about relations within management.

In January 1985, we were visited by Alex Goiricelaya and Isabel Lagarreta of FAGOR's Department of Personnel. They worked particularly with Kane, assessing the extent to which management-training materials used in the United States could be adapted for use in Mondragón.

In February, Kane returned to Mondragón with Fred Freundlich to work with the people in personnel on the first stages of their new program. Freundlich remained through July to work on this and other projects. Later in February, Greenwood went to Mondragón to plan the July seminar and the field research activities the FAGOR team would undertake to provide data for that seminar.

Early in May, Alex Goiricelaya and Isabel Lagaretta returned to Cornell with José Luis Gonzalez and Ino Galparsoro, personnel director of Copreci, to continue working with Kane on plans for management training. During this period, Kane arranged for them to visit people in personnel at IBM, Xerox, and Corning Glass Works.

In mid-May, Kathleen and I spent two weeks in Mondragón, along with Sally Klingel, who stayed on for the July seminar, working on surveys of several of the cooperatives. Later in May, the Cornell contingent was reinforced for ten weeks by two graduate students. Peter Taylor worked on a study of the evolution of FAGOR, and Carmen Aibar studied the evolution of its constitution and bylaws.

In June, Professor William Kaven of Cornell's School of Hotel Administration spent two weeks in Mondragón working with their personnel people on cases to be used in management training.

Greenwood returned in July for the intensive seminar on FAGOR. As the people in Mondragón worked with Greenwood, they became increasingly committed to the value of what we were calling participatory action research. In fact, the focus of their report shifted from a study of FAGOR to a description and evaluation of the research process they were developing with us. General Manager Mongelos supported this research, and for the first time, in 1986, FAGOR included an appropriation for social research in its personnel department budget.

WRITING THE BOOK

This book developed in two distinct stages. Except for information we gathered during the weeks we spent in Mondragón in 1975, our account of the early years of the complex is based primarily on the field research and doctoral thesis of Ana Gutiérrez-Johnson. There are important exceptions. We have used Larrañaga's biography of Don José María, published in 1981, which Ana first brought to our attention, to strengthen the story of the evolution of the complex, as well as the excellent book about the founder by Azurmendi (1984).

In 1985, we learned how Don José María launched the Caja Laboral Popular despite the objections of his associates. We also gathered substantial new information regarding the creation and early development of the social council and the policy of allocating members' shares of profits to their capital accounts. We also clarified how the policy of pooling profits and losses within ULARCO was developed.

We are particularly indebted to Ana Gutiérrez-Johnson for her early interviews with two of the Ulgor pioneers, Alfonso Gorroñogoitia and José María Ormaechea, and for sharing with us what she learned from her extensive reading on the history and culture of the Basques. Our interpretation of Basque culture and history has been further strengthened by Davydd Greenwood and reading materials he suggested.

Since Ana worked so closely with me from 1975 to 1982, it is impossible to determine exactly which ideas were hers and which mine. She deserves particular credit for pointing out the importance of the *equilibrio* principle in guiding the development of the cooperatives. Ana phrased it in terms of the contrast between digital and analogic reasoning. Digital reasoning frames choices in either/or zero-sum terms, whereas analogic reasoning frames the choices in terms of both/and, guiding the actors toward balancing interests and needs.

For the story of Mondragón since 1979, we have relied primarily on our own field interviews and on documents, supplemented by the work of other researchers.

My collaboration with Kathleen King Whyte has evolved over many years. Although Kathleen's professional background was as an artist, she has always had a lively interest in social sciences and has been in-volved in most of my field explorations. She has provided a very impor-tant balance betwen a strong interest in my work and a critical evaluation of its weaknesses. She helped me edit my earlier books and edited *Higher Yielding Human Systems for Agriculture* (Whyte and Boyn-ton 1984) for Cornell's Center for International Studies. In *Learning from the Field: A Guide from Experience* (1984), she is identified as my collaborator.

With the exception of the trip in November 1985, Kathleen par-ticipated with me in all of the interviews in Mondragón, and many of the ideas in this book have evolved out of our discussions over the years.

Throughout the time we were conducting our personal research, we tried to provide some interpretations of Mondragón to the people in the complex who had helped us by submitting to interviews and guiding us to documents, but the exchange was markedly one-sided. We were learn-ing more about Mondragón than they were learning from us.

Following our 1983 visit, we sent translations of our preliminary reports to some of the key people we had interviewed, in the hope that they would correct errors and provide other interpretations we needed to con-sider. Only one out of the eight reports produced any written response. María Angeles Amenabar, administrative secretary to the Governing Council of Zubiola, made extensive corrections and additions to my report on the first stages of the struggle to reorganize Zubiola. More than a key informant, María Angeles Amenabar was a close friend of Tomasa Zabaleta, who had become our best friend in Mondragón. Amenabar had stayed at our home with Tomasa during their visit in the 1970s and had joined us on weekends in Tomasa's apartment during our visits in 1983 and later. She had also arranged for our 1983 visit to Zubiola and to other cooperatives in the URKIDE group and had proved to be the key to our learning the history of Zubiola. In 1986, she told us the story of Zubiola's second reorganization and gave us a copy of the report on that process that she had written for Zubiola and URKIDE.

As an institutional collaborative relationship developed between Cornell and FAGOR, our book came to be a component of the overall program. The most important step in this direction was taken by Greenwood as he planned the July 1985 seminar. The seminar was built on three elements: a critical review of foreign literature on Mondragón, lectures and discussions with Greenwood on social research methods and social theory, and the writing of their study of Ulgor. As part of the foreign literature segment, draft chapters of this book were included. Only a few of the participants could read English, but they reported to the others, and as a result, we got extensive and very valuable criticisms and suggestions. Some weeks before, I had written a preliminary paper entitled "A Conceptual Scheme for Understanding Mondragón," which Greenwood thought would be helpful for the seminar. Those participants who could read English agreed and had it translated. Their discussions of the paper encouraged us to believe that our interpretations were on the right track. Finally, the participants decided to focus their study of Ulgor on the events before, during, and after the 1974 strike and on the difficult period of economic and social adjustment of the 1980s. The July 1985 seminar resulted in a 116-page monograph on Ulgor, which we have found extraordinarily valuable in writing our book, especially its review of the 1974 Ulgor strike.

Other people provided very useful comments and suggestions on the 1985 draft of our book. Alex Goiricelaya made exceedingly detailed notes for corrections and referred us to additional information. Iñaki Gorroño and María Jesús Zabaleta in the Caja provided very valuable feedback on the chapters dealing with the bank. Davydd Greenwood not only read and criticized the 1985 version but provided invaluable advice and criticisms on all of the drafts. Furthermore, when he returned to Mondragón in July 1986, he set aside time to have an extended discussion of the manuscript with Alex Goiricelaya and José Luis Gonzalez. Greenwood tape-recorded this discussion, which provided a most useful record. The chapters dealing with the development of agribusiness and of Eroski were sent to Iñaki Imasa, general technical secretary of Eroski, who provided valuable feedback.

We are indebted to José Ramon Elorza for helping us trace Arizmendi's early thoughts on the social council and to Norma Bernstein Tarrow for background information on higher education in the Basque country.

We also wish to thank Joseph Blasi, who reviewed the manuscript and provided many useful suggestions.

We received substantial help on the bibliography from David Ellerman, Constance Finlay, Eva Kronik, and Carla Weiss.

Finally, we are indebted to Erica Fox of ILR Press for her skill and diligence in editing, which went far beyond what has become customary these days.

On Translating Quotations

The translation of material from Spanish was handled in different ways depending on the time period being discussed and the nature of the quotations. Except for the notes on interviews with Don José María, our field notes, and the documentary materials gathered up to 1979, we have used Ana Gutiérrez-Johnson's translations. Interview quotations from Don José María and passages in his writings included in Azurmendi's book (1984) were translated by Ana María Perez-Girones.

I have done my own translations of the interviews and documentary materials Kathleen and I gathered from 1979 on. We have depended on Perez-Girones and Gutiérrez-Johnson for the corrections of the translations but have rephrased some segments to make them read more smoothly. When I was in doubt about the correct translation of a word or phrase dealing with a matter of some importance, I checked with Davydd Greenwood, whose knowledge of Spain, the Basques, and Spanish is far superior to mine.

Problems and Potentialities of Mondragón Research

Mondragón presents unusual problems for the researcher. The complex is a unique set of organizations. There are no familiar models with which to compare it; nothing can be taken for granted by extrapolating from organizational behavior research elsewhere. Furthermore, the member organizations and interorganizational relations of the complex are constantly evolving and changing. Anyone who encounters Mondragón only briefly is likely to emerge with a static picture and with the impression that its structures and processes have changed very little over the years. In fact, the complex is notable for its dynamism. One is thus left with the question of how much of what one observes today was predetermined by the structures and policies established in the early years.

For the researcher, the open communication system of Mondragón is an enormous advantage. Its members have the right to a wealth of information, and the written records are unusually rich. The reports of the social councils, for example, do not simply indicate the problems discussed and the decisions or recommendations made but rather give a full account of the arguments in favor and opposed for any issue of importance. It would be difficult to gain access to the minutes of meetings of the board of directors, executive committee, and so on of a private firm in the United States. And, assuming we could secure access, we would probably find the written reports sanitized and no evidence of differences of opinion.

The spirit of organizational self-criticism prevailing in Mondragón enormously strengthens the ability of the researcher to probe beneath the surface toward a greater level of understanding. Although they must sometimes find this process painful, Mondragón people take pride in their ability to resolve conflicts of interests and ideas and in their willingness to discuss them openly. This spirit is further exemplified in the monthly publication *Trabajo y Unión*. Because the purpose of this publication, like that of any house organ, is to promote commitment to the organization, as well as to provide information, it is not surprising that *Trabajo y Unión* generally presents a favorable interpretation of Mondragón. At the same time, it appears far more frank and open in discussing deficiencies and problems than one would find in house organs of American private firms.

We have benefited from an extraordinary degree of collaboration and involvement of Mondragón people in the development of this book. Our experience, however, should not encourage those following us to assume that they will be similarly well received. We had the advantage of being the first English-speaking visitors who could also converse in Spanish. On our first visit in 1975, through arrangements with Javier Retegui, director of the Escuela Politécnica Profesional, we were met at the Bilbao airport by Manuel Quevedo, director of Ikerlan, and one of his associates. We had hardly settled in to Hostal Txerrita when he brought Don José María to greet us and begin our orientation to the early development of Mondragón.

As the complex has become increasingly well known around the world, Mondragón has become flooded with international visitors, ranging from those who are simply curious and want to report that they have been there to serious students who want to study some aspect of the cooperatives. On one of our later visits, we received a phone call from a fellow American who had been told of our presence. She had come to Europe for a meeting that had been canceled and had arrived at Mondragón without any advance preparation. She asked me, "Could I tag along with you on the next tour?" I had to tell her that there was no such thing as a tour of the cooperatives.

Later, one of our Mondragón associates received a letter from an American professor who was completely unknown to him. The professor proposed to spend his sabbatical year in Mondragón studying the cooperatives and had requested help in finding a place to live and in arranging for his research. He seemed to assume that Mondragón people would be flattered by the attention he proposed to give them. That might have been true up to the mid-1970s when foreign visitors were exceedingly rare.

By now the situation has been dramatically transformed. To be sure, Mondragón people take pride in the still-growing worldwide interest in their cooperatives, but leaders recognize that this international recognition can carry a heavy cost. This situation also poses problems for people at Cornell University who have been involved with Mondragón. As our involvement has become known in the academic world and among activists in the cooperative movement, people frequently look to us for advice and help on studying some aspect of the complex. Although we would like to help colleagues and friends, we have not been appointed gatekeepers for any Mondragón cooperatives; nor would it be appropriate for us to assume that role.

To help both Mondragón people and foreign researchers deal with the growing interest in the complex, Davydd Greenwood and I have been discussing with our associates the need to institutionalize the process of visiting and studying so as to minimize the drain on the time of Mondragón people and to enable them to choose from among the growing number of requests to visit. This way, Mondragón would most likely receive some benefits from study visits, instead of simply providing service to the outside world. Mondragón people are not opposed to serving the outside world, but they do not see themselves as missionaries, and they must give primary attention to their own interests and needs.

WILLIAM FOOTE WHYTE

Bibliography

Aldabaldetrecu, F., and J. Gray
   1967   "De L'Artisanat Industriel au Complexe Coopératif: L'Experience de
           Mondragón." Paris: Centre de Recherches Cooperatives.

Alleva, Ernest L., Jr.
   1983   "The Justification of Workers' Self-Management." Ph.D. diss., Co-
           lumbia University.

Amsden, Jon
   1972   *Collective Bargaining and Class Conflict in Spain.* London: Weidenfeld
           and Nicolson.

Aranzadi, Dionisio
   1976   *Cooperativismo Industrial Como Sistema, Empresa y Experiencia.* Bilbao,
           Spain: Universidad de Deusto.

Argyris, Chris, Robert Putnam, and Diana McLain Smith
   1986   *Action Science.* San Francisco: Jossey-Bass.

Ash, M.
   1979   "Reflections on Mondragón." *Town and Country Planning* 47:11–14.

Axworthy, Christopher S.
   1986   "Mondragón: A Less Favorable Assessment." In *Radical Perspectives
           on Social Problems*, edited by Frank Lindenfeld. Dix Hills, N.Y.:
           General Hall.

Azurmendi, Joxe
   1984   *El Hombre Cooperativo: Pensamiento de José María Arizmendiarrieta.*
           Mondragón: Caja Laboral Popular.

Barton, D.
   1982   "Mondragón: Experiment or Prototype?" *Accountancy* 93:125–26.

Bellas, C. J.
   1975   "Industrial Demcracy through Worker Ownership: An American
           Experience." In *Self-Management: Economic Liberation of Man*, edited
           by Jaroslav Vanek. Hammondsworth, England: Penguin Books.

Benson, C.
  1980   "Purely for Profit?" *Employee Relations* 2:2–5.

Berger, Lisa, and Chris Clamp
  1983   "Striking Similarities: Spain." *Workplace Democracy* 10:4, 6–8.

Bradley, Keith, and Alan Gelb
  1981   "Motivation and Control in the Mondragón Experiment." *British Journal of Industrial Relations* 19:211–31.
  1982a   "The Mondragón Cooperatives: Guidelines for a Cooperative Economy?" In *Participatory and Self-Managed Firms*, edited by D. C. Jones and J. Svejnar. Lexington, Mass.: Lexington Books.
  1982b   "The Replicability and Sustainability of the Mondragón Experiment." *British Journal of Industrial Relations* 20:20–33.
  1983   *Cooperation at Work: The Mondragón Experience.* London: Heinemann Educational Books.
  1985   *"Mixed Economy" versus Cooperative Adjustment: Mondragón's Experience through Spain's Recession.* Report no. DRD122. Washington, D.C.: World Bank.
  1987   "Cooperative Labour Relations: Mondragón's Response to Recession." *British Journal of Industrial Relations* 25:77–97.

Caja Laboral Popular
  1967   *Una Experiencia Cooperativa.* Mondragón: Caja Laboral Popular.
  1979   *Nuestra Experiencia Cooperativa.* Mondragón: Caja Laboral Popular.

Campbell, A.
  1980   *Mondragón 1980.* London: Industrial Common Ownership Movement.

Campbell, A., and B. Foster
  1980   *The Mondragón Movement.* ICOM Pamphlet 5. London: Industrial Common Ownership Movement.

Campbell, Alistair, C. Keen, G. Norman, and R. Oakeshott
  1977   *Worker-Owners: The Mondragón Achievement.* London: Anglo-German Foundation for the Study of Industrial Society.

Caro Baroja, Julio
  1974   "La Tradicion Técnica del Pueblo Vasco." In *Vasconiana* 3:103–79. San Sebastián, Spain: Editorial Txertoa.

Centre for the Study of Co-operatives
  1987   *Worker Cooperatives for the Creation and Maintenance of Employment*, Proceedings of the International Conference on Cooperatives, Montreal, 1984.

Clamp, Christine Anne
1983   "Mondragón Meets the Recession." *Workplace Democracy* 10(2):10–11.
1984   "Managing Cooperation at Mondragón." In *Proceedings of the National Employee-Ownership and Participation Conference.* Greensboro, N.C.: Guilford College.
1986   "Managing Cooperation at Mondragón." Ph.D. diss., Boston College.

Clutterbuck, D.
1974   "Where Industrial Co-operatives Reign in Spain. *International Management* 29:35–40.

Coates, Ken, and Tony Topham
1968   *Workers' Control.* Revised edition. London: Panther Books.

Collins, Orvis, David G. Moore, and Darab B. Unwalla
1964   *The Enterprising Man.* East Lansing: Michigan State University.

Co-operatives Research Unit, Open University
1982   *Mondragón Co-operatives—Myth or Model.* Milton Keynes, England: Co-operatives Research Unit, Open University.

Cort, John
1982   "The Marvels of Mondragón." *Commonweal* (June 18):369–71.

de Arroiabe, Simon Mz.
1984   "Caja Laboral Popular: 25 Años." *Trabajo y Unión* (June–July):4–5.

del Arco, José Luis
1982   *El Complejo Cooperativo de Mondragón.* Madrid: Asociación de Estudios Cooperativos.

Eaton, J.
1978a   *The Mondragón Cooperatives.* London: Centre for Alternative Industrial and Technological Systems (CAITS).
1978b   "The Relevance of Mondragón to Britain." *Political Quarterly* 49:478–83.
1979   "The Basque Workers' Cooperatives." *Industrial Relations Journal* 10:32–40.

Elena Diaz, Fernando
1973   *Quince Años de la Experiencia de la Zona de Mondragón.* No. 476. Madrid: Información Comercial Española, Ministerio de Economia y Hacienda.

Ellerman, David F.
1982   *The Socialization of Entrepreneurship: The Empresarial Division of the Caja Laboral Popular.* Somerville, Mass.: Industrial Cooperative Association.

1984a   "Entrepreneurship in the Mondragón Cooperatives." *Review of Social Economy* 42:272–94.

1984b   *Management Planning with Labor as a Fixed Cost: The Mondragón Annual Business Plan Manual.* Somerville, Mass.: Industrial Cooperative Association.

1984c   *The Mondragón Cooperative Movement.* Case 1-384-270. Cambridge, Mass.: Harvard University Business School.

1984d   "Theory of Legal Structure: Worker Cooperatives." *Journal of Economic Issues* 18:861–91.

Fishman, Robert Michael
1985   "Working Class Organization and Political Change: The Labor Movement and the Transition to Democracy in Spain." Ph.D. diss., Yale University.

García, Quintin
1970   *Les Coopératives Industrielles de Mondragón.* Paris: Editions Ouvrieres.

Gardner, David
1982   "Co-operative Experiment a Success." *Financial Times* (June 10).

Gorrono, Iñaki
1975   *Experiencia Cooperativa en el Pais Vasco.* Durango, Spain: Leopoldo Zugaza.

1985–   "L'Experience Cooperative de Mondragón." *Cooperatives et Developpe-*
86   *ment* 17:2.

Goyder, M.
1979   "The Mondragón Experiment." *Personnel Management* 11:24–27.

Greenwood, Davydd
1976   *Unrewarding Wealth: Commercialization and the Collapse of Agriculture in a Spanish Basque Town.* New York: Cambridge University Press.

1984   *The Taming of Evolution: The Persistence of Nonevolutionary Views in the Study of Humans.* Ithaca, N.Y.: Cornell University Press.

Gui, Benedetto
1984   "Basque versus Illyrian Labor-Managed Firms: The Problem of Property Rights." *Journal of Comparative Economics* 8:168–81.

Gunther, Richard, Giacomo Sani, and Goldie Shabad
1986   *Spain after Franco: The Making of a Competitive Party System.* Berkeley: University of California Press.

Gutiérrez-Johnson, Ana
1976   "Cooperativism and Justice: A Study and Cross-Cultural Comparison of Preferences for Forms of Equity among Basque Students of a Cooperative School-Factory." M.S. thesis, Cornell University.

1978   "Compensation, Equity, and Industrial Democracy in the Mondragón Cooperatives." *Economic Analysis and Workers' Self Management* 12:267–89.
1982   "Industrial Democracy in Action: The Cooperative Complex of Mondragón." Ph.D. diss., Cornell University.
1984   "The Mondragón Model of Cooperative Enterprise." *Changing Work* 1:35–41.

Gutiérrez-Johnson, Ana, and William F. Whyte
1977   "The Mondragón System of Worker Cooperatives." *Industrial and Labor Relations Review* 31:18–30.

Gutierrez-Marquez, Antonio
1985   "The Creation of Industrial Cooperatives in the Basque Country." Ph.D. diss., University of Chicago.

Industrial Cooperative Association
1984   "Report on a Study Visit to Mondragón." Unpublished manuscript.

Información Comercial Española
1972   *El Cooperativismo Industrial de Mondragón.* No. 467–68. Madrid: Información Comercial Española, Ministerio de Economia y Hacienda.

Jackobs, S.
1979   "Community, Industrial Democracy, and the Cooperatives of Mondragón." B.A. thesis, Harvard University.

Jacobs, Jane
1984   *Cities and the Wealth of Nations.* New York: Random House.

Jay, P.
1977a   "St. George and Mondragón." *Times* (London) (Apr. 7).
1977b   "Til We Have Built Mondragón." *Times* (London) (Apr. 14).

Job Ownership Ltd.
1982   *Lagun-Aro: The Non-Profit Making Social Welfare Mutuality of the Mondragón Co-operatives.* London: Job Ownership.

Johnson, Ana Gutiérrez. *See* Gutiérrez-Johnson, Ana.

Jones, Derek C.
1980   "Producer Co-operatives in Industrialized Western Economies." *British Journal of Industrial Relations* 18:141–54.

Kroeber, A. L., and C. Kluckhohn
1952   "Culture: A Critical Review of Concepts and Definitions." Peabody Museum Papers No. 47.

Larrañaga, Jesús
  1981   *Buscando un Camino: Don José María Arizmendi-Arrieta y la Experiencia Cooperativa de Mondragón*. Bilbao, Spain: R & F.
  1982   "José Ayala: Con la Muerte a Cuestas." *Trabajo y Unión* (Oct.):8–9.

Larrañaga, Juan
  1986   *El Consejo Social: Pasado, Presente y Futuro*. Mondragón: Caja Laboral Popular.

Lazes, Peter, and Tony Costanza
  1984   *Xerox Cuts Costs without Layoffs through Union-Management Collaboration*. Labor-Management Cooperation Brief. Washington: U.S. Department of Labor.

Leighton, Alexander H.
  1984   "Then and Now: Some Notes on the Interaction of Person and Social Environment." *Human Organization* 43:189–97.

Logan, C.
  1979   "The Mondragón Cooperative Model: A Critical Appraisal." *Public Enterprise* 16:7–8.

Mendicute, José Antonio
  1987   "ETEO, Junto con Eskola, en la Enseñanza de Técnicas de Gestion." *Trabajo y Unión* (Apr.):40–41.

Milbrath, Robert
  1983   "Lessons from the Mondragón Cooperatives." *Science for the People* 15:3–11, 28–29.
  1984   "Long-Run Accumulation of Capital in a Cooperative Sector: Simulation Analysis Based on the Case of Mondragón." In *Proceedings of the National Employee-Ownership and Participation Conference*. Greensboro, N.C.: Guilford College.
  1986   "Institutional Development and Capital Accumulation in a Complex of Basque Worker Cooperatives (Spain)." Ph.D. diss., University of Michigan.

Mollner, Terence Jerome
  1982   "The Design of a Nonformal Education Process to Establish a Community Development Program Based upon Mahatma Gandhi's Theory of Trusteeship." Ph.D. diss., University of Massachusetts.
  1984   "Mondragón: A Third Way." *Review of Social Economy* 42:260–71.

Nairn, Allan
  1984   "Mondragón: Where Workers Call the Shots. An Alternative to Multinationals." *Multinational Monitor* 5:9–13.

National Center for Employee Ownership
   1988   *The Employee Ownership Report* 7 (Jan.-Feb.).

Norkett, Paul C.
   1983   "Management Accounting for Co-operatives." *Management Accounting* 61:30–32.

Oakeshott, Robert
   1973   "Mondragón: Spain's Oasis of Democracy." *Observer (London) Supplement* (Jan. 21).
   1978a   *The Case for Workers' Co-ops.* London: Routledge & Kegan Paul.
   1978b   "Industrial Cooperatives: The Middle Way." *Lloyds Bank Review* (Jan.):44–58.
   1978c   "The Mondragón Model of Participation." *Industrial and Commercial Training* 10:50–56.
   1978d   *The Prospect and the Conditions for Successful Co-operative Production.* London: Cooperative Union Ltd.
   1981   "European Co-operatives: Perspectives from Spain." In *Prospects for Workers' Co-operatives in Europe* 2:S1–S22. Brussels: Commission of the European Communities.

Ochoteco Aguirre, Pedro
   1985– "La Methode de Création de Nouvelles Coopératives a Partir de la
   86   Caja Laboral Popular." In *Cooperatives et Developpement, Revue du Ciriec*, edited by Benoit Levesque.

Olibarri, Ignacio
   1984   "Tradiciones Cooperativas Vascas." In *Euskal Herria: Historia y Sociedad*, edited by Joseba Intxausti. Mondragón: Caja Laboral Popular.

Ormaechea, José María
   1986   *El Hombre que yo Conocí.* Mondragón: Fundación Gizabidea.

Ornelas-Navarro, Jesús Carlos
   1980   "Producer Cooperatives and Schooling: The Case of Mondragón." Ph.D. diss., Stanford University.
   1982   "Cooperative Production and Technical Education in the Basque Country." *Prospects* 13:467–75.

Pérez de Calleja, Basterrechea A.
   1975   *The Group of Cooperatives at Mondragón in the Spanish Basque Country.* Mondragón: Caja Laboral Popular.

Piore, Michael J., and Charles F. Sabel
   1983   "Italian Small Business Development: Lessons for U.S. Industrial Policy." In *American Industry in International Competition: Government Policies and Corporate Strategies*, edited by John Zysman and Laura Tyson. Ithaca, N.Y.: Cornell University Press.

Riaza, Ballesteros, et al.
　1968　　*Cooperativas Industriales de Production. Experiencias y Futuro.* Bilbao, Spain: Ediciones Deusto.

Rothschild-Whitt, Joyce
　1979　　"The Collectivist Organization: An Alternative to Rational-Bureaucratic Models." *American Sociological Review* 44:509–27.

Royal Arsenal Cooperative Society Ltd.
　1980　　*Mondragón: The Basque Cooperatives.* London: Royal Arsenal Cooperative Society Ltd.

Saive, Marie-Anne
　1980　　"Mondragón: An Experiment with Co-operative Development in the Industrial Sector." *Annals of Public and Co-operative Economy* 51:223–55.
　1981　　"Cooperative Doctrine and Rent in Mondragón." *Annals of Public and Co-operative Economy* 52:369–79.

Schön, Donald A.
　1983　　*The Reflective Practitioner.* New York: Basic Books.

Shostak, Arthur
　　　　　"Robust Unionism." Unpublished manuscript.

Sperry, Charles W.
　1985　　"What Makes Mondragón Work?" *Review of Social Economy* 43:345–56.

Spinks, N.
　1981　　"The Acceptable Face of Worker Capitalism." *Accountant* 185:164–66.

Tarrow, Norma Bernstein
　1985　　"The Autonomous Basque Community of Spain: Language, Culture and Education." In *Cultural Identity and Educational Policy*, edited by Colin Brock and Witold Tulasiewicz. London: Croom Helm.

Tetrault, Ives, et al.
　1979　　*Coopératives Ouvrieres de Production. Coopératives Forestieres. Coopératives Industrielles. France et Mondragón.* Québec: Gouvernement du Québec.

Thomas, Henk
　1980　　"The Distribution of Earnings and Capital in the Mondragón Cooperatives." *Economic Analysis and Workers' Management* 14:363–92.
　1985　　"The Dynamics of Social Ownership: Some Considerations in the Perspective of the Mondragón Experience." *Economic Analysis and Workers' Management* 19:147–60.

Thomas, Henk, and Chris Logan
1980a   *Mondragón: An Economic Analysis*. London: George Allen and Unwin.
1980b   *Mondragón Producer Cooperatives*. The Hague: Institute of Social Sciences.
1982   "The Performance of the Mondragón Cooperatives in Spain." In *Participatory and Self-Managed Firms*, edited by D. C. Jones and J. Svejnar. Lexington, Mass.: Lexington Books.

Vines, S.
1981   "A Mondragón for Wales?" *Observer (London)* (Feb. 8).

Weitzman, Martin L.
1984   *The Share Economy: Conquering Stagflation*. Cambridge, Mass.: Harvard University Press.

Wellens, John
1978   "Worker Owners: The Mondragón Achievement." *Industrial and Commercial Training* 10:57–59.

White, D.
1984   "Successful Basque Co-operatives: The Unorthodox Survivor." *Financial Times* (May 22).

Whyte, William Foote
1982   "Social Inventions for Solving Human Problems." *American Sociological Review* 47:1–13.
1986   "Philadelphia Story." *Society* (Mar.-Apr.):36–44.

Whyte, William F., and Joseph Blasi
1980   "From Research to Legislation on Employee Ownership." *Economic and Industrial Democracy* 1:395–415.
1982   "Worker Ownership, Participation and Control: Toward a Theoretical Model." *Policy Sciences* 14:137–63.

Whyte, William F., and Damon Boynton, eds.
1984   *Higher Yielding Human Systems for Agriculture*. Ithaca, N.Y.: Cornell University Press.

Whyte, William F., Tove Helland Hammer, Christopher B. Meek, Reed Nelson, and Robert N. Stern
1983   *Worker Participation and Ownership: Cooperative Strategies for Strengthening Local Economies*. Ithaca, N.Y.: ILR Press.

Whyte, William F., with Kathleen King Whyte
    1985   *Learning from the Field: A Guide from Experience.* Beverly Hills, Calif.: Sage Publications.

Workplace Democracy
    1985   "Worker Ownership in North Carolina." *Workplace Democracy* 12(1):2–3.

Zwerdling, D.
    1980   "Mondragón of Spain." In *Workplace Democracy.* New York: Harper and Row.

Index

About the Authors

WILLIAM FOOTE WHYTE is an emeritus professor in the New York State School of Industrial and Labor Relations at Cornell University and the research director of Cornell's Programs for Employment and Workplace Systems. The author of *Street Corner Society* and *Learning from the Field: A Guide from Experience*, he holds a Ph.D. in sociology from the University of Chicago and has written extensively for both journals and books on the sociology of the workplace. He has served as president of the American Sociological Association, the Industrial Relations Research Association, and the Society for Applied Anthropology.

KATHLEEN KING WHYTE has worked professionally as an editor and artist. She collaborated with William Foote Whyte on the field research for *Making Mondragón* and *Learning from the Field*.

317